BARRON'S

THE TRUSTED NAME I

T0283760

AP® Q&A

Psychology

600

QUESTIONS
AND ANSWERS

ROBERT McENTARFFER, PH.D.

Lincoln Public Schools, Lincoln, Nebraska

KRISTIN WHITLOCK, M.ED.

Davis High School, Kaysville, Utah

Weber State University, Ogden, Utah

AP® is a registered trademark of the College Board, which is not affiliated with Barron's and was not involved in the production of, and does not endorse, this product.

Acknowledgments

We would like to thank Kristen Girardi and Michele Sandifer for their diligent, professional, and kind help during the process of creating this book. Thanks to our families for giving us the time and support we need, and to our friends in the AP Psychology teacher community (you know who you are!). Finally, thanks to our AP Psychology students for helping us become better teachers.

AP® is a registered trademark of the College Board, which is not affiliated with Barron's and was not involved in the production of, and does not endorse, this product.

© Copyright 2023, 2020 by Kaplan North America, LLC, d/b/a Barron's Educational Series

All rights reserved.
No part of this publication may be reproduced or distributed in any form
or by any means without the written permission of the copyright owner.

Published by Kaplan North America, LLC, d/b/a Barron's Educational Series
1515 W Cypress Creek Road
Fort Lauderdale, FL 33309
www.barronseduc.com

ISBN: 978-1-5062-8801-7

10 9 8 7 6 5 4 3 2 1

Kaplan North America, LLC, d/b/a Barron's Educational Series print books are available at special quantity discounts to use for sales promotions, employee premiums, or educational purposes. For more information or to purchase books, please call the Simon & Schuster special sales department at 866-506-1949.

Contents

Introduction and Explanation of the Book

If you are reading this introduction, you are probably preparing to take the AP Psychology exam. If so, congratulations! The content assessed on this exam can help us understand ourselves and empathize with others. Psychology is a fascinating field, and studying for the AP Psychology exam will help you make sure you understand and can apply these concepts in potentially useful ways. High school and college psychology teachers work hard every year to try to make sure that the AP Psychology exam is a reliable and valid test of your knowledge of college-level psychology content (and if you don't know what the terms "reliable" and "valid" mean yet, you will soon!).

The purpose of this book is to help you practice multiple-choice items that are as similar as possible to the multiple-choice items you will see on the actual AP Psychology exam. We are experienced AP Psychology teachers who have been involved with the AP Psychology exam for over 20 years. We used everything we know about AP Psychology content and the AP Psychology exam to create over 600 multiple-choice items (whew!) that will help you practice exactly the kinds of items you will see on the exam.

It is also important that you know what you will not find in this book: the purpose of this book is not to help teach you the content covered on the exam. Hopefully you had the opportunity to participate in an AP Psychology course at your school, and that class included access to a college-level introductory psychology textbook. If you are looking for other resources that can help you review the content involved in the AP Psychology exam, Barron's *AP Psychology Premium* may be a useful resource. The purpose of this book is to help you review examples of the kinds of multiple-choice items you will encounter on the exam and practice answering many different kinds of questions.

This Q & A book focuses on one part of the AP Psychology exam: the 100 multiple-choice items you will see on the test. Your performance on these multiple-choice items will determine two-thirds of your overall score on the exam, so if you use this book to become an expert at answering these kinds of questions, you will improve your score (and learn a lot about important psychology concepts!). The other part of the AP Psychology exam is the Free-Response Question (FRQ) section. The FRQs will ask you to write about how psychological concepts apply to specific situations. For more information about the FRQ portion of the exam, refer to that chapter in Barron's *AP Psychology Premium*—it includes sample FRQs and answers along with tips about how to write your answers.

Finally, we want to explain why we wrote this book in the way we did. Our first step was to do some research on AP Psychology multiple-choice items. We analyzed past AP Psychology exams in order to better understand the multiple-choice items that appear on the exam. We analyzed hundreds of actual AP Psychology multiple-choice items, and this analysis uncovered categories of items that no other exam preparation book addresses. We used these categories to write the questions for this book, and if you understand and practice items in each of these categories, you will be much better prepared for the AP exam.

While writing this book, College Board revised the AP Psychology exam and course description. We looked through these changes carefully and made sure that the items we wrote aligned with the new course description. One change was the focus on specific course skills. We have written questions from each skill category so you will have lots of opportunities to practice. We have also included information with each question that will help you see how that item aligns with the new course description (for more information, see the "Revised Course Description" section below).

THE ANALYSIS

You already know that you can expect multiple-choice questions from specific units to appear on the AP exam. The following table shows the breakdown of multiple-choice items in this book based on specific topics. This breakdown also mirrors the proportion of items from each chapter on the AP exam.

Unit	Chapter	Number of Items	Percentage of Items
1. Scientific Foundations	History and Approaches	18	3%
	Methods	48	8%
2. Biological Bases of Behavior	Biological Bases of Behavior	54	9%
	States of Consciousness	18	3%
3. Sensation and Perception	Sensation and Perception	48	8%
4. Learning	Learning	48	8%
5. Cognitive Psychology	Cognition	54	9%
	Testing and Individual Differences	36	6%
6. Developmental Psychology	Developmental Psychology	48	8%

Unit	Chapter	Number of Items	Percentage of Items
7. Motivation, Emotion, and Personality	Motivation and Emotion	48	8%
	Personality	42	7%
8. Clinical Psychology	Abnormal Psychology	48	8%
	Treatment of Psychological Disorders	36	6%
9. Social Psychology	Social Psychology	54	9%

But there is another way to think about the different "types" of multiple-choice items you will be answering. We examined almost 400 released items from four of the most recently publicly released AP exams to see if they fell into specific "categories" or "types." Through this analysis we determined that AP Psychology items can be categorized into the following groups:

Stimulus	3% of items
Definitions	42% of items
Scenarios	28% of items
Names	11% of items
Research Methods	9% of items
Perspectives	7% of items

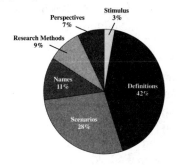

A Note About the Categories

Many of the released AP Psychology questions we analyzed could be placed into more than one category. AP Psychology questions often require knowing the definition of a term, or analyzing a scenario, but also involve names of famous psychologists or different research methods or psychological perspectives. As we categorized items we used our judgment to place each item into the category we felt was most appropriate. It's not important that every item is in the "right" category—the purpose of this book is to give you experience answering many questions in each category. As you work your way through the book, don't worry if you encounter an item in a "Definition" section that seems like it could also be in the "Scenario" section, or vice versa. This book provides you with dozens of questions in each of these categories, so you'll become an expert in thinking through every type of item, and that expertise will help you on the actual AP Psychology exam!

Also, as you work through this book you'll find some items that ask about the same concept in different ways. Two or three definition items may ask about the same concept—one item may ask you to identify the right definition, and the next item may ask you to match the right term to a definition. We purposely included these "variations" of similar items so that you can gain experience answering different kinds of items about the same concept.

Revised Course Description

The new AP Psychology Course Description outlines the content included in the nine units used in this book (see the Table of Contents) and a description of skills students should learn during their AP Psychology class:

- Skill 1: Concept Understanding—students should be able to recognize definitions of and apply important concepts. Specifically, students should practice defining/applying concepts (Skill 1a), using concepts to explain behavior in context (Skill 1b), and apply theories and psychological perspectives in context (Skill 1c).
- Skill 2: Data Analysis—students should be able to interpret and analyze numerical data.
- Skill 3: Scientific Investigation—students should be able to analyze/critique examples of psychological research studies and conclusions from those studies.

Based on the new AP Psychology Course Description, you can expect that 75–80% of the multiple-choice questions will be Skill 1 questions, 8–12% will focus on Skill 2, and 12–16% will be Skill 3 questions.

In order to help you practice these skills, we "keyed" every one of the 600 multiple-choice items to the skills. In the Answers section of this book, you will find an explanation of the correct answer to the question, why the incorrect answers are incorrect, and which skill (Skill 1a, 1b, 1c, Skill 2, or Skill 3) is most applicable for that question.

We used our experience and best judgment to categorize the questions according to these skills. You will find that often questions we have labeled as "Definitions" fit into the Skill 1a category where you will be asked to define or apply a specific concept. Scenario questions are most likely Skill 1b or 1c. The way to distinguish them is to look for what the question focuses on. If the Scenario question asks only about a specific concept, it is a Skill 1b. If the Scenario question asks about a theory or a psychological perspective, it is a Skill 1c. Questions that ask you to analyze data, figure simple statistics, or read a chart are most likely Skill 2 questions. If you are analyzing a study, either real or fictional, for some element of research design (e.g., identifying the independent variable, addressing the weakness of a study, or ethical concerns), it is most likely a Skill 3 question. Questions that refer to specific psychologists may cross all three skill categories.

EXPLANATIONS OF THE CATEGORIES AND EXAMPLE ITEMS

Note that the example items in this section are NOT released items from previous AP Psychology exams. We wrote these example items to help you better understand each category.

Stimulus

Some of the items we analyzed used a stimulus to provide context or information that you need to use when answering the item. We predict that there will be more of these kinds of items on future tests and that students will be required to answer several questions about each stimulus. At the beginning of each chapter, you'll find a stimulus and either one or a series of items tied to that stimulus. The stimulus might be an explanation of a research study, a diagram, a data table, or some other psychology-related information. Although you won't encounter many of these Stimulus items on the test, you should look through these items carefully and practice answering several questions about the same stimulus.

Example

Use the data table below to answer questions 1–3.

	Mean	SD
Group A	2.43	.30
Group B	3.45	.29

If Group A is the control group and Group B is the experimental group, which statement below is most accurate about the impact of the independent variable in this experiment?

(A) Group A is a larger sample because its SD is slightly higher, although the Group A mean is significantly lower.
(B) The independent variable may have increased performance since the mean of Group B is higher and the variance of each group is about equal.
(C) There is likely a high correlation between the independent variable in Group A and Group B.
(D) The independent variable must have been operationally defined incorrectly because if the means are different, the SD must be very different, too.
(E) The independent variable worked more effectively in Group B than it did in Group A.

(B) If Group B is the experimental group, that group experienced the independent variable. Since the mean for Group B is higher, Group B may have increased performance (or whatever the dependent variable is in this experiment). SD stands for standard deviation, which is a measure of variance. The data table doesn't provide any information about sample size (answer A) or about correlation information (answer C). Standard deviations can be very different across groups even if the means are different (answer D). Answer E is incorrect because only the experimental group, which is Group B, would experience the independent variable.

Course Skill: This question is a Skill 2 because you are asked to draw conclusions about research based on data provided in the chart.

How to prepare for Stimulus items: The first step is to study the stimulus carefully since you will use it to answer several items. The stimulus will always include clues. Rely on these clues when answering each question. Feel free to make notes on the stimulus, circling information or details that you think may be important. As you answer each item, look back at the stimulus and check each answer to see if your answer makes sense given the information provided.

Definitions

We were surprised by this category as we completed the analysis. As AP Psychology teachers, we told our students that they shouldn't expect multiple-choice items on the AP Psychology exam that focused only on defining terms. We were surprised when we found that almost half the items we examined primarily tested the students' knowledge of term definitions. These items did not include a scenario, an example, or researcher names. Instead, they tried to measure the students' ability to recall, recognize, and think about the specific definitions of psychological vocabulary.

Note that definition items are definitely not simple questions. Questions in this category do not just ask you to identify or recognize a correct definition of a term. Instead, they require that you demonstrate a deep understanding of the definition (rather than simply memorizing the definition). The question requires you to choose the correct term or definition based on a specific aspect or use of a term in context. In addition, sometimes incorrect answer choices are included that may appear correct to students. Remember, though, that each item is written to have one and only one truly correct answer.

Example

Conditioning occurs most quickly when which of the following is used?

(A) Variable-ratio
(B) Variable-interval
(C) Continuous reinforcement
(D) Punishment
(E) Negative reinforcement

(C) Continuous reinforcement always results in the quickest learning. In continuous reinforcement, organisms are given reinforcement after each desired behavior, resulting in fast conditioning. Answer choices A and B list different schedules of reinforcement. These are effective but not as fast as continuous reinforcement. Answer choices D and E are different kinds of conditioning, not different reinforcement schedules.

Course Skill: This is a Skill 1a question as it focuses on knowing about a specific concept, that is, continuous reinforcement.

How to prepare for Definition items: As you study psychological vocabulary, make sure you go beyond simply memorizing the textbook definition of terms. Rewriting the definitions in your own words can be effective. Write examples of how psychological theories impact your own life. Doing so can create vivid examples that help you remember specific terms in the context of your life. Writing these examples is "deep processing," a concept from the Cognition (memory) chapter. Deep processing increases the chances you will be able to answer questions about these terms on the exam.

Scenarios

About one-third of the items in past tests included a scenario in the stem of the question. These scenarios were short descriptions of a fictional study, an example of human thinking or behavior using fictional names, or occasionally five different examples presented as possible answers to the question. These Scenario items were the most direct examples of one of the goals of the AP Psychology exam: to measure students' ability to APPLY psychological terms to examples across different contexts.

Example

Esme practices the viola every day over the summer without fail, even though no one is tracking her practice hours and she doesn't have orchestra rehearsal or private lessons during summer break. Which of the following explains Esme's dedication?

(A) Heuristics
(B) Algorithms
(C) Extrinsic motivation
(D) Intrinsic motivation
(E) Overconfidence

(D) The term that most closely matches Esme's practicing behavior is answer D, intrinsic motivation. This type of motivation describes behaviors that people perform because they want to, behaviors that are motivated by internal desires and preferences rather than external rewards or punishments. Answer choices A and B describe problem-solving techniques, not motivations. Answer choice C is incorrect because Esme does not receive either an external reward or a punishment for practicing. Answer choice E is not relevant to this scenario because it does not involve Esme being either confident or overconfident.

Course skill: This is a Skill 1b question because it assesses whether you can apply the concept, intrinsic motivation, to a real-world scenario.

How to prepare for Scenario items: Use the Scenario items in this book to practice reading scenarios carefully. The scenarios include details that are usually key to understanding the correct answer. Look at the terms/vocabulary used in the scenarios—they often give you a clue about what concept the question is trying to assess. A scenario that includes either the word *conditioning* or the term *positive reinforcement* is most likely trying to assess your understanding of behaviorism and operant conditioning. Another useful technique is to develop your own scenarios for the psychological concepts you're studying. If you can develop your own scenario for a concept, you will remember how that concept applies to a real-life example and gain practice analyzing the kinds of scenarios used in this type of item.

Names

About 10% of the items in previous AP exams referred to specific names from either the history of psychology or current researchers. Being familiar with these individuals and their research will obviously help you answer Name items correctly. If you encounter an item that includes a name you're not familiar with, do not despair! Many of these items do not completely depend on your ability to recall information about an individual. You can often figure out the answer (or at least eliminate a couple of possible wrong answers) using context clues from the question. The other terms or vocabulary used in the question can provide context clues that help you narrow down possible correct and incorrect answers even if you aren't familiar with the name mentioned in the item. For example, in the question below, if you do not remember anything about Jean Piaget, you still might be able to choose the right answer if you notice that the question asks about cognitive developmental stages and then remember that the formal operations stage is associated with young adulthood.

Example

Which of the following cognitive developmental stages described by Jean Piaget most likely describes the thought processes of young adults?

(A) Formal operations
(B) Concrete operations
(C) Postconventional reasoning
(D) Preoperational thinking
(E) Identity versus role confusion

(A) Answer A matches the young adult age range (adolescence and above) described by Piaget. Answer choices B and D describe Piaget's stages experienced by younger children. Answer C refers to a stage in Kohlberg's moral reasoning theory. Choice E refers to a stage in Erikson's social development theory.

Course Skill: This is a Skill 1a question. Even though it asks about Jean Piaget's theory, it is focusing only on one part of the theory, that is, the formal operations stage. If it were a Skill 1c, the question would include information concerning each stage of Piaget's cognitive theory of development.

How to prepare for Name items: The names of many important psychological researchers are included in the AP Psychology curriculum. Hopefully you became familiar with many of these names during your AP Psychology class (and by studying your college-level psychology textbook). Using flash cards can be an efficient way to associate individual researchers with their particular theories, vocabulary terms, and concepts. Note that, in the book Barron's *AP Psychology Premium*, we included a chapter that may help you with Name items. We narrowed down the long list of possible names to the "Fabulous 15." Focusing your study on these 15 names will be a good use of your time. These psychology researchers are the most important and are more likely to appear in AP Psychology multiple-choice items than other researchers.

Research Methods

About 10% of the items in previous AP exams required students to have knowledge of research methods, usually the experimental method. Some of the items required students to critique an example of a study (finding flaws, analyzing researchers' conclusions, and so on). Other items required students to identify specific elements from an example study, such as identifying the independent variable of a study or how the dependent variable is operationally defined.

Research Method items are often similar to the Scenario items described above. However, Research items always involve specific knowledge of research methodology. This specific knowledge is usually vocabulary related to the experimental method. Some of these items require you to have statistical knowledge. Understanding statistical analysis conceptually is almost always more important than being able to compute specific statistics. Calculators are not allowed during the exam, so you won't be required to do complex numerical calculations.

Example

In an experiment, which term refers to the variable a researcher manipulates, making the experimental group different from the control group?

(A) Dependent
(B) Confounding
(C) Independent
(D) Random
(E) Control

(C) The independent variable, answer choice C, is the variable a research manipulates, making the experimental group different from the control group. Choices A, B, and E describe different kinds of variables involved in the experimental method. Answer D refers to either random sampling or random assignment, not to a type of variable.

Course Skill: Even though this is a question regarding research methods, it would be categorized as a Skill 1a primarily because it is a definition of an independent variable. If the question asked you to identify the independent variable in a real or fictional study, it would be categorized as a Skill 3 question.

How to prepare for Research Method items: Study the experimental method carefully to make sure you understand terms like independent variable, dependent variable, operational definition, random sampling, random assignment, and other associated terms. In addition, think carefully about what each kind of research method can prove. Specifically, think about differences between correlation and causation. Remember that only experiments can prove cause. Developing your own short examples of experiments and labeling these elements can be helpful. In addition to studying the experimental method, you should practice differentiating among other kinds of research methods. Practice recognizing and thinking about the differences among the experimental method and other kinds of research, like case study, naturalistic observation, and correlational studies.

Perspectives

A few items (about 7%) involve the major psychological perspectives. These perspectives describe the different "lenses" that psychologists currently use to think about human thought and behavior. These perspectives are associated with specific terminology, the names of researchers, and research methodology in some cases.

Example

Clinical therapists who use the behavioral perspective to help clients change unwanted behaviors are most likely to use which of the following techniques?

(A) Helping someone understand her or his own unhealthy thinking patterns
(B) Analyzing dreams and other evidence of unconscious thinking
(C) Changing the existing reinforcements or punishments for the behavior
(D) Exploring the feelings associated with the undesired behavior
(E) Relating past events in the client's life to the current undesired behavior

(C) The behavioral perspective involves using rewards and punishments as referred to in choice C. The other answer choices do not involve rewards, punishments, or other kinds of conditioning, making them incorrect.

   Course Skill: This is a Skill 1a question because it asks you to apply what you know about the behavioral perspective to the work of a clinician. If this question included a real-world scenario (e.g., "Dr. Michael focuses on changing her client's actions by…"), it would be categorized as a Skill 1c.
   How to prepare for Perspective items: Make sure you thoroughly understand the major perspectives on psychology and, more importantly, that you can USE these perspectives to analyze human behaviors. One effective study method is to choose an example of your own behavior (a bad habit, a superstition, a choice you recently made, and so on) and try to explain it from various perspectives. As you practice the Perspective items in this book, you may start to notice that some perspectives use specific key terms or phrases that help provide clues about what perspective is being tested. Remember the following examples of different perspectives and associated vocabulary:

- Behaviorism: conditioning, positive/negative reinforcement, stimulus, response (note that these terms would help you answer the example item above)
- Cognitive: scheme, encoding, recall/recognition, mental interpretation
- Psychodynamic: unconscious, repression, defense mechanism
- Biological psychology: neurotransmitters, endocrine system, genetic predisposition

QUESTIONS

History and Approaches

Answers for Chapter 1 are on pages 195–198.

STIMULUS

Use the following excerpt from a blog post by PsychGuy42 to answer questions 1–3.

> "The history of psychology isn't long, but it's eventful: it starts with one group of professors who decide to test how people perceive the world by getting them to describe their sensory experiences. But soon after that another group decides that we shouldn't even talk about 'thinking' anymore because that can't be measured, and we should only describe behaviors. Then a different group decides that thinking might just be important after all, and in fact maybe we should even research how people around the world think and behave rather than just people in Europe and the U.S. Makes me wonder how psychologists will change this science next time around?"

1. **Which of the following is the most accurate statement about the history of psychology described in the excerpt?**

   (A) Psychology is an ancient science tracing its roots back to the Persians.
   (B) The science of psychology began with a group of professors who researched human perception.
   (C) The science of psychology has focused on the study of observable behaviors since the beginning.
   (D) Biopsychology and the study of the brain are increasingly central to the science of psychology.
   (E) Psychology began with Freud's observations about human perception and descriptions of sensory experiences.

2. **Which important contemporary psychological perspective is not mentioned in the excerpt?**

   (A) Cognitive
   (B) Functionalism
   (C) Structuralism
   (D) Biological
   (E) Behaviorism

3. Which major disagreement between two psychological perspectives is described in the excerpt?

(A) Biological versus evolutionary psychology
(B) Trait theory versus humanism
(C) Role playing versus dissociation theory
(D) Psychoanalysis versus psychotherapy
(E) Behaviorism versus cognitive psychology

DEFINITIONS

4. Researchers analyzed the types of requests that most likely motivate individuals to donate their time to aid organizations. These researchers are most likely engaged in what kind of research?

(A) Basic research
(B) Introspection
(C) Factor analysis
(D) Applied research
(E) Linkage analysis

5. Which of the following statements describes how a cognitive psychologist might explain why a student experiences test anxiety?

(A) Students who experience repeated failures will react to tests with anxiety.
(B) Increased heart rates and blood pressure are often interpreted as anxiety.
(C) Unresolved unconscious conflicts emerge in stressful situations as anxiety.
(D) Students who grow up in a family or school culture that emphasizes grades over learning may be more anxious about tests.
(E) If students interpret low grades as a personal failure, they may experience increased test anxiety.

6. Researchers in which of the following psychological perspectives would be most interested in investigating different kinds of stimuli that cause physiological responses?

(A) Humanistic
(B) Behaviorist
(C) Cognitive
(D) Sociocultural
(E) Psychodynamic

7. The various psychological perspectives are not mutually exclusive. Many researchers use a combination of psychological perspectives to explain thinking and behavior. Which of the following combinations of psychological perspectives might a researcher be most likely to use when investigating the relationship between how we think about events and what we were rewarded and punished for in the past?

   (A) Humanistic and psychoanalytic
   (B) Sociocultural and structuralism
   (C) Cognitive and behaviorism
   (D) Biological and behavior genetics
   (E) Evolutionary and functionalism

8. What makes positive psychology different from other psychological perspectives/movements?

   (A) Positive psychology focuses on personality traits such as openness and extroversion rather than on negative personality attributes.
   (B) Most other psychological perspectives justify their theories using the experimental method, while positive psychology primarily uses case studies.
   (C) Positive psychology is exclusively used by clinical psychologists rather than other career areas.
   (D) All the psychological perspectives focus on explaining human behavior, while positive psychology attempts to explain human thinking.
   (E) Positive psychology focuses on human flourishing rather than on treating psychological disorders or researching issues related to deficiencies in human thinking and behavior.

9. Which of the following topics would a clinical psychologist most likely be interested in?

   (A) The processes involved as sensations become perceptions
   (B) Factors that influence conditioning of nonhuman animals
   (C) Psychological disorders common in different cultures
   (D) Statistical principles of experimental methodology
   (E) Reliability and validity issues involved in personality testing

10. What makes psychoanalysis unique among the historical psychological movements?

    (A) The psychoanalytic movement was the first time talk therapy was used to help alleviate mental issues.
    (B) Other psychological movements used case studies and other anecdotal research methods, while psychoanalysts used experimentation.
    (C) Psychoanalysis focused on measuring behaviors rather than on internal mental states, like emotion.
    (D) As a group, psychoanalysts were among the first psychologists to recognize the need to study across different cultural groups.
    (E) The psychoanalytic movement focused on human strengths rather than on weaknesses.

11. Which historical psychological movement is best summarized by the idea "in order to be a science, psychology needs to focus exclusively on what can be measured about humans rather than on unmeasurable internal cognitive states"?

    (A) Structuralism
    (B) Behaviorism
    (C) Gestalt psychology
    (D) Behavior genetics
    (E) Psychometrics

SCENARIOS

12. Dr. Gopnik demonstrated that infants show fear when presented with a toy snake but not when shown a toy bunny. She suggests that fear of objects that can be dangerous to us, like snakes, are biologically predisposed and allowed our ancestors to survive. Dr. Gopnik's view is most consistent with which of the following psychological perspectives?

    (A) Behavioral
    (B) Humanistic
    (C) Evolutionary
    (D) Cognitive
    (E) Psychodynamic

13. Dr. Brunsman's research focuses on the impact of testing accommodations on the accuracy of measurements regarding students' reading achievement levels. Which of the following psychological career areas is the most appropriate label for Dr. Brunsman's research?

    (A) Developmental psychology
    (B) Human factors psychology
    (C) Social psychology
    (D) Psychometric psychology
    (E) Humanistic psychology

14. Dr. Keith spent much of his career researching how operant conditioning principles can be used to modify behaviors in positive ways. Late in his career, he changed his research to focus on whether or not these principles impact behaviors in the same way in different countries. Which psychological perspective best matches Dr. Keith's late-career research?

    (A) Sociocultural perspective
    (B) Behaviorism
    (C) Cognitive psychology
    (D) Humanistic perspective
    (E) Functionalism

15. Steve, your college roommate, tells you he wants to research how people throughout history became the "best they could be." He is fascinated by self-sacrificing people like Gandhi and Martin Luther King Jr. who devoted most of their lives to making others' lives better. He asks you what area of psychology he could research in order to find out more about these self-sacrificing historical figures. What area would you recommend?

    (A) Cognitive perspective
    (B) Behavior genetics
    (C) Personality psychology
    (D) Humanistic perspective
    (E) Gestalt psychology

NAMES

16. Sigmund Freud's perspective on psychology was most dependent on which of the following concepts?

    (A) Conformity
    (B) Repression
    (C) Naturalistic observation
    (D) Overjustification effect
    (E) Experimentation

17. Wilhelm Wundt presented subjects with an object, such as a piece of fruit, and asked them to describe their thoughts or perceptions of it, such as the object's color, its shape, and how it felt when touched. What did Wundt call this method?

    (A) Random assignment
    (B) Free association
    (C) Active listening
    (D) Shaping
    (E) Introspection

PERSPECTIVES

18. Dr. Leary conducts a study investigating whether the hormone oxytocin can be used to treat individuals who abuse opioids. Which psychological perspective is most applicable to Dr. Leary's study?

    (A) Humanistic
    (B) Behavioral
    (C) Evolutionary
    (D) Biological
    (E) Psychodynamic

Methods

Answers for Chapter 2 are on pages 199–210.

STIMULUS

Use the following data chart to answer questions 19–21.

Student	Classes Missed in a Semester	Grade Point Average
1	4	1.5
2	3	2.5
3	0	3.8
4	1	3.5
5	2	2.5
6	1	3.0
7	5	1.0
8	7	1.5
9	5	2.5
10	3	2.75

19. Researchers were interested in the relationship between the number of classes high school students missed during a semester and students' grade point averages. Which of the following scatter plots best represents the data presented in the chart?

(A)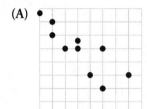

(B)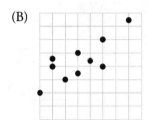

(C)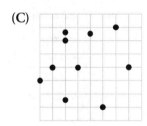

(D)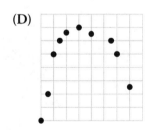

(E)

20. Based on the data presented in the chart, which of the following best describes the relationship between the number of classes missed during a semester and grade point average?

    (A) Positive
    (B) Perfect
    (C) Negative
    (D) Random
    (E) Significant

21. Which of the following newspaper headlines would be most appropriate in reporting the findings of this study?

    (A) "Missing Classes in High School Causes Bad Grades"
    (B) "Increased School Absences Benefit High School Students!"
    (C) "School Absenteeism Decreases High School Grade Point Averages"
    (D) "More Absences from School Linked to Poor Grades"
    (E) "Researchers Find No Link Between High School Attendance and Grades"

DEFINITIONS

22. Which of the following allows psychologists to generalize research findings to the intended population?

    (A) Replication
    (B) Random assignment
    (C) Double-blind technique
    (D) Use of a placebo
    (E) Random sampling

23. Theories

    (A) are statements of precise procedures used in a research study.
    (B) describe the characteristics of a sample.
    (C) are random methods used to sort participants into different groups.
    (D) are requirements in place to protect the welfare of research subjects.
    (E) organize and integrate information understood about a specific phenomenon.

24. In research, a specific testable prediction is a(n)

    (A) correlation
    (B) meta-analysis
    (C) theory
    (D) hypothesis
    (E) independent variable

25. Which of the following best illustrates the use of an operational definition?

    (A) "Students listening to music during class will have lower grade point averages than students who do not listen to music during class."
    (B) "Alcohol affects judgment."
    (C) "Happiness in college students is negatively impacted by the number of classes taken during a semester."
    (D) "Adults are more likely to experience empty nest syndrome later in life."
    (E) "Twelve-year-old children who watch violence on television will demonstrate less aggressive behavior if the characters are cartoons."

26. Which of the following is central for the replication of a research study?

    (A) Random sampling of research subjects
    (B) Operational definitions of procedures
    (C) Random assignment of participants into experimental or control conditions
    (D) Use of the double-blind procedure
    (E) Debriefing of participants

27. Of the following, what is a major drawback of using a case study?

    (A) The results cannot be generalized to a large population.
    (B) The particular wording of questions can affect the results.
    (C) Neither the researcher nor the subject knows what condition the subject has been assigned to.
    (D) Since case studies are conducted quickly, they may lead to inaccurate conclusions.
    (E) Manipulating certain variables is not ethical.

28. Naturalistic observation

    (A) requires the manipulation of variables to isolate cause and effect.
    (B) involves the in-depth investigation of individuals in unusual circumstances.
    (C) provides a large amount of information on many cases.
    (D) shows whether two variables are related.
    (E) allows for careful examination of behavior in native environments.

29. When conducting survey research, what must a researcher do to generalize the results to the population?

    (A) Randomly assign participants to groups
    (B) Use the double-blind technique
    (C) Operationally define the procedures used
    (D) Randomly sample participants
    (E) Obtain informed consent

30. Which of the following allows researchers to determine how well one variable predicts the presence of another variable?

    (A) Random assignment
    (B) Case studies
    (C) Correlational studies
    (D) Surveys
    (E) Statistical significance

31. A visual representation of a correlation is called a

    (A) normal curve
    (B) factor analysis
    (C) histogram
    (D) statistical significance
    (E) scatter plot

32. A correlation coefficient of +.70 indicates that

    (A) there is an inverse relationship between the two variables.
    (B) there is a very weak relationship between the two variables.
    (C) the finding is statistically significant.
    (D) as one variable increases, another variable increases.
    (E) the data are normally distributed.

33. Which of the following correlation coefficients reflects the weakest relationship between two variables?

    (A) −1.00
    (B) +.20
    (C) −.50
    (D) +.75
    (E) −.80

34. **Correlational studies**

    (A) compare individuals of different ages at a specific time.
    (B) use statistical procedures that combine the results of many research studies.
    (C) measure how spread out the numbers are from the mean.
    (D) determine how likely it is that research results occurred by chance.
    (E) reveal relationships between variables but do not prove cause and effect.

35. A researcher is interested in the relationship between age and height in children from infancy to 18 years old. What type of correlation would you predict would be found between these variables?

    (A) Negative
    (B) Perfect
    (C) Positive
    (D) Illusory
    (E) Significant

36. Which of the following best illustrates an illusory correlation?

    (A) A high school football player wears his lucky socks for every game because his team hasn't lost since he started wearing them.
    (B) After staring at a flag of green stripes against a yellow background, a man sees red stripes against a blue background when he shifts his gaze to a white surface.
    (C) You feel uncomfortable when you let someone copy off your paper after you have previously expressed that cheating is wrong.
    (D) A woman perceives color, motion, form, and depth simultaneously when observing a car driving down her street.
    (E) A person knows that juice poured from a short, wide glass remains the same amount when poured into a tall, thin glass.

37. Which of the following is the only method that allows a researcher to establish a cause-and-effect relationship?

    (A) Correlational studies
    (B) Case studies
    (C) Naturalistic observations
    (D) Surveys
    (E) Experimentation

38. Which of the following is unique to experimental design?

    (A) Random sampling
    (B) Positive correlations
    (C) Operational definitions
    (D) Random assignment
    (E) Descriptive statistics

39. In order to control for experimenter bias, researchers will often use

    (A) random assignment
    (B) inferential statistics
    (C) the double-blind technique
    (D) split-half reliability
    (E) random sampling

40. Which of the following measures of central tendency is most influenced by extreme scores?

    (A) Median
    (B) Range
    (C) Mode
    (D) Mean
    (E) Standard deviation

41. If the difference between the means of two groups is statistically significant, what does this mean?

    (A) The findings are important and will impact our understanding of a specific psychological phenomenon.
    (B) The scores in the distributions for the two groups are normally distributed.
    (C) Outliers have skewed the distribution of the scores for the different groups.
    (D) The two variables have a positive correlation.
    (E) The difference between the groups is not likely due to chance.

SCENARIOS

Use the following scenario to answer questions 42–44.

Researchers believe that an over-the-counter supplement may be useful in reducing memory impairment in older adults. They randomly assign 40 adults between the ages of 50 and 90 years who had mild memory impairments to receive either a placebo or 90 milligrams of the supplement twice daily for 18 months. At six-month intervals, researchers conduct various memory tests.

42. What type of research method is used to study the impact of the supplement on memory ability?
    (A) Survey
    (B) Case study
    (C) Naturalistic observation
    (D) Correlation
    (E) Experimentation

43. In the study described above, which of the following is the independent variable?
    (A) The supplement
    (B) The results of the memory tests
    (C) Adults between the ages of 50 and 90
    (D) The group that receives the placebo
    (E) The time periods between administration of the tests

44. Why is it important that the individuals participating in the study are randomly assigned to either the group that receives the supplement or to the group that receives the placebo?
    (A) This increases the likelihood that the two groups are the same so that any differences between the two groups are due to the manipulation.
    (B) Without random assignment, data collection could be inconsistent and the results could be inaccurate.
    (C) Keeping the researchers blind helps prevent their own expectations from influencing the results of the study.
    (D) This method helps participants make a knowledgeable decision about whether or not they want to be a part of the study.
    (E) If the study can be repeated, the researchers will have more confidence in the results.

45. Researchers were interested in whether drinking from a colored cup influenced perception of the sweetness of hot chocolate. Participants were divided into groups that received hot chocolate in either an orange-colored cup or a white cup. Researchers found that those who received colored cups found the hot chocolate to be sweeter. Those drinking hot chocolate from the orange cups

    (A) were participants in the control group.
    (B) were receiving the dependent variable.
    (C) were subjects in the experimental group.
    (D) were randomly sampled into this group.
    (E) were members of a placebo group.

46. In an experiment, investigators randomly assigned subjects to one of two groups. In the first group, subjects attended an event and used media to record it. In the second group, subjects attended the same event but did not use media to record it. Subjects were then asked to recall the event. Researchers found that the group not using media remembered the event more accurately. What was the independent variable in this experiment?

    (A) Use of media
    (B) Recall accuracy of the experience
    (C) Number of subjects
    (D) Type of personal experience
    (E) Enjoyment of the experience

47. Researchers were interested in the impact of age on memory recall. Thirty 25-year-olds and 75-year-olds were asked to rehearse a list of 15 unrelated nouns 20 times. Participants were then tested on their recall of the list. What is the dependent variable in this experiment?

    (A) The number of participants
    (B) The list of 15 unrelated nouns
    (C) The number of words recalled
    (D) The number of rehearsals of the list
    (E) The ages of the participants

48. A researcher found that the closer students sat to the front of the classroom, the higher their final grades in the course. This finding reflects a(n)

    (A) inverse relationship.
    (B) statistically significant result.
    (C) positive correlation.
    (D) negative skew.
    (E) placebo effect.

Use the following scenario to answer questions 49 and 50.

In a study investigating stereotyping, African American students, who were aware of a negative stereotype regarding their academic performance, were randomly assigned into one of two groups. Those in Group A were exposed to an encouraging message from an African American role model. Students in Group B were not exposed to such a message. Members of both groups completed a test comprised of items from the SAT exam. Researchers found that those exposed to the positive message earned higher test scores. At the conclusion of the study, students' names and their corresponding test scores were sent to all participants.

49. Why can researchers conclude there is a cause-and-effect relationship between the independent and dependent variables in the study described in the scenario?

    (A) The descriptive research methods used allowed researchers to maintain control of potential confounding variables.
    (B) The subjects were randomly assigned to either an experimental or a control group.
    (C) Researchers found a positive correlation between hearing a positive message and test scores.
    (D) Researchers found that students in Group A had higher test scores than those in Group B.
    (E) Researchers operationally defined the dependent variable.

50. In the study described in the scenario, how did researchers violate the current ethical guidelines regarding research participation?

    (A) Subjects were deceived and should have been debriefed at the conclusion of the study.
    (B) Researchers' values might affect their observations and interpretation of the results.
    (C) It wasn't fair that only members of one group received the encouraging message.
    (D) Researchers should have kept participants' names and test scores confidential.
    (E) SAT exams lack reliability and should not have been used to measure academic performance.

51. A preschool teacher measured the amount of time students engaged in positive social play. The following is the distribution of scores: 5, 10, 10, 10, 15, 25, 25, 30. What was the mean amount of time students engaged in positive social play?

    (A) 10 minutes
    (B) 12.5 minutes
    (C) 15 minutes
    (D) 16.25 minutes
    (E) 25 minutes

52. Six babies were born on the same evening in a local hospital. The following is the distribution of their birth weights (in grams): 3,866; 3,838; 3,837; 3,783; 3,746; 3,500; 1,745. What statistical measure would give the most accurate information about the variation in the data?

    (A) Mode
    (B) Mean
    (C) Standard deviation
    (D) Correlation coefficient
    (E) p value

53. A high school teacher collected the final test scores of students in her Honors United States History course. She found that the scores were normally distributed with a mean of 70 and a standard deviation of 10. What percentage of her students passed the exam with a score of 60 or above?

    (A) 34%
    (B) 68%
    (C) 84%
    (D) 95%
    (E) 99.7%

54. Researchers investigated whether students who distributed their study time earned higher grades on their final exams. Students were randomly assigned to two conditions. Group A (n = 35) studied a list of vocabulary words 15 minutes a night for 10 days. Group B (n = 35) studied the same list of words for 2.5 hours the night before the exam. Researchers found that in Group A, the mean test score was 80. In Group B, the mean test score was 70. Researchers determined that the results were statistically significant. What does statistical significance mean in the context of this study?

    (A) The p value is < .05.
    (B) The difference between groups is due to the manipulation of the independent variable.
    (C) The results are important.
    (D) The differences between the groups are not likely to have occurred by chance.
    (E) There is a strong positive correlation between distributed practice and ability to recall information.

NAMES

55. Sigmund Freud was contacted by the father of Little Hans, a 5-year-old with a phobia of horses. Freud analyzed Hans's dreams, statements, and emotional reactions. Then Freud concluded that Hans's fear of horses came from his Oedipal conflict. Horses symbolized Hans's father. Freud believed that Hans was having sexual fantasies about his mother and feared his father's retaliation. Thus, Little Hans displaced his fear of his father onto horses. What type of research method did Freud most likely use to draw his conclusions?

    (A) Survey
    (B) Case study
    (C) Naturalistic observation
    (D) Correlation
    (E) Experimentation

56. Research participants in Stanley Milgram's experiment were told it was an investigation into the effects of punishment on learning when it really concerned obedience to an authority figure. Based on today's ethical standards, what would Milgram be required to do because of this deception?

    (A) Obtain informed consent before beginning the study.
    (B) Keep information about participants confidential.
    (C) Attain approval from an Institutional Review Board (IRB).
    (D) Debrief participants at the conclusion of the study.
    (E) Protect participants from undue discomfort.

57. In 1953, 27-year-old H. M. had most of his hippocampus removed in an attempt to control his epileptic seizures. After surgery, H. M. lost the ability to form new memories. In the decades that followed, researchers tried to understand the role of the hippocampus in forming memory by conducting numerous studies. In studying H. M., researchers were

    (A) replicating earlier work.
    (B) conducting a case study.
    (C) pioneering the work on the retention curve.
    (D) determining a correlation coefficient.
    (E) operating a double-blind experiment.

58. In Elizabeth Loftus's groundbreaking experiment on memory, participants watched films of traffic accidents. Afterward, participants were asked to describe what had happened and were asked specific questions. Some groups were asked, "How fast were the cars going when they smashed into each other?" Others were asked, "How fast were the cars going when they contacted each other?" What is the independent variable in this experiment?

    (A) The films of the traffic accidents
    (B) The age of the participants
    (C) The speed reported by the participants
    (D) The number of participants in each group
    (E) The wording of the questions

RESEARCH METHODS

59. In a correlational study, researchers found that the more time students spent on social media, the lower their overall grades were. The relationship between these two variables is

    (A) a positive correlation.
    (B) a causal relationship.
    (C) a negative correlation.
    (D) statistically significant.
    (E) a reliable finding.

60. Psychologists were interested in whether or not individuals talking on the phone would be more likely to strike traffic cones while driving on a course than those who were not talking on the phone. This testable prediction would most likely be called a(n)

    (A) naturalistic observation.
    (B) hypothesis.
    (C) illusory correlation.
    (D) random sample.
    (E) theory.

61. Zajonc proposed that being watched by others generates physiological arousal that increases the probability that while performing a highly practiced task, a person will make fewer mistakes, but when doing an unpracticed task, a person will make more errors. Zajonc's proposal helps organize and explain human behavior as well as predict future actions. His explanation would most likely be called a(n)

    (A) hypothesis.
    (B) operational definition.
    (C) replication.
    (D) theory.
    (E) case study.

62. When is it appropriate to use a correlational study instead of experimentation?

    (A) When a researcher wishes to discover a cause-and-effect relationship
    (B) When a researcher wants to generalize from a small sample to a population
    (C) When a researcher is concerned about the impact of the placebo effect on the results of the study
    (D) When a researcher cannot randomly assign subjects to different conditions due to ethical concerns
    (E) When a researcher wants to establish if the results are statistically significant

Use the following scenario to answer questions 63–65.

Researchers Craik and Tulving showed 24 participants a list of 60 words and then asked them questions that included, "Was the word in upper or lower case?" which tests shallow structural processing or "Does the word _____ fit into this sentence?" which tests deeper semantic processing. The researchers found that participants recalled more words that required deeper processing.

63. Although the results supported the researchers' hypothesis, because of the small sample size critics might question this study's

    (A) replicability.
    (B) illusory correlation.
    (C) generalizability.
    (D) heritability.
    (E) ethics.

64. Critics of the study described above point out that learning lists of words is not necessarily how we learn information in our daily lives, making this task artificial. Such concerns raise questions about the

    (A) framing of this study.
    (B) validity of this study.
    (C) reliability of this study.
    (D) statistical significance of this study.
    (E) heritability of this study.

PERSPECTIVES

65. The research interests of Craik and Tulving are most consistent with which of the following psychological perspectives?

(A) Psychodynamic
(B) Behavioral
(C) Cognitive
(D) Neuroscience
(E) Social-cultural

66. Sigmund Freud suggested that traumatic experiences are repressed in the unconscious mind. He believed that although repressed feelings and memories are no longer accessible to our direct awareness, they fuel our behaviors and can lead to mental illness. From a scientific standpoint, why are Freud's ideas questioned today?

(A) There is no correlation between traumatic experiences and personal well-being.
(B) Freud's ideas are statistically significant, but they lack cohesiveness.
(C) Case studies, which are the basis of Freud's theories, are not considered valid research methods today.
(D) Testing Freud's assertions empirically would be difficult.
(E) Freud's ideas do not link behavior with the functions of the brain.

Biological Bases of Behavior

Answers for Chapter 3 are on pages 210–222.

STIMULUS

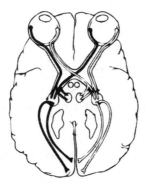

67. The image of a flower is projected to the left visual field, while the image of a basket is projected to the right visual field. In a right-handed split-brain patient, what would you predict would occur?

(A) Using his or her left hand, the person would be able to draw a picture of a basket.

(B) When asked what he or she saw, the person would say, "I saw a basket."

(C) Using his or her right hand, the person would pick up a flower from an array of objects.

(D) Because of the damage to the optic nerve, the person would be unable to respond.

(E) When asked what he or she saw, the person would say, "I saw a flower."

DEFINITIONS

68. Which part of the neuron receives the neurotransmitters from other cells and then combines that information?

    (A) Dendrites
    (B) Myelin sheath
    (C) Axon
    (D) Terminal branches
    (E) Vesicles

69. Which of the following is the nerve fiber in a neuron that conducts electrical impulses from the soma?

    (A) Dendrite
    (B) Terminal branch
    (C) Vesicle
    (D) Axon
    (E) Glial cell

70. How is the myelin sheath involved in the process of neural firing?

    (A) It provides support and nourishment for the neurons.
    (B) It contains the nucleus that directs all functions necessary for the cell's survival.
    (C) It is the junction between cells.
    (D) It is where excess neurotransmitters are reabsorbed and repackaged.
    (E) It insulates the cell and speeds up neural transmission.

71. When a neuron depolarizes, what does it produce that travels down the length of the axon?

    (A) Refractory period
    (B) Reflex
    (C) Action potential
    (D) Inhibitory impulse
    (E) Agonist

72. Which of the following surround and support neurons, provides insulation between cells, and participates in signal transmission?

    (A) Agonists
    (B) GABA
    (C) Interneurons
    (D) Glial cells
    (E) Receptor sites

73. Once a neuron reaches threshold, regardless of having a strong or a weak stimulus, it will always fire at the same intensity. This is referred to as

    (A) the difference threshold.
    (B) an all-or-none response.
    (C) the refractory period.
    (D) reuptake.
    (E) Weber's law.

74. Which of the following is the location in the neuron from which neurotransmitters are released into the synapse?

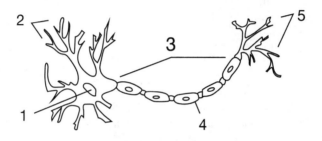

    (A) 1
    (B) 2
    (C) 3
    (D) 4
    (E) 5

75. No two neurons touch one another as they are separated by

    (A) a myelin sheath.
    (B) a synapse.
    (C) glial cells.
    (D) antagonists.
    (E) vesicles.

76. The process of neurotransmitters binding with the receptor sites is most like

    (A) a toilet flushing after the handle is pressed.
    (B) dominoes falling one by one.
    (C) a key fitting into a lock.
    (D) pushing a car's gas pedal to make the vehicle travel faster.
    (E) hitting a nail with a hammer.

77. **Excitatory impulses**

    (A) increase the likelihood that an action potential is initiated.
    (B) block a neurotransmitter's action at the synapse.
    (C) return the axon to its resting state.
    (D) produce a strong neural message.
    (E) cause the degradation of excess neurotransmitters at the synapse.

78. **Which of the following neurotransmitters plays an essential role in our experience of pain?**

    (A) Dopamine
    (B) Serotonin
    (C) Norepinephrine
    (D) Acetylcholine
    (E) Endorphins

79. **The central nervous system is comprised of**

    (A) the brain and spinal cord.
    (B) the hypothalamus and pituitary gland.
    (C) sensory and motor neurons.
    (D) the autonomic and somatic nervous systems.
    (E) the limbic and endocrine systems.

80. **Which of the following is responsible for initiating the fight or flight response?**

    (A) Parasympathetic nervous system
    (B) Endocrine system
    (C) Hippocampus
    (D) Sympathetic nervous system
    (E) Medulla

81. **Which brain scan measures the amount of glucose in various areas of the brain, allowing researchers to generate a picture of the brain's activity levels?**

    (A) Electroencephalogram (EEG)
    (B) Positron emission tomography (PET)
    (C) Magnetic resonance imaging (MRI)
    (D) Functional magnetic resonance imaging (fMRI)
    (E) Magnetoencephalography (MEG)

82. Which of the following are located in the brainstem?

    (A) Hippocampus and amygdala
    (B) Thalamus and hypothalamus
    (C) Corpus callosum
    (D) Cerebellum
    (E) Medulla and pons

83. Which of the following regions is associated with regulating heart rate, breathing, and other autonomic functions?

    (A) Thalamus
    (B) Hippocampus
    (C) Prefrontal cortex
    (D) Amygdala
    (E) Medulla

84. Which of the following relays sensory information to the cerebral cortex?

    (A) Hypothalamus
    (B) Pons
    (C) Reticular formation
    (D) Thalamus
    (E) Somatosensory cortex

85. The reward center of the brain is most associated with which of the following regions?

    (A) Thalamus
    (B) Cerebellum
    (C) Hypothalamus
    (D) Reticular formation
    (E) Amygdala

86. Which of the following includes the primary visual cortex?

    (A) Frontal lobe
    (B) Temporal lobe
    (C) Optic chiasm
    (D) Parietal lobe
    (E) Occipital lobe

87. Which of the following is responsible for integrating information from the primary sensory areas in the cortex?

    (A) Corpus callosum
    (B) Association areas
    (C) Limbic system
    (D) Somatosensory cortex
    (E) Wernicke's area

88. Which of the following is the band of fibers that connects the right and left hemispheres and that allows the brain to communicate internally?

    (A) Optic chiasm
    (B) Broca's area
    (C) Corpus callosum
    (D) Somatosensory cortex
    (E) Association areas

89. If the brain is damaged, it may reorganize itself and create new neural pathways to compensate. This is called

    (A) long-term potentiation.
    (B) dual processing.
    (C) blind sight.
    (D) plasticity.
    (E) lesioning.

90. The left hemisphere typically specializes in

    (A) spatial reasoning.
    (B) moving the left hand.
    (C) initiating reflexes.
    (D) language comprehension and speech production.
    (E) instigating the fight or flight response.

SCENARIOS

91. Which neurotransmitter would be most directly responsible for allowing Kaitlyn to swing her tennis racket?

    (A) GABA
    (B) Acetylcholine
    (C) Endorphins
    (D) Serotonin
    (E) Norepinephrine

92. Naloxone is a medication used to reverse opioid overdose. It works by binding to opioid receptors and then reversing and blocking the effects of opioids. Naloxone is a(n)

    (A) agonist.
    (B) endorphin.
    (C) reuptake inhibitor.
    (D) antagonist.
    (E) stimulant.

93. While walking home late at night, you see a shadow move into your peripheral vision. You suddenly feel your heart pounding, and you start sweating. Which of the following has been activated, initiating body responses to help you deal with this potential threat?

    (A) Parasympathetic nervous system
    (B) Reflex arc
    (C) Sympathetic nervous system
    (D) Limbic system
    (E) Central nervous system

94. Henry has been experiencing severe headaches, problems with maintaining balance, memory loss, and nausea. His physician suspects that Henry may have a brain tumor. Which of the following would be the most appropriate technique to determine if a tumor is present?

    (A) Triarchic abilities test
    (B) Electroencephalogram (EEG)
    (C) Lesioning
    (D) Magnetic resonance imaging (MRI)
    (E) Transcranial magnetic stimulation (TMS)

95. Carl had a tumor attached to his cerebellum. Once the tumor was removed, he experienced a number of major changes in his day-to-day functioning. Which of the following would be expected after the removal of part of Carl's cerebellum?

    (A) Inability to form new memories
    (B) Difficulty seeing a portion of the visual field
    (C) Numbness on his left side
    (D) Trouble in recognizing facial expressions related to distress
    (E) Uncoordinated and jerky movements

96. Clive Wearing, an English musician, suffered brain damage from a viral infection. As a result, he lost the ability to form any new memories. Which part of Clive's brain was damaged?

    (A) Cerebellum
    (B) Hypothalamus
    (C) Frontal lobe
    (D) Hippocampus
    (E) Somatosensory cortex

97. Allison walked outside into the heat of a summer day. As a result, Allison's blood temperature increased, causing certain cells in her brain to increase their neural firing. Consequently, Allison began sweating to release the heat. What brain region functions to maintain Allison's internal temperature?

    (A) Hippocampus
    (B) Amygdala
    (C) Hypothalamus
    (D) Temporal lobe
    (E) Somatosensory cortex

98. When researchers electrically stimulated a region of a cat's brain, the previously calm animal became aggressive and threatening. Which region of the brain was most likely stimulated?

    (A) Amygdala
    (B) Pons
    (C) Medulla
    (D) Cerebellum
    (E) Thalamus

99. James stayed up late studying for an exam but was able to stay alert in class. What part of James's brain helped him pay attention and stay alert even when he was feeling sleepy?

    (A) Cerebellum
    (B) Corpus callosum
    (C) Medulla
    (D) Hypothalamus
    (E) Reticular formation

100. The image of your friend's face that is on the retinas in your eyes is sent to your brain through the optic nerve. Before you can perceive your friend's face, though, the image must be received and transmitted to the visual cortex by the

    (A) hypothalamus.
    (B) corpus callosum.
    (C) spinal cord.
    (D) thalamus.
    (E) pons.

101. Fiona is deciding what college she should attend in the fall. She made a list of all of the pros and cons for every school she's considering. As she deliberately and consciously weighs each choice, which brain region is primarily activated?

    (A) Temporal lobe
    (B) Prefrontal cortex
    (C) Limbic system
    (D) Reticular formation
    (E) Parietal lobe

102. Stimulation of the somatosensory cortex would most likely lead to which of the following?

    (A) Moving your right hand to pick up a pencil
    (B) Hearing your favorite song on the car radio
    (C) Increased heart rate and feeling your fingers tingling before a job interview
    (D) Feeling your hair brushing against your forehead
    (E) Turning to pay attention to a car backfiring as it drives past

103. Which of the following best demonstrates the concept of brain plasticity?

    (A) Railroad worker Phineas Gage reportedly experienced a change in personality after an accident where a metal rod passed through his frontal lobe.
    (B) After researchers implanted electrodes into the motor cortex of a paralyzed patient, Gayle was able to control a prosthetic hand with her thoughts.
    (C) Donald, who is a split-brain patient, is able to draw a circle with his left hand and simultaneously draw a square with his right hand.
    (D) Four-year-old Jill, whose left hemisphere was removed due to seizures, regained use of her right hand after intensive therapy.
    (E) A reduction in Parkinson's tremors occurred when embedded electrodes provided electrical impulses to specific targets in Charlie's brain.

104. Aidan has red hair, but both of his parents have brown hair. Aidan has inherited
    (A) two dominant genes.
    (B) two recessive genes.
    (C) one dominant gene and one recessive gene.
    (D) one dominant gene only.
    (E) one recessive gene only.

NAMES

105. Physician Paul Broca saw a patient called Tan. The patient was called this because after his stroke, it was the only word he could say. Broca suspected that a specific area of Tan's brain had been damaged. Where is the region that Broca proposed was responsible for the production of speech?
    (A) The corpus callosum
    (B) The right temporal lobe
    (C) The right parietal lobe
    (D) The left frontal lobe
    (E) The cerebellum

106. Evolutionary psychologists attempt to explain the existence of beneficial psychological traits as the products of natural selection. Which of the following researchers was a primary contributor to this perspective?
    (A) Walter Penfield
    (B) Wilhelm Wundt
    (C) John Locke
    (D) Edward Titchener
    (E) Charles Darwin

107. The research of Roger Sperry and Michael Gazzaniga established that
    (A) being raised in stimulating environments leads to changes in neural structure.
    (B) areas of the body that require fine motor control, such as the hands, took up more space in the motor cortex.
    (C) bumps on the skull were associated with specific traits.
    (D) the building blocks of the nervous system were neurons.
    (E) the left and right hemispheres specialize in specific tasks, such as language ability.

108. Stroke patients may be able to produce fluent speech, but the phrases lack meaning. Which area of the brain has most likely been damaged?

    (A) Limbic system
    (B) Broca's area
    (C) Somatosensory cortex
    (D) Wernicke's area
    (E) Thalamus

109. Thomas Bouchard, in the Minnesota Twin Study, reunited many twins separated at birth to study the impact of genetics on their cognitive and personality traits. Which of the following findings supports the hypothesis that genes play an important role in the development of differences in human traits, such as intelligence?

    (A) Monozygotic twins are less similar than fraternal twins on intelligence test scores.
    (B) Identical twins reared apart are as similar to one another as identical twins reared together.
    (C) There has been a steady increase in performance on intelligence tests, known as the Flynn effect.
    (D) Identical twins tend to be treated more similarly by parents, peers, and others than do fraternal twins.
    (E) If people choose mates similar to themselves, fraternal twins could share more than 50% of their genes as they would receive similar genes from their parents.

110. Giacomo Rizzolatti wired monkeys with electrodes implanted next to the motor cortex to monitor neural activity involved in formulating plans and performing physical actions. He found that when a monkey put a peanut into its mouth, these neurons would fire. He also found that when the monkeys watched either other monkeys or humans put a peanut in their mouths, the same neurons would fire. Rizzolatti found what is now referred to as

    (A) synaptic receptors.
    (B) mirror neurons.
    (C) glial cells.
    (D) interneurons.
    (E) agonists.

RESEARCH METHODS

Use the following scenario to answer questions 111–114.

Rosenzweig investigated the impact of the environment on the cerebral cortex. Twelve sets of 3 male laboratory rats, each set from the same litter, were randomly assigned to different environments. Each group was supplied with adequate food and water. One member of each group was assigned to a different sort of cage: a standard cage with other rats, a small impoverished cage where the rat was isolated, or an enriched cage with other rats and multiple toys. Researchers found that the cerebral cortexes in the rats raised in the enriched cage were heavier and thicker.

111. **What research method did Rosenzweig employ in his research? How do you know?**
    (A) This was a correlational study; researchers investigated the relationship between two variables.
    (B) This was a naturalistic observation; the rats were carefully observed in their environment.
    (C) This was an experiment; the rats were randomly assigned to different conditions.
    (D) This was a longitudinal study; the same group of rats were studied and tested over a long period of time.
    (E) This was a case study; researchers collected extremely detailed information on a small sample.

112. **In Rosenzweig's research, what is the independent variable?**
    (A) The sex of each rat
    (B) The measured differences of the cerebral cortexes
    (C) The nourishment provided
    (D) The different cage environments
    (E) The natural intelligence of the rats

113. After the rats in Rosenzweig's research lived in the varying environments, their brains were autopsied and studied. The inspection was done in random order with each rat being assigned a number so that the person doing the examination would not know if the rat was raised in an enriched, standard, or impoverished condition. Which of the following is the best explanation as to why researchers would use this technique?

    (A) This technique allows the study to be replicated by other researchers.
    (B) This technique equalizes any differences among the different rats in each group.
    (C) This technique allows researchers to generalize their results to the larger population.
    (D) This technique allows the researchers to determine if the results were statistically significant.
    (E) This technique helps control for experimenter bias.

114. Critics of Rosenzweig's research suggested that the differences in the cerebral cortex may have been due to the handling the "enriched" rats received twice a day when researchers took the rats from the cage and changed the available toys. In this case, handling could have

    (A) been a dependent variable.
    (B) increased confidence in the internal validity of the study.
    (C) acted as a confounding variable.
    (D) led to a negative correlation.
    (E) been a placebo.

115. A biological psychologist interested in the role of the hippocampus in memory might surgically remove the hippocampus from a rat's brain and then assess the rat's ability to complete a variety of memory tasks. The technique of destroying cells to measure their impact on brain functioning is called

    (A) electroconvulsive therapy (ECT).
    (B) a lobotomy.
    (C) lesioning.
    (D) split-brain.
    (E) neurogenesis.

116. Biological psychologists may use indirect methods to assess brain damage. A patient was shown a drawing of a house and asked to copy it. The drawing below shows the original (model) drawing on the left and the patient's drawing on the right. Based on the patient's copy, which of the following appears to have sustained damage?

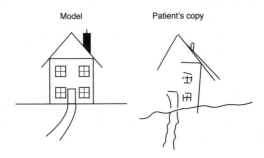

Model   Patient's copy

(A) The optic nerve
(B) The reticular formation
(C) The right hemisphere
(D) The cerebellum
(E) The limbic system

PERSPECTIVES

117. A psychologist who suggests that low levels of serotonin and norepinephrine are associated with depression would most likely be considered a(n)

(A) evolutionary psychologist.
(B) cognitive psychologist.
(C) developmental psychologist.
(D) biological psychologist.
(E) health psychologist.

118. Which of the following would a biological psychologist focus on when understanding happiness?

(A) Using a more positive explanatory style
(B) Finding out why life is worth living and experiencing flow
(C) The role of dopamine in producing feelings of pleasure
(D) Determining if a person has an internal or an external locus of control
(E) Comparing oneself to others

119. If a psychologist uses functional magnetic resonance imaging (fMRI) as a part of his or her research, with what perspective does the psychologist most likely identify?

    (A) Cognitive
    (B) Evolutionary
    (C) Behavioral
    (D) Biological
    (E) Psychodynamic

120. Psychologists who study the influence of genes and environment on individual differences in behavior are called

    (A) evolutionary psychologists.
    (B) social-cultural psychologists.
    (C) psychiatrists.
    (D) cognitive psychologists.
    (E) behavior geneticists.

States of Consciousness

Answers for Chapter 4 are on pages 222–226.

STIMULUS

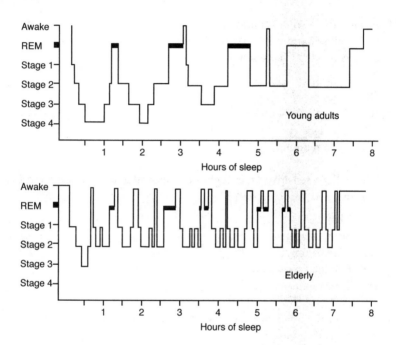

121. Which of the following best represents the information presented in the figure above?

   (A) During a typical night, younger people go through the sleep cycle more often than older people.
   (B) Older people spend less time during a typical night's sleep in NREM-3 than younger people.
   (C) Younger people are awakened more during the night than older people.
   (D) REM sleep comes right after NREM-3 sleep in both younger and older people.
   (E) Older people spend less time in lighter sleep than do younger people.

DEFINITIONS

122. **Which of the following best describes the circadian rhythm?**

    (A) False sensory experiences that happen during stage 1 sleep
    (B) The period of time when large, slow delta waves are produced
    (C) The sleep stage when bursts of activity are produced in the brain
    (D) During REM sleep when new neural connections are strengthened
    (E) A biological process that cycles between sleepiness and wakefulness

123. **As an individual drifts into stage 1 sleep, he or she might experience vivid hallucinations of images or sounds or might feel that his or her still body is moving. These sensations are referred to as**

    (A) delusions.
    (B) apnea.
    (C) manifest content.
    (D) hypnagogic.
    (E) REM rebound.

124. **Which light-sensitive brain region is responsible for activating circadian rhythms and inducing sleep?**

    (A) Medulla
    (B) Suprachiasmatic nucleus
    (C) Cerebellum
    (D) Reticular formation
    (E) Somatosensory cortex

125. **Which of the following best describes the process of consolidation that occurs in REM sleep?**

    (A) A period of increased production of human growth hormone by the pituitary gland
    (B) The time during which the brain attempts to make sense of random neural signals produced by the pons
    (C) When the production of ghrelin, a hormone that stimulates hunger sensations, increases
    (D) When recent memories are stored in long-term memory (LTM) by strengthening new neural connections
    (E) When REM increases in frequency and duration after deprivation

126. Why is REM sleep considered paradoxical?

    (A) The brain is highly active, but motor function is virtually absent.
    (B) After REM sleep deprivation, there is a tendency to spend more time in REM sleep during the next day's sleep cycle.
    (C) Delta waves are present during REM.
    (D) Infants spend more of their time asleep in REM than do adults.
    (E) REM sleep seems to be more important for promoting creative thinking.

127. With continued use, a person may experience a gradual decrease in his or her reaction to a drug. This is called

    (A) withdrawal.
    (B) diathesis stress.
    (C) tolerance.
    (D) generalization.
    (E) plasticity.

128. Which of the following is used primarily for pain relief?

    (A) Depressants
    (B) Stimulants
    (C) Hallucinogens
    (D) Narcotics
    (E) Inhalants

SCENARIOS

129. Kathy had a vivid dream of seeing brightly colored jeweled rings on each of her fingers. When she awoke, she consulted an online dream dictionary that suggested each jewel represented a value in herself that others admire. According to Sigmund Freud, this explanation represents

    (A) the manifest content of the dream.
    (B) a flashbulb memory.
    (C) the latent content of the dream.
    (D) her prototype of the concept.
    (E) top-down processing.

130. Kate is relaxed, has her eyes closed, and is lying in bed ready to sleep. If Kate's brain waves were being monitored on an electroencephalograph (EEG), what type of brain waves would you most likely see?

    (A) Theta
    (B) Delta
    (C) Alpha
    (D) Beta
    (E) Sleep spindles

131. Tack experiences sudden attacks of sleepiness where he falls to the ground and is unable to move. Tack most likely has

    (A) sleep apnea.
    (B) night terrors.
    (C) narcolepsy.
    (D) insomnia.
    (E) restless leg syndrome.

132. Kenneth abused prescription narcotics after knee surgery left him in constant pain. With the supervision of his doctor, he stopped taking the drugs. Within 24 hours, Kenneth experienced muscle aches, agitation, insomnia, sweating, and vomiting. These symptoms indicate that

    (A) Kenneth was psychologically addicted to the narcotics.
    (B) narcotics speed up Kenneth's central nervous system.
    (C) narcotics are not addictive.
    (D) Kenneth had a physical dependence on the drugs.
    (E) Kenneth will be unable to stop taking the drugs.

NAMES

133. Which of the following theorists first suggested that the unconscious mind is a reservoir of unacceptable thoughts, feelings, and wishes that directs our behavior?

    (A) Carl Jung
    (B) Carl Rogers
    (C) Karen Horney
    (D) Sigmund Freud
    (E) John Allan Hobson

RESEARCH METHODS

Use the following scenario to answer questions 134 and 135.

Researchers are investigating the impact of alcohol on judgment. Male subjects, aged 21–40, drank alcohol until they reached a blood alcohol content of 0.08%. Subjects were then asked to take 9 steps, heel to toe, along a straight line, turn, and walk back. The researchers observed to see if the subjects took an incorrect number of steps.

134. Which of the following is the operational definition of the dependent variable?

(A) Blood alcohol content of 0.08%
(B) Alcohol consumed
(C) The number of incorrect steps taken
(D) Age of the subjects
(E) Judgment

135. Subjects may come into this study having preconceived notions about how alcohol affects their behavior. This belief could impact the number of mistakes made in the subsequent task. How might researchers best control for this belief?

(A) Make sure that subjects drink the same amount of alcohol.
(B) Randomly sample the participants from the population.
(C) Randomly assign subjects to an experimental or to a placebo group.
(D) Use a correlational study instead of an experiment.
(E) Replicate the study.

PERSPECTIVES

136. Judith had a dream of being in a room full of stacked pancakes where she must eat her way out. Her analyst suggested that dreaming of pancakes indicates that Judith has several multilayered problems in her life that she needs to address. Her analyst's suggestion best reflects the focus of which of the following psychological perspectives?

(A) Behavioral
(B) Psychodynamic
(C) Humanistic
(D) Evolutionary
(E) Biological

137. Hobson and McCarley suggested that dreams occurred because the pons sent random signals to the cortex during REM that were integrated by the frontal lobe. Such an explanation for the existence of dreams reflects which of the following psychological perspectives?

    (A) Cognitive
    (B) Psychodynamic
    (C) Behavioral
    (D) Evolutionary
    (E) Biological

Sensation and Perception

Answers for Chapter 5 are on pages 226–236.

STIMULUS

Use the following description to answer questions 138–141.

"Think about what your brain and body are doing right now: somehow these letters are getting from the page into your brain [1], and you are comprehending that the letters make words that make sense. [2] While you are reading, you might feel cold or notice that your shoes are too tight [3], and somehow all those messages from the outside world are getting into your brain [4] so that you can deal with the world."

138. Look at the part of the excerpt marked with the number [1]. Which of the following sentences best describes what is happening at this point in the excerpt?

    (A) Perceptions are encountered by our brains and interpreted because of our past experiences.

    (B) Human brains are wired to understand language, so the letters are interpreted by our brains.

    (C) Light reflected from the page passes through the pupil and is projected onto the retina.

    (D) The process starts in the language center of the brain, which directs the eye to look at and understand the letters.

    (E) The person in the excerpt is likely to be a visual learner since he or she comprehends the letters so quickly and efficiently.

139. Look at the part of the excerpt marked with the number [2]. Which of the following terms is most appropriate for the process described at this point in the excerpt?

    (A) Sensation

    (B) Transduction

    (C) Potentiation

    (D) Perception

    (E) Adaptation

140. Look at the part of the excerpt marked with the number [3]. What part of the brain is mostly likely involved in the perceptions described at this point in the excerpt?

    (A) Motor cortex
    (B) Broca's area
    (C) Ventromedial hypothalamus
    (D) Frontal lobe
    (E) Somatosensory cortex

141. Look at the part of the excerpt marked with the number [4]. All the sensations described in the excerpt pass through which of the following brain structures before being sent to their final locations in the brain?

    (A) Thalamus
    (B) Parietal lobe
    (C) Synaptic gap
    (D) Central nervous system
    (E) Amygdala

DEFINITIONS

142. Which of the following is the best example of a sensation?

    (A) Light entering the eye and activating rods and cones in the retina
    (B) Feature detectors firing in the occipital lobe in response to impulses from the eye
    (C) Autonomic nervous system activation because of a perceived threat
    (D) Dopamine passing through a synaptic gap and activating the next neuron
    (E) The brain interpreting energy or chemical signals from the outside world

143. The following statement is an example of which term?

    "That bird in the tree made noise, and those sound waves traveled through the air and into my ear, where the sound waves moved neural cells in the cochlea."

    (A) Perception
    (B) Sensory adaptation
    (C) Trichromatic theory
    (D) Sensation
    (E) Convergence

144. Which of the following is the best example of a perception?

    (A) Light entering the eye through the pupil and activating neurons in the retina
    (B) Feature detectors firing in the occipital lobe in response to seeing a circle on a page
    (C) Sympathetic nervous system activation because of a friend jumping out at you from around a corner
    (D) Dopamine passing through a synaptic gap and activating the next neuron
    (E) One of the five senses firing because of a chemical or energy stimulus

145. As you read this question, your brain is using what you know about the English language to make meaning out of the letters on this page. What is this an example of?

    (A) Bottom-up processing
    (B) Selective attention
    (C) Top-down processing
    (D) Opponent-process theory
    (E) Monocular cues

146. You encounter a piece of abstract art at the museum, and it looks completely different from any art you've seen before. You are struggling to figure out what the artist was trying to represent in this piece of art. Which of the following perceptual processes might be most applicable to this example?

    (A) Bottom-up processing
    (B) Selective attention
    (C) Top-down processing
    (D) Opponent-process theory
    (E) Kinesthetic sense

147. You can tell if someone is whispering because you can see his or her lips moving, but the person is too far away for you to hear the sounds of the whispers. Which of the following terms would be the most useful if you tried to explain this phenomenon?

    (A) Difference threshold
    (B) Sensory adaptation
    (C) Vestibular sense
    (D) Weber's law
    (E) Absolute threshold

148. **Which of the following is the best definition of difference threshold?**

    (A) The minimum amount of energy or chemicals detectable by our senses
    (B) How much a sensation needs to change in order for us to detect that change
    (C) When our brain uses past knowledge or "rules" to help us interpret sensations
    (D) The difference between excitatory and inhibitory neurotransmitters, which determines if a neuron fires
    (E) How much our perception of a sensation decreases if we are constantly exposed to that stimulus

149. **We are bombarded with many stimuli all the time. Which of the following concepts would you use to explain to someone why we consciously perceive only a few of these stimuli?**

    (A) Bottom-up processing
    (B) Kinesthesis
    (C) Blind spot
    (D) Selective attention
    (E) Figure-ground

150. **You may be deep in thought as you try to answer this question, and you may not be aware of other events occurring around you. Which psychological term best explains this phenomenon?**

    (A) Absolute threshold
    (B) Selective attention
    (C) Mindfulness
    (D) Precognition
    (E) Perception

151. **Which of the following lists the parts of the eye most relevant to the processing of visual sensations?**

    (A) Cornea, cochlea, lens, pupil
    (B) Iris, fovea, frontal lobe, visual cortex
    (C) Gate-control theory, Broca's area, optic chiasm
    (D) Medulla, optic nerve, feature detectors
    (E) Pupil, lens, retina, rods, cones, optic nerve

152. **Which of the following is the most useful analogy for the role the pupil plays in the process of vision?**

(A) A telescope, bringing light into focus
(B) A movie screen with light projected onto it
(C) A smartphone, interpreting incoming messages in useful ways
(D) A curtain, opening or closing to let in the right amount of light
(E) A "contrast" button on a keyboard, adding or taking away light to make an image more clear

153. **Which of the following is the most useful analogy for the role the lens plays in the process of vision?**

(A) A telescope, bringing light into focus
(B) A movie screen with light projected onto it
(C) A smartphone, interpreting incoming messages in useful ways
(D) A curtain, opening or closing to let in the right amount of light
(E) A "contrast" button on a keyboard, adding or taking away light to make an image more clear

154. **Which of the following is the most useful analogy for the role the retina plays in the process of vision?**

(A) A telescope bringing light into focus
(B) A movie screen with light projected onto it
(C) A smartphone, interpreting incoming messages in useful ways
(D) A curtain, opening or closing to let in the right amount of light
(E) A "contrast" button on a keyboard, adding or taking away light to make an image more clear

155. **What causes the "blind spot" in the eye?**

(A) The occipital lobe doesn't have enough feature detectors to "cover" the entire retina, so some spots in the retina are, in effect, blind.
(B) Eyes are spaced apart on the human face, so there is a small space in the middle that falls between the visual fields; this is the blind spot.
(C) The place where the optic nerve attaches in the retina of each eye doesn't contain rods or cones; this is the blind spot in each eye.
(D) Every person is born with a small number of defective receptor cells in the retina of each eye; these cells can't fire reliably, creating the blind spot.
(E) Even though human eyes function well, human consciousness won't allow people to see some stimuli, creating blind spots unique to each person based on his or her past experiences.

156. In the back of each eye, the optic nerve connects to one of the important structures in the eye. What is that structure, and what phenomenon does this connection cause?

    (A) Retina; blind spot
    (B) Lens; retinal disparity
    (C) Iris; color constancy
    (D) Cornea; glaucoma
    (E) Pupil; binocular vision

157. Which of the following is an example of the process of transduction?

    (A) Sound waves entering the ear and moving the eardrum
    (B) Chewing food and absorbing chemicals into the tongue
    (C) Tipping your head back while practicing yoga
    (D) Light activating rods and cones, firing neurons in the optic nerve
    (E) Neurons in the prefrontal cortex firing in response to making a difficult decision

158. In every example of sensation and perception, either energy or chemicals are turned into neural impulses. What is this process called?

    (A) Transduction
    (B) Bottom-up processing
    (C) Convergence
    (D) Perceptual set
    (E) Action potential

159. Which of the following terms is the most clear stage or process that marks where the process of sensation ends and where perception begins?

    (A) Kinesthesis
    (B) Gestalt
    (C) Depolarization
    (D) Transduction
    (E) Dissociation

160. Where does transduction occur in the ear?

    (A) Tympanic membrane
    (B) Hammer
    (C) Cochlea
    (D) Anvil
    (E) Thalamus

161. Which two theories, when combined, best explain how humans perceive color?

    (A) Gestalt and vestibular theories
    (B) Trichromatic and opponent-process theories
    (C) Bottom-up and top-down theories
    (D) Figure-ground and signal detection theories
    (E) Absolute threshold and difference threshold theories

162. Which sensation and perception theory can most easily explain the phenomena of color afterimages?

    (A) Binocular vision
    (B) Retinal disparity
    (C) Trichromatic theory
    (D) Opponent-process theory
    (E) Color constancy

163. Some psychological concepts are very similar. Which of the following concepts is most similar to the cocktail party effect?

    (A) Identity formation
    (B) Spotlight syndrome
    (C) Selective attention
    (D) Egocentrism
    (E) Self-reference effect

SCENARIOS

164. You and your friends go to an art opening because the gallery promised to "show art like no one has seen before—you won't know what you are looking at, but your conception of art will be expanded." Which of the following perceptual principles will you most likely use since the art will be very abstract and unfamiliar?

    (A) Top-down processing
    (B) Signal detection theory
    (C) Selective attention
    (D) Opponent-process theory
    (E) Bottom-up processing

165. Professor Benjamin holds up a pound of feathers and a one-pound weight. He says, "If these two identical weights felt the same, we wouldn't need the science of psychology; we would need only physics." Professor Benjamin is probably trying to make a point about which of the following processes?

    (A) Perception
    (B) Sensation
    (C) Transduction
    (D) Kinesthesis
    (E) Vestibular

166. You are at a party with your friend Fred. The DJ is playing music you don't really like, and she's playing it very loudly. Fred shouts to you, "I THINK SHE IS ACTUALLY PLAYING THIS SONG LOUDER THAN THE LAST ONE!" You shout back, "HOW CAN YOU ACTUALLY TELL?" Which sensation principle determines whether or not Fred might actually be able to tell whether this song is louder than the last one?

    (A) Signal detection theory
    (B) Difference threshold
    (C) Binocular cues
    (D) Trephination
    (E) Perceptual set

167. The vice principal of your school, Mr. Drumknott, explains the school dress code to you (again) and then asks you if you understand. You feel embarrassed and admit to Mr. Drumknott that you don't understand because you didn't really hear what he said. Which of the following terms might help best explain why you didn't perceive the sensation of Mr. Drumknott's voice and words?

    (A) Transduction
    (B) Difference threshold
    (C) Selective attention
    (D) Projection
    (E) Operant conditioning

168. Someone challenges you to explain exactly what you are seeing right now and how you are seeing it. Which of the following terms are you most likely to use in your answer?

    (A) Sensation, threshold, selective attention, transduction
    (B) Optic nerve, cochlea, hair cells, Gestalt
    (C) Monocular cues, binocular cues, convergence, perception
    (D) Pupil, lens, retina, optic nerve
    (E) Signal detection theory, opponent-process theory, trichromatic theory

169. Someone challenges you to explain exactly what you are hearing right now and how you are perceiving what you're hearing. Which of the following terms are you most likely to use in your answer?

    (A) Eardrum, cochlea, hair cells, temporal lobe
    (B) Auditory nerve, thalamus, frontal lobe, temporal lobe
    (C) Pitch, tone, cochlea, transduction
    (D) Signal detection, bottom-up processing, receptor cells
    (E) Frequency, amplitude, brainstem, auditory cortex

170. You are watching the final round of the gymnastics championship at your school. The captain of the team, Sybil Ramkin, just finished an amazing routine on the uneven bars. As you watch her, you wonder how she knows where she is in space as she flips around the bar and how she makes sure she's in the right position to land perfectly on her feet. Which two sensory systems are most responsible for Sybil Ramkin's performance?

    (A) Vestibular system and sense of touch
    (B) Kinesthesis and vision
    (C) Hearing (inner ear) and gustation
    (D) Proprioception and olfaction
    (E) Transduction and kinesthesis

171. You are hanging out with your nephew Rufus at the park. Suddenly, Rufus looks at you excitedly and says, "Did you hear that? Someone is playing that song you like over in the neighborhood," while he points out into the neighborhood. You don't hear anything, but you smile and nod to be polite. Which perceptual principle explains why Rufus heard the song but you did not?

    (A) Difference threshold
    (B) Proprioception
    (C) Absolute threshold
    (D) Transduction
    (E) Structuralism

172. You are lying on your back in the park, staring at the clouds. Suddenly, you realize that a group of clouds to the left looks exactly like the face of your school mascot. What area of sensation and perception research and thinking might be most interested in perceptual issues related to you seeing your school mascot in the clouds?

    (A) Functionalists
    (B) Structuralists
    (C) Psychodynamic
    (D) Gestalt
    (E) Naturalistic observation

173. You are invited to an art class by one of your friends. She tells you that the art class will be a lot of fun because it will focus on how to portray depth more accurately in pencil and charcoal drawings. Which of the following perceptual principles is most relevant to this art class?

    (A) Binocular cues
    (B) Top-down processing
    (C) Retinal disparity
    (D) Bottom-up processing
    (E) Monocular cues

174. Leonard is on a trip to a debate tournament in a small, rural town he's never visited before. When he gets out of the van, Leonard immediately smells a strong odor of manure. Leonard wonders how anyone lives in the town with the constant smell of manure. What psychological principle explains why residents of the town do NOT constantly perceive that smell?

    (A) Sensory adaptation
    (B) Habituation
    (C) Perceptual set
    (D) Dissociation
    (E) Defense mechanism

175. When he was growing up, Samuel visited his aunt's house every day after school. His aunt had a large portrait titled *Lord Havelock* hanging over the fireplace. When his aunt first acquired the portrait, it startled Samuel. After a few weeks, he eventually stopped noticing and seeing it when he visited his aunt. What psychological principle explains why Samuel stopped seeing the portrait?

    (A) Sensory adaptation
    (B) Habituation
    (C) Blind spot
    (D) Occipital lobe
    (E) Perceptual omission

176. Mr. Slant, who bills himself as a "mental psychological stage performer," claims to be able to see "auras" that are in the infrared and ultraviolet spectrum. Which of the following psychological principles would researchers test in Mr. Slant in order to check his claim?

    (A) Difference threshold
    (B) Proprioception
    (C) Absolute threshold
    (D) Transduction
    (E) Structuralism

NAMES

177. The research of which two psychologists established the basis for the difference threshold?

    (A) Hubel and Wiesel
    (B) Skinner and Watson
    (C) Bandura and Beck
    (D) Weber and Fechner
    (E) Seligman and Peterson

178. Which two psychologists helped establish how the brain physiologically reacts to visual stimuli?

    (A) Hubel and Wiesel
    (B) Gazzaniga and Sperry
    (C) Eagleman and Ramachandran
    (D) Weber and Fechner
    (E) Gage and Wearing

179. **During brain surgery to remove a tumor in a patient's occipital lobe, a surgeon implants several very small microphones to listen for neurons firing as the patient looks at visual stimuli. The work of which researchers established the basis for this medical practice?**

(A) Nation and Benjamin
(B) Weber and Fechner
(C) Sternberg and Gardner
(D) Gazzaniga and Sperry
(E) Hubel and Wiesel

RESEARCH METHODS

180. **A researcher is interested in what factors influence which sensations we perceive and which sensations we don't notice. She decides to design an experiment to test her theory that distraction determines which visual stimuli are remembered. Which of the following is the researcher most likely to choose as an independent variable for her experiment?**

(A) Transduction
(B) Selective attention
(C) Absolute threshold
(D) Perceptual constancy
(E) Sensory habituation

181. **Which of the following is likely to be an operational definition of absolute threshold that a researcher might use during a study?**

(A) The random assignment to experimental or control conditions
(B) How intensely (bright, loud, etc.) the stimuli are presented during the experiment
(C) The minimum amount of stimulus a participant perceives in 50% of the trials
(D) The precise definitions of the operations involved in the methodology of the study
(E) Removing the influence of top-down processing, resulting in more accurate measurements of perceptions

182. Would it be possible to assign participants randomly to the experimental group and to the control group in a study about color blindness?

(A) Yes; random assignment is always possible if the sample is chosen carefully.

(B) Yes; random assignment is always used in the experimental method.

(C) It is impossible to determine whether random assignment can be used before the experiment begins.

(D) No; since the study is about color blindness, that trait would determine the group the participant is assigned to.

(E) No; random assignment is possible only when a researcher works with a team so that no one knows who is assigned to the control group and to the experimental group.

PERSPECTIVES

183. A patient reports that she is having trouble perceiving objects in her right visual field. She says that she's "not blind—I can see stuff on the right side, but I just can't tell what it is until I look at it dead on." Which of the psychological perspectives might be most useful when trying to explain the cause of this visual difficulty?

(A) Biological perspective

(B) Evolutionary perspective

(C) Psychoanalytic perspective

(D) Cognitive perspective

(E) Sociocultural perspective

184. The concept of perceptual set is most relevant to which psychological perspective?

(A) Biological

(B) Evolutionary

(C) Psychoanalytic

(D) Cognitive

(E) Humanist

185. Sociocultural psychologists would be most interested in research about how people from different cultures differ in their use of which of the following perceptual clues?

(A) Monocular cues

(B) Blind spot

(C) Transduction

(D) Absolute threshold

(E) Difference threshold

STIMULUS

Use the following information to answer questions 186–189.

The table below describes the behaviors of a rat named Sniffy. The psychologist working with Sniffy was investigating how giving or taking away food pellets related to whether Sniffy stood on her hind legs or not. In each of the four conditions listed in the table, Sniffy received a food pellet or a food pellet was taken away, and Sniffy stood on her hind legs or she didn't.

	Sniffy Received a Food Pellet	One of Sniffy's Food Pellets Was Taken Away
Sniffy Stood on Her Hind Legs	1	2
Sniffy Didn't Stand on Her Hind Legs	3	4

186. In the cell marked with the number 1, what kind of conditioning most likely took place?

(A) Negative reinforcement
(B) Classical conditioning
(C) Positive reinforcement
(D) Negative punishment
(E) Positive punishment

187. In the cell marked with the number 2, what kind of conditioning most likely took place?

(A) Negative reinforcement
(B) Classical conditioning
(C) Positive reinforcement
(D) Negative punishment
(E) Positive punishment

188. **In the cell marked with the number 3, what kind of conditioning most likely took place?**

    (A) Negative reinforcement
    (B) Classical conditioning
    (C) Positive reinforcement
    (D) Negative punishment
    (E) Positive punishment

189. **In the cell marked with the number 4, what kind of conditioning most likely took place?**

    (A) Negative reinforcement
    (B) Classical conditioning
    (C) Positive reinforcement
    (D) Negative punishment
    (E) Positive punishment

Use the following scenario to answer questions 190–193.

> A friend came to visit Dana and knocked on the door. After Dana opened the door, her dog Phinny saw the "stranger" and barked like crazy. This happened the next few times that a "stranger" knocked on Dana's door. Now Phinny barks whenever she hears anything that sounds like someone is knocking on the door.

190. **In this example, what is the unconditioned stimulus?**

    (A) Hearing a knock
    (B) Barking
    (C) Opening the door
    (D) Seeing a stranger
    (E) Generalization

191. **In this example, what is the conditioned stimulus?**

    (A) Hearing a knock
    (B) Barking
    (C) Opening the door
    (D) Seeing a stranger
    (E) Generalization

192. Which of the following is both the unconditioned response as well as the conditioned response?

   (A) Hearing a knock
   (B) Barking
   (C) Opening the door
   (D) Seeing a stranger
   (E) Generalization

193. The scenario says, "Now Phinny barks whenever she hears anything that sounds like someone is knocking on the door." This is an example of which of the following learning principles?

   (A) Discrimination
   (B) Spontaneous recovery
   (C) Extinction
   (D) Reinforcement
   (E) Generalization

DEFINITIONS

194. What type of conditioning involves pairing a neutral stimulus with a stimulus that already causes an automatic response?

   (A) Operant conditioning
   (B) Classical conditioning
   (C) Positive reinforcement
   (D) Negative reinforcement
   (E) Conjoined conditioning

195. What type of conditioning involves either providing or taking away a stimulus after an organism responds and then watching to see if the organism repeats that response?

   (A) Operant conditioning
   (B) Classical conditioning
   (C) Positive reinforcement
   (D) Negative reinforcement
   (E) Secondary reinforcement

196. **Which type of conditioning is most like the common practice of providing rewards for desired behaviors?**

    (A) Observational learning
    (B) Classical conditioning
    (C) Positive conditioning
    (D) Advantage learning
    (E) Operant conditioning

197. **Which of the following summaries best describes classical conditioning?**

    (A) Adding a stimulus or removing a stimulus after a response in order to influence an organism's behaviors
    (B) Waiting until an organism does something close to what the researcher wants it to do and giving the organism a reward
    (C) Finding a stimulus that automatically causes a response and pairing that with a new stimulus
    (D) Determining what the unconditioned response the researcher wants to condition and then figuring out the best reinforcement
    (E) Experimenting with the most effective, traditional schedule of reinforcement

198. **Which of the following summaries best describes operant conditioning?**

    (A) Examine how an organism interprets an event, and then modify the event to better match the organism's cognitive interpretation of the event.
    (B) Rewarding an organism will strengthen the researcher's relationship with that organism, and the organism will be more likely to do what the researcher wants.
    (C) When a researcher finds a stimulus that automatically causes an organism to do something, he or she pairs that stimulus with a new, neutral stimulus.
    (D) A researcher figures out what he or she wants the organism to do and then gives the organism something it wants when it gets close to that behavior.
    (E) Punish an organism via conditioned stimuli until the behavior conforms to desired parameters.

199. What term would a behaviorist use for an external event or object that elicits a behavior in an organism?

    (A) Punishment
    (B) Stimulus
    (C) Instinct
    (D) Response
    (E) Reinforcement

200. Which of the following is the best definition of a stimulus?

    (A) An external event or object that elicits a behavior in an organism
    (B) An external object that increases the chance an organism will repeat a behavior
    (C) Energy or a chemical that activates one of the human senses
    (D) A physical reaction or behavior elicited by an external event or object
    (E) An external object that decreases the chance an organism will repeat a behavior

201. Which term would a learning researcher use for a physical reaction or behavior elicited by an external event or object?

    (A) Punishment
    (B) Stimulus
    (C) Instinct
    (D) Response
    (E) Reinforcement

202. Which of the following is the best definition of a response?

    (A) A cognitive interpretation or a memory of an event
    (B) An external event or object that elicits a behavior in an organism
    (C) A long-term change in behavior caused by past experiences
    (D) External energy or chemicals that are changed into neural impulses
    (E) A physical reaction or behavior elicited by an external event or object

203. Which term describes something that automatically causes a physical reaction?

    (A) Conditioned stimulus
    (B) Unconditioned stimulus
    (C) Conditioned response
    (D) Unconditioned response
    (E) Behavioral contingency

204. Which term describes something a behaviorist would pair with an unconditioned stimulus in order to produce a classically conditioned response?

    (A) Conditioned stimulus
    (B) Positive reinforcement
    (C) Conditioned response
    (D) Unconditioned response
    (E) Negative reinforcement

205. Which of the following lists all the elements of classical conditioning?

    (A) Stimulus, reinforcement, response
    (B) Primary reinforcement, secondary reinforcement, continuous reinforcement, acquisition
    (C) Unconditioned stimulus, conditioned stimulus, unconditioned response, conditioned response
    (D) Behavior, generalization, acquisition, discrimination, response
    (E) Behavioral response, shaping, observational learning, modeling, latent learning, cognition

206. Which of the following is likely to occur when the conditioned stimulus is presented many times without the unconditioned stimulus?

    (A) Discrimination
    (B) Shaping
    (C) Spontaneous recovery
    (D) Extinction
    (E) Overjustification

207. Spontaneous recovery can happen only after which of the following stages of classical conditioning?

    (A) Generalization
    (B) Extinction
    (C) Punishment
    (D) Reinforcement
    (E) Deindividuation

208. Sometimes organisms begin to respond with the conditioned response to stimuli that are similar to the original conditioned stimulus. Which term below is the opposite of this process?

(A) Generalization
(B) Behaviorism
(C) Structuralism
(D) Overjustification
(E) Discrimination

209. Which of the following concepts would early behaviorists NOT be interested in researching?

(A) Acquisition
(B) Discrimination
(C) Cognition
(D) Extinction
(E) Shaping

210. Which of the following terms applies to both classical and operant conditioning?

(A) Unconditioned stimulus and conditioned response
(B) Generalization and discrimination
(C) Shaping and reinforcement
(D) Cognitive map and latent learning
(E) Observational and vicarious learning

211. To a behaviorist, what is the most important difference between reinforcement and punishment?

(A) Reinforcement increases the chances that a behavior will be repeated, and punishment decreases those chances.
(B) Organisms interpret reinforcements as rewards, and they interpret punishments as aversive.
(C) The major difference between reinforcements and punishments is the frequency of application.
(D) Reinforcements are generally less effective at modifying behavior in the long term.
(E) Punishments are used when behaviors need to be eliminated, while reinforcements are used when behaviors need to be decreased or just controlled.

212. Which of the following are two of the factors that differentiate schedules of reinforcement?

    (A) Frequency and amplitude
    (B) Positive and negative
    (C) Complete and partial
    (D) Interval and ratio
    (E) Cognitive and behavioral

213. How can you tell the difference between a conditioned response and an unconditioned response?

    (A) A conditioned response is elicited by the conditioned stimulus alone.
    (B) An unconditioned response occurs each time the conditioned stimulus is detected.
    (C) Conditioned responses are less frequent but more intense than unconditioned responses.
    (D) Unconditioned responses are caused by operant conditioning, and conditioned responses are caused by classical conditioning.
    (E) The unconditioned responses can be elicited only by primary reinforcers.

SCENARIOS

214. Professor Wilikins is demonstrating principles of learning to her class. She gently blows air into the eye of a student volunteer while saying the word "puff," and the puff of air makes the student blink. After three pairings, the student blinks when Professor Wilikins says "puff" but does not blow any air toward the student. What psychological principle is Professor Wilikins demonstrating?

    (A) Operant conditioning
    (B) Semantic conditioning
    (C) Latent learning
    (D) Expectancy effect
    (E) Classical conditioning

215. Dr. Hix has been working with a client for weeks in an effort to help him reduce his smoking habit. The client calls and is excited because he hasn't smoked for seven days in a row. Dr. Hix says, "That's great! Please check the reinforcement chart we made to see which reward you should give yourself." What kind of conditioning is Dr. Hix using to help this client?

    (A) Fixed-ratio schedule
    (B) Classical conditioning
    (C) Operant conditioning
    (D) Aversive conditioning
    (E) Positive punishment

216. My dog, Watch, looks up and starts salivating whenever she hears me pick up her dog bowl from the floor. If this response is classically conditioned, what is most likely the unconditioned stimulus?

    (A) Watch salivating
    (B) Watch looking up
    (C) The sound of the food bowl
    (D) Previous training about food
    (E) The smell of dog food

217. Mrs. Ridcully, a dog trainer, is struggling to train a dog to learn a new trick. Mrs. Ridcully classically conditioned the dog to sit whenever she whistled. However, the dog responds only to Mrs. Ridcully's specific whistle, not to the whistle of the dog's owner (who hired Mrs. Ridcully to train the dog). What operant principle is causing this difficulty?

    (A) Instinctive drift
    (B) Selective attention
    (C) Proactive interference
    (D) Discrimination
    (E) Extinction

218. Mr. Stibbons is frustrated with how much his son cries every time Mr. Stibbons tells him "no." Mr. Stibbons lectured his son for 20 minutes yesterday when this happened. Today, though, when Mr. Stibbons told his son "no," his son repeated the same crying behavior as before. What can we conclude based on this example?

    (A) The son keeps crying because he thinks he is the center of attention.
    (B) No classical conditioning relationship exists between frustration and crying.
    (C) Mr. Stibbons's lecture is probably not a punishment for his son.
    (D) The negative reinforcement of the lecture is not working.
    (E) Mr. Stibbons needs to use a positive reinforcement.

219. Mrs. Whitlow's third-period class is very noisy. The students constantly talk and are disruptive whenever Mrs. Whitlow tries to teach a lesson. However, Mrs. Whitlow notices that whenever she has students use their laptops during class, the students stop talking and the disruptive behaviors stop. Mrs. Whitlow starts to use the student laptops more during class. Which of the following terms best describes how Mrs. Whitlow's behavior was conditioned?

    (A) Negative reinforcement
    (B) Positive reinforcement
    (C) Aversion training
    (D) Positive modeling
    (E) Engagement strategy

220. When Ms. Brevis decides to train her cat to jump up into her lap on command, she uses cat treats to reinforce the jumping behavior. Later, though, Ms. Brevis notices that her cat is gaining weight because of the treats. What technique can Ms. Brevis use to maintain the desired behavior but avoid giving too many treats?

    (A) Classical conditioning instead of operant conditioning
    (B) Insight learning after initial conditioning
    (C) Negative reinforcement replacing the positive reinforcement
    (D) Spontaneous recovery after extinction
    (E) Fixed-ratio schedule of reinforcement

221. Mrs. Ogg, a computer programmer, is working on a project for a casino. The casino manager asked her to program a video poker machine to make sure that players win only after they get a winning hand and only after they have been playing for somewhere between 10 and 23 minutes. Which schedule of reinforcement best matches the program Mrs. Ogg is writing?

(A) Fixed-ratio schedule
(B) Variable-interval schedule
(C) Fixed-interval schedule
(D) Variable-ratio schedule
(E) Variable-frequency schedule

222. Dr. Reiman is developing the new summer reading program for children at her library. A few other librarians suggest giving the children ice cream coupons for every book they read. Dr. Reiman decides against this idea because she is concerned that giving rewards might decrease the children's intrinsic motivation to read. What learning principle supports Dr. Reiman's decision?

(A) Overjustification effect
(B) Primary reinforcement
(C) Secondary reinforcement
(D) Latent learning effect
(E) Proactive interference

223. Jason watches his brother Shawn sneak downstairs to play video games after they were both supposed to be in bed. Their parents don't wake up. Shawn comes back upstairs an hour later, says that playing the games was a lot of fun, and does not get in trouble. A few nights later, Jason sneaks downstairs to play video games. What kind of learning most influences Jason in this scenario?

(A) Positive reinforcement
(B) Vicarious reward
(C) Observational learning
(D) Obedience training
(E) Permissive parenting style

224. Olaf is the ringmaster at a local circus. He specializes is training small dogs to do amazing tricks, such as pulling open a file cabinet, getting out a file, balancing a sugar bowl on the nose, and serving Olaf a plate of salmon. You ask Olaf how he trains the dogs. He responds, "It's not that hard. I just wait to reward them when they do anything even close to what I want them to do, then reward them each time they get a little closer, and eventually I get them to do exactly what I want." What behavioral technique is Olaf describing?

    (A) Generalization
    (B) Conservation
    (C) Structuralism
    (D) Shaping
    (E) Functionalism

NAMES

225. Which of the following researchers was most involved with the earliest research into classical conditioning?

    (A) Ivan Pavlov
    (B) John Watson
    (C) Robert Rescorla
    (D) John Garcia
    (E) B. F. Skinner

226. Which of the following psychologists is most associated with operant conditioning research?

    (A) Ivan Pavlov
    (B) John Watson
    (C) Robert Rescorla
    (D) John Garcia
    (E) B. F. Skinner

227. Which of the following psychologists is most associated with establishing the behaviorist perspective as a dominant force in psychological thinking?

    (A) Ivan Pavlov
    (B) John Watson
    (C) Robert Rescorla
    (D) John Garcia
    (E) B. F. Skinner

228. **Which researcher is the most likely author of this quote?**

"Psychology as the behaviorist views it is a purely objective experimental branch of natural science. Its theoretical goal is the prediction and control of behavior. Introspection forms no essential part of its methods, nor is the scientific value of its data dependent upon the readiness with which they lend themselves to interpretation in terms of consciousness."

(A) Ivan Pavlov
(B) John Watson
(C) Robert Rescorla
(D) John Garcia
(E) Albert Bandura

229. **Which of the following researchers would have been most interested in cognitive interpretations of external events?**

(A) Albert Bandura
(B) John Watson
(C) B. F. Skinner
(D) John Garcia
(E) Ivan Pavlov

RESEARCH METHODS

230. **A researcher wants to investigate which conditioned responses are developed by children who grow up in extremely stressful homes. Which of the following research methods would the researcher need to use?**

(A) Experiment
(B) Survey
(C) Correlation
(D) Case study
(E) Random assignment

231. Esmerelda is a psychology graduate student researching different kinds of positive reinforcements on the behavior of pigeons. She randomly separates the pigeons into two groups. Birds in group A get a food pellet for pecking the target disk. Birds in group B get sweet-flavored water for pecking the target disk. What is the most likely operational definition of the dependent variable in this study?

    (A) The amount of food or flavored water each pigeon consumes
    (B) The number of pigeons in group A versus the number in group B
    (C) The number of times a pigeon pecks the target disk
    (D) The operant-conditioned responses resulting from the positive reinforcements
    (E) The difference in the amount of time pigeons in group A spent in the Skinner box versus the amount of time those in group B spent in the Skinner box

PERSPECTIVES

232. One of the most common current psychological therapies combines principles of behaviorism (like positive reinforcement) with talk therapy that focuses on how clients interpret past events and the actions of others. What is this approach to treatment called?

    (A) Behavioral psychotherapy
    (B) Rational emotive treatment
    (C) Reciprocal determinism
    (D) Humanistic behavioral therapy
    (E) Cognitive-behavioral therapy

233. Which of the following combinations of psychological perspectives emphasizes measuring observable phenomena carefully?

    (A) Humanism and psychoanalysis
    (B) Behaviorism and neuroscience
    (C) Cognitive and evolutionary
    (D) Structuralism and social-cultural
    (E) Incrementalism and psychometrics

Cognition

Answers for Chapter 7 are on pages 247–262.

STIMULUS

234. The graph below best illustrates which of the following?

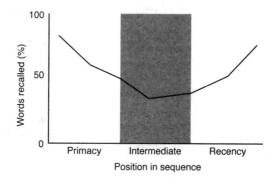

(A) The spacing effect
(B) The impact of elaborative rehearsal on recall
(C) Hermann Ebbinghaus's forgetting curve
(D) The effect of visual imagery on retention
(E) The serial position effect

DEFINITIONS

235. What are the three memory processes of the information-processing model?

(A) Sensory, short-term, long-term
(B) Shallow, intermediate, deep processing
(C) Recall, recognition, relearning
(D) Encoding, storage, retrieval
(E) Space, time, frequency

236. **Where are stored memories integrated with the information that is currently being processed?**

    (A) Iconic memory
    (B) Explicit memory
    (C) Working memory
    (D) Echoic memory
    (E) Broca's area

237. **Which of the following is an example of an explicit memory?**

    (A) Robert can play a song on the piano without having to look at his fingers.
    (B) Jessica can text her friend without having to think about where the letters are located.
    (C) Pari can shift gears in her car and, at the same time, have a conversation with a passenger.
    (D) McRae recalls the winning season his football team had during his senior year in high school.
    (E) James can automatically do a flip turn in the swimming pool.

238. **Which of the following refers to sensory memories that are devoted to storing auditory information?**

    (A) Iconic
    (B) Implicit
    (C) Explicit
    (D) Working
    (E) Echoic

239. **Which of the following is an example of chunking?**

    (A) Mentally placing items from your shopping list at specific points in your house and then later taking a mental walk around your house to help you recall where you put them
    (B) Grouping items on a shopping list as "frozen foods," "dairy," "fruits and vegetables," or "bakery"
    (C) Visually connecting items from your shopping list with a numbered list of rhyming words, such as "one is a bun" and "two is a shoe"
    (D) Rehearsing the items on your list for 5 minutes each day on Monday through Friday before your shopping trip on Saturday
    (E) Writing new lyrics to one of your favorite songs using the items on your shopping list

240. **Which region of the brain is primarily responsible for the formation of new memory?**

    (A) Hippocampus
    (B) Amygdala
    (C) Cerebellum
    (D) Frontal lobe
    (E) Hypothalamus

241. **Hearing the words "student," "bus," "desk," and "backpack" led to research participants more easily recalling the word "school," even though that word was not specifically mentioned. This demonstration best illustrates which of the following?**

    (A) Source amnesia
    (B) Priming
    (C) Chunking
    (D) Flashbulb memory
    (E) Echoic memory

242. **Which of the following examples most accurately illustrates mood congruent memory?**

    (A) Megan accidentally left her grocery list at home. As she tried to recall it while at the store, she could remember the first and last few items but had difficulty remembering items in the middle.
    (B) After Brian's stroke, he could remember details from important events in his past but had difficulty forming new memories.
    (C) Lillian could recall exactly where she was and what her elementary school teacher said when the teacher announced to the class that President John F. Kennedy had been assassinated.
    (D) While feeling sad after breaking up with her boyfriend, Jen was flooded with memories of other heartbreaking events in her life.
    (E) When Angie studied her notes for her United States history class, she tried to tie the events to places she had recently visited on a family trip.

243. **What is the primary difference between explicit memory and implicit memory?**

    (A) Explicit memory refers to information already stored in long-term memory, and implicit memory is the ability to form new memories.
    (B) Explicit memories are stored in the cerebellum, while implicit memories are stored throughout the cerebral cortex.
    (C) Explicit memory is primarily encoded semantically, and implicit memory is encoded based on visual or auditory cues.
    (D) Explicit memories are primarily echoic, while implicit memories are primarily iconic.
    (E) Explicit memories must be deliberately and consciously recalled, while implicit memories are automatically and unconsciously recalled.

244. **Which of the following is the most accurate example of a procedural memory?**

    (A) Recalling the names of all 50 states in the United States
    (B) Quizzing yourself on psychology terms before your big final exam
    (C) Riding your bicycle to school
    (D) Reciting a Shakespearean sonnet you've memorized for your English final exam
    (E) Telling your best friend about all the places you visited on your summer vacation

245. **Which of the following is limited to holding approximately 7 units of information for up to 30 seconds?**

    (A) Echoic memory
    (B) Iconic memory
    (C) Short-term memory
    (D) Semantic memory
    (E) Long-term memory

246. **The ability to focus on one aspect of the environment and block out others is called**

    (A) framing.
    (B) confirmation bias.
    (C) homeostasis.
    (D) mental set.
    (E) selective attention.

247. The best example of a category is referred to as a

     (A) concept.
     (B) prototype.
     (C) phoneme.
     (D) morpheme.
     (E) schema.

248. Answering questions on a multiple-choice exam requires that you narrow down your choices to one correct answer. This process is a good example of

     (A) trial and error.
     (B) functional fixedness.
     (C) divergent thinking.
     (D) incubation.
     (E) convergent thinking.

249. Making delicious chocolate chip cookies requires that you carefully follow the steps of a recipe. This best illustrates the use of

     (A) trial and error.
     (B) mental set.
     (C) an algorithm.
     (D) belief perseverance.
     (E) a heuristic.

250. Which of the following is the best example of the use of a heuristic?

     (A) Following the step-by-step instructions to fix a washing machine
     (B) Brainstorming ideas for your next short-story assignment in English class
     (C) Trying on and discarding multiple pairs of shoes to find just the right pair to wear with a new outfit
     (D) Deciding that the 7-foot-tall man you saw at the grocery store must have played professional basketball
     (E) Wearing broken glasses because you didn't think about using a paper clip to fix them

251. Which of the following is the best example of confirmation bias?

(A) When your car won't start, the first thing you check is your battery to see if you've left the lights on, just like you did last week.

(B) When solving a math problem, you approach it the same way you've always done, even though it takes more time than using a different method and is ultimately not working.

(C) When it's time to hang a new picture on the wall, you can't find a hammer so you use the heel of your shoe.

(D) Although the members of Brett's baseball team had batting averages around 0.300 and his average was a poor 0.218, Brett still couldn't understand why the coach couldn't see what a great hitter he was.

(E) Zoe believes climate change is a hoax. When writing a report, Zoe ignored data that supported climate change and focused on sources that supported her beliefs.

252. Executives are designing an advertising campaign for a new ice cream. One ad claims that the ice cream is "20% fat," while the other asserts that the product is "80% fat free." A sample of consumers in a market research study show a preference for the ice cream that is "80% fat free." The consumers' preference reflects the

(A) spacing effect.

(B) framing effect.

(C) spotlight effect.

(D) bystander effect.

(E) placebo effect.

253. What's the difference between an algorithm and a heuristic?

(A) When you use an algorithm, a solution is always guaranteed. However, using heuristics doesn't always lead to successful problem solving.

(B) Finding a solution takes more time when you use a heuristic than when you use an algorithm.

(C) When you use an algorithm, you have a sudden realization of how to solve a problem. This doesn't happen when you use a heuristic.

(D) Heuristics require that you follow a step-by-step procedure, while algorithms are mental shortcuts.

(E) Using a heuristic is more likely to lead to creative thinking than is using an algorithm.

254. When asked to decide what leads to more deaths in the United States per year, tornadoes or lightning strikes, most people say tornadoes. However, lightning strikes actually lead to more deaths. Because tornadoes receive more nationwide attention and press, these may impact people's impressions. This example best illustrates

    (A) the representativeness heuristic.
    (B) belief perseverance.
    (C) the availability heuristic.
    (D) confirmation bias.
    (E) divergent thinking.

255. The words "dine" and "dime" sound exactly the same except for the sounds "n" and "m." These sounds are different

    (A) phonemes.
    (B) morphemes.
    (C) prototypes.
    (D) memes.
    (E) mnemonics.

256. The words "antibody" and "antisocial" both contain the prefix "anti-," which means "opposite." A prefix is an example of

    (A) babbling.
    (B) a phoneme.
    (C) grammar.
    (D) a morpheme.
    (E) a prototype.

257. Saeed learned to speak Farsi as a child and immigrated to the United States when he was a teenager. As an adult, he is fluent in English but has difficulty pronouncing the "th" sound in the words "mother" and "father." When did Saeed lose the ability to discriminate and produce specific phonemes not found in his native language?

    (A) When he was prelinguistic
    (B) When he was cooing
    (C) When he was babbling
    (D) At the one-word stage
    (E) At the two-word stage

SCENARIOS

258. Micah has been practicing a piece for his piano recital for months. While playing, Micah has found that he can think about what happened at school and not lose his place in the piece. Micah's ability best illustrates which of the following?

    (A) Automatic processing
    (B) Framing
    (C) Cognitive dissonance
    (D) Stimulus generalization
    (E) Effortful processing

259. While Allison was watching a storm over the lake, a flash of lightning lit up the dark skies. Even though the flash of light disappeared from the sky quickly, Allison could still briefly "see" the light. It appears that this information was being held in Allison's

    (A) iconic memory.
    (B) short-term memory.
    (C) eidetic memory.
    (D) implicit memory.
    (E) flashbulb memory.

260. Audra is taking a multiple-choice test in her psychology class. Such a test is considered an example of

    (A) a recall test.
    (B) an implicit memory test.
    (C) a test of recognition.
    (D) an iconic memory test.
    (E) mood congruent memory.

261. Carrie finds that she remembers more when she studies 10 minutes each night instead of cramming the night before a test for 3 hours. Carrie is taking advantage of

    (A) the serial position effect.
    (B) the spacing effect.
    (C) semantic encoding.
    (D) the testing effect.
    (E) chunking.

262. Researchers found that when a rat's hippocampus was removed a few hours after the animal had learned where to find a treat, the memory for the event did not form. What process has primarily been disrupted?

(A) Chunking
(B) Serial processing
(C) Priming
(D) Consolidation
(E) Convergent thinking

263. Researchers used a ribbon to tie the ankle of a 3-month-old to a mobile hanging above a crib. The infant quickly learned that kicking his leg would make the mobile turn. When tested later, the infant kicked more when placed into the same crib. This finding best supports which of the following?

(A) Serial position effect
(B) Retroactive interference
(C) Infantile amnesia
(D) Context-dependent memory
(E) Retrograde amnesia

264. Sara is studying for her psychology test. Which of the following methods is most likely to help her encode the information into long-term memory?

(A) Repeating each concept 10 times
(B) Grouping the concepts based on the letter each word starts with
(C) Making flash cards of each word and its definition
(D) Creating personal examples and connections to the newly learned information
(E) Rewriting the concepts in different colors of ink

265. When you see your friend at lunch, she says, "I heard the best joke from my brother yesterday!" Then she tells you the same joke that you had told her yesterday. Your friend is most likely experiencing

(A) mood congruent memory.
(B) encoding failure.
(C) source amnesia.
(D) retrieval failure.
(E) retrograde amnesia.

266. Cade accepted an invitation for a blind date. His date described herself as having a medium build with long, dark hair. As he waits to meet her at the coffee shop, he focuses only on people who match that description and ignores anyone who doesn't. This best illustrates

   (A) cognitive dissonance.
   (B) social facilitation.
   (C) mere exposure effect.
   (D) selective attention.
   (E) reciprocity norm.

267. Which of the following is the best example of inattentional blindness?

   (A) Images disappear when they are projected on the part of the retina where the optic nerve leaves the eye.
   (B) You do not notice that your best friend is wearing a different shirt at the end of the school day than he wore during first period.
   (C) While sitting in a movie theater, the words "Buy popcorn" flash so quickly on the screen that you don't process them consciously. However, the message unconsciously influences you to get a snack.
   (D) You get in a car accident because you were texting and didn't notice that the car in front of you stopped.
   (E) When continually staring at a stabilized image of a triangle, parts of the image begin to fade and reappear.

268. Merle refuses to get a yearly flu shot because she believes that she will get the flu from the vaccine, even though her doctor has explained that the virus is inactive and cannot make her sick. Merle's resistance best illustrates which of the following?

   (A) Belief perseverance
   (B) Framing
   (C) Cognitive dissonance
   (D) Trial and error
   (E) Misinformation effect

269. Which of the following best illustrates telegraphic speech?

   (A) "Mine!"
   (B) "I love you, Daddy."
   (C) "Mommy goed to the store."
   (D) "Mommy up!"
   (E) "My dolly is cold."

270. A stroke patient heard the following sentence, "The boy wore a brown belt." Afterward, the patient had difficulty in correctly answering the question, "What color was the belt?" Which brain area has most likely been impacted by damage caused by the stroke?

(A) Broca's area
(B) The motor cortex in the frontal lobe
(C) Wernicke's area
(D) The somatosensory cortex
(E) The amygdala

271. In a study conducted by Dan Simons and Daniel Levin, a confederate holding a map asked a random pedestrian for directions. As they talked, two people holding a door walked in between them. During the interruption, the confederate was replaced by one of the people holding the door. Fifty percent of pedestrians failed to notice they were talking to a different person. Which of the following concepts best explains their findings?

(A) Belief perseverance
(B) Change blindness
(C) Episodic memory
(D) Mental set
(E) Source amnesia

272. Researchers have found that over 90% of American drivers believe they are better-than-average drivers. This belief can make them engage in more risky behaviors. This demonstrates the widespread impact of

(A) mental set.
(B) hindsight bias.
(C) source amnesia.
(D) overconfidence.
(E) the misinformation effect.

NAMES

273. When research participants were asked to listen to a series of 15 numbers and then recall them, most remembered 7 numbers. This finding best supports the research of which of the following psychologists?

(A) George Miller
(B) Hermann Ebbinghaus
(C) Alan Baddeley
(D) Richard Atkinson and Richard Shiffrin
(E) Eric R. Kandel and James H. Schwartz

274. Hermann Ebbinghaus studied lists of nonsense words, such as BAZ and LUR. He was interested in investigating the impact of the passage of time on memory retention. Which of the following best represents his findings?

(A)

(B)

(C)

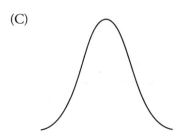

(D)

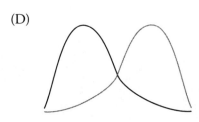

(E)

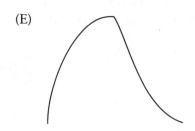

275. Which of the following psychologists demonstrated how easily misleading information can be incorporated into our memories, leading to the creation of false recollections?

(A) Hermann Ebbinghaus
(B) Mary Cover Jones
(C) Alan Baddeley
(D) George Miller
(E) Elizabeth Loftus

276. Benjamin Lee Whorf believed that if a language does not have a way to communicate about the past, those who speak that language cannot think about the past. His belief is referred to as

(A) aphasia.
(B) linguistic determinism.
(C) the language acquisition device.
(D) a critical period.
(E) receptive language.

277. Wolfgang Köhler challenged a chimpanzee, Sultan, to solve a number of problems. For example, Sultan was placed into a cage with fruit placed outside of his reach. He could reach a stick, but it was too short to reach the fruit. After surveying the situation, Sultan suddenly used the shorter stick to pull a longer stick to him and then used that longer stick to get the fruit. Köhler demonstrated Sultan's use of

(A) mental set.
(B) framing.
(C) an algorithm.
(D) insight.
(E) the availability heuristic.

278. Who suggested that all humans have the inborn ability to learn grammar rules?

(A) B. F. Skinner
(B) Paul Broca
(C) Carl Wernicke
(D) Noam Chomsky
(E) Benjamin Lee Whorf

RESEARCH METHODS

Use the following information to answer questions 279 and 280.

> In an experiment, researchers Loftus and Palmer (1974) asked a sample of 45 students from the University of Washington to watch a film of a car accident. Afterward, participants were asked either one of two questions: "About how fast were the cars going when they smashed into each other?" or "About how fast were the cars going when they hit each other?"

279. Loftus and Palmer found that participants who heard the word "smashed" estimated greater speeds. Which of the following is the dependent variable?

    (A) The number of participants
    (B) The location of the school the students attended
    (C) The wording of the questions asked
    (D) The reported speed of the cars
    (E) The educational level of the participants

280. In Loftus and Palmer's experiment, participants were all students at the University of Washington. As a result, these subjects may not be representative of the general population. For example, students may be younger, have higher intelligence test scores, or have better memories than people in the average population. Such a concern best illustrates which of the following?

    (A) Confirmation bias
    (B) Experimenter bias
    (C) Interviewer bias
    (D) Sampling bias
    (E) Hindsight bias

281. Researchers asked college females to judge the attractiveness of male faces on a 9-point scale. While looking at each face, participants were presented with either a pleasant or unpleasant scent. Participants rated the faces as being less attractive when presented with an unpleasant scent. What is the independent variable in this study?

    (A) The gender of the participants
    (B) The ability of the participants to recall the faces
    (C) Exposure to either a pleasant or an unpleasant scent
    (D) The attractiveness rating given to each picture
    (E) The educational level of the subjects

282. Researchers asked 10- and 12-year-old children to write text messages describing ten scenarios (for example, telling a friend that children missed the bus and would be late). Participants who used more textisms, such as abbreviations or symbols, tended to score more highly on a reading task. What is the primary reason why researchers should be cautious before concluding that using textisms causes greater reading ability?

    (A) This is a correlational study, so the subjects have not been randomly assigned to differing conditions to determine if a possible cause-and-effect relationship is present.
    (B) Using children in research is unethical because they cannot give researchers their informed consent prior to participating in the experiment.
    (C) In an experiment, confounding variables, like age, should be controlled or they would make it difficult to determine if a cause-and-effect relationship exists.
    (D) This is an experiment conducted in an artificial environment. To know if there is cause and effect, researchers need to consider text messages written by children in their everyday lives.
    (E) This is a case study, which is a descriptive research method and cannot be used to determine cause and effect.

283. Participants in a research study played a game where they were given the numbers 2, 4, 6. Participants were then asked to propose three other numbers to see if they could determine the rule behind the given numbers. Researchers found that the majority of their participants proposed sets of numbers such as "4, 8, 10," "6, 8, 12," or "20, 22, 24" based on their hypothesis that the rule was a "sequence of even numbers." Once the participants felt they knew the rule, they proposed only sequences that supported their incorrect beliefs. The correct rule was just three increasing numbers, meaning that 7, 9, 11 satisfies the rule. This research study best demonstrates

    (A) insight.
    (B) confirmation bias.
    (C) functional fixedness.
    (D) framing.
    (E) misinformation effect.

Use the following information to answer questions 284 and 285.

H. M. underwent brain surgery to stop his epileptic seizures. However, he experienced severe amnesia as a result. To investigate his remaining abilities, researchers asked H. M. to trace the outline of a 5-pointed star while watching his hand in a mirror.

284. H. M. could not remember doing the task. However, his performance improved. These findings suggest that

    (A) people have implicit and explicit memory systems.
    (B) deep processing leads to better memory retention than does shallow processing.
    (C) retrograde amnesia appears to be caused by damage to the hippocampus.
    (D) selective attention is vital to the encoding of new memories.
    (E) proactive interference hinders the ability to recall new information.

285. Which of the following was used in the long-term study of H. M.'s memory abilities?

    (A) Correlational study
    (B) Cross-sectional study
    (C) Case study
    (D) Survey
    (E) Randomization

PERSPECTIVES

286. Dr. Simonds is a psychologist interested in the techniques students use to improve their memory for class content. Dr. Simonds is most likely which type of psychologist?

    (A) Biological
    (B) Cognitive
    (C) Evolutionary
    (D) Sociocultural
    (E) Psychodynamic

287. B. F. Skinner believed that children learn language by associating words with meanings. The association is formed when a child is positively reinforced for saying a word or phrase correctly. B. F. Skinner's ideas best represent which of the following psychological perspectives?

    (A) Cognitive
    (B) Social-cultural
    (C) Sociocultural
    (D) Behavioral
    (E) Psychodynamic

288. As children acquire language, they overregularize grammatical rules, such as saying "tooths" instead of "teeth" or "foots" instead of "feet." This ability changes how which of the following perspectives views language development?

    (A) Cognitive
    (B) Behavioral
    (C) Evolutionary
    (D) Biological
    (E) Humanistic

Testing and Individual Differences

Answers for Chapter 8 are on pages 263–272.

STIMULUS

289. Most intelligence tests have a mean of 100 and a standard deviation of 15. Based on this information and on the IQ score distribution shown below, approximately what percentage of individuals are categorized as intellectually disabled?

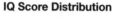

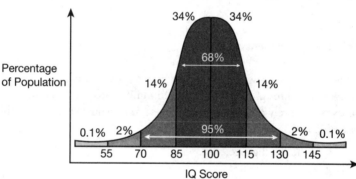

IQ Score Distribution

(A) 0.1
(B) 2.1
(C) 14
(D) 16.1
(E) 34

DEFINITIONS

290. Intelligence that is reflected in tests of mental ability, as suggested by Charles Spearman, is called

(A) practical intelligence.
(B) multiple intelligences.
(C) crystallized intelligence.
(D) general intelligence (*g*).
(E) the Flynn effect.

291. Factor analysis

    (A) is a statistical procedure that allows researchers to identify clusters of abilities.
    (B) is used to sample from the population randomly.
    (C) allows researchers to determine if the difference in group scores is statistically significant.
    (D) is used to compute the standard deviation for a distribution of test scores.
    (E) is used to determine the reliability of intelligence tests.

292. Howard Gardner suggested that an individual who excels at mentally manipulating objects and enjoys creating and interpreting visual images exhibits which of the following types of intelligence?

    (A) Bodily-kinesthetic
    (B) Crystallized
    (C) Spatial
    (D) Practical
    (E) Logical-mathematical

293. Robert Sternberg suggested that we have a type of intelligence that is not learned through training, is not found in books, and requires the individual to rely on personal experience to solve new problems. This triarchic intelligence is referred to as

    (A) analytic intelligence.
    (B) general intelligence.
    (C) creative intelligence.
    (D) emotional intelligence.
    (E) practical intelligence.

294. Which of the following is most similar to Spearman's concept of g?

    (A) Interpersonal intelligence
    (B) Analytical intelligence
    (C) Emotional intelligence
    (D) The Flynn effect
    (E) Existential intelligence

295. Of the following, who demonstrates a high level of emotional intelligence?

(A) Ken, an architect, enjoys the challenge of designing functional and beautiful buildings.

(B) Rik, a professional basketball player, is known for his agility and ability to handle the ball.

(C) Jane, a writer, reviews local concerts and musicals for the local news.

(D) Jim, a psychologist, investigates the relationship between brain development and learning.

(E) Elizabeth, an office manager, skillfully handles conflicts among employees.

296. An achievement test

(A) quantifies the abilities associated with high levels of emotional intelligence.

(B) assesses the skills associated with Sternberg's concept of creative intelligence.

(C) figures the standard deviation in a distribution of intelligence test scores.

(D) determines the reliability of an assessment tool.

(E) measures an individual's level of knowledge or skill in a specific area.

297. Which of the following refers to the measure of a person's intellectual attainment based on the age at which it takes the average person to achieve that same level?

(A) Aptitude

(B) Mental age

(C) Criterion

(D) Intrapersonal intelligence

(E) General intelligence

298. If an 8-year-old child does as well as the average 10-year-old child on an intelligence test, the 8-year-old child would have an IQ of

(A) 80

(B) 100

(C) 110

(D) 125

(E) 150

299. If an intelligence test is pretested with a representative sample, the test is

    (A) undergoing factor analysis.
    (B) being evaluated for its content validity.
    (C) determining heritability of intelligence.
    (D) undergoing a check on its reliability.
    (E) being standardized.

300. For an intelligence test with normally distributed scores, with a mean of 100, and with a standard deviation of 15, approximately what percentage of the population scored 70 and above?

    (A) 34
    (B) 50
    (C) 68
    (D) 84
    (E) 98

301. The Flynn effect refers to the

    (A) negative impact of a test taker's expectations on performance.
    (B) relative impact of nature and of nurture on intelligence.
    (C) increase of intelligence test scores over time.
    (D) difference between cross-sectional and longitudinal testing of intelligence at different ages.
    (E) ability to predict school achievement based on a comparison of mental and chronological ages.

302. If an individual takes the same test multiple times and the scores are consistent, the test is considered to be

    (A) valid.
    (B) standardized.
    (C) heritable.
    (D) reliable.
    (E) positively skewed.

303. The ability to think abstractly, reason quickly, identify patterns, and integrate information is referred to as

    (A) crystallized intelligence.
    (B) practical intelligence.
    (C) fluid intelligence.
    (D) intrapersonal intelligence.
    (E) savant syndrome.

304. Richard Lewontin designed a demonstration where genetically diverse seeds were planted into two different environments. He allowed them to grow to their full heights. One environment had barely enough light, water, and nutrients for the plants to survive. The other environment was ideal for plant growth. Lewontin suggested that the differing heights of the plants within one of the environments had to be due to the genetic differences in the seeds, and not the environment. This demonstration was developed to illustrate which of the following concepts?

    (A) Statistical significance
    (B) Heritability
    (C) Factor analysis
    (D) Predictive validity
    (E) Grit

SCENARIOS

305. When Sue's glasses broke while she was at school, she used a paper clip to hold them together until she could get them fixed. According to Robert Sternberg, Sue's solution shows a high level of which of the following intelligences?

    (A) Practical
    (B) Analytical
    (C) Bodily-kinesthetic
    (D) Spatial
    (E) Creative

306. Researchers found that when managers were trained to be more self-aware, to demonstrate empathy toward employees, and to manage their own and other's emotions more effectively, workers were more motivated and worked harder. These researchers linked work performance and

    (A) emotional intelligence.
    (B) creative intelligence.
    (C) analytical intelligence.
    (D) linguistic intelligence.
    (E) general intelligence.

307. Students in Mrs. Nielsen's third-period psychology class had 25 minutes to answer a free-response question, while students in her fourth-period class had only 15 minutes to answer the same question. To ensure that any differences in test scores were due to students' ability and not due to the time given, in the future Mrs. Nielsen should

    (A) make sure to use questions that reflect only the content covered in her class.
    (B) standardize the test.
    (C) administer a similar exam two weeks later and compare the students' scores.
    (D) conduct a split-half reliability test.
    (E) use the double-blind technique.

308. Mrs. Coburn wanted to determine if students interested in taking AP Psychology would be successful in the course. So, she designed the Psychology Abilities Test (PAT) and administered it to all of her incoming students. If the test has predictive validity,

    (A) Mrs. Coburn will find a positive correlation between PAT scores from the beginning and the end of the school year.
    (B) the mean, median, and mode of the PAT scores will be the same number.
    (C) the instructions, number of questions, and allotted time to take the test will be the same for every student.
    (D) students' responses on the PAT will accurately distinguish between fluid and crystallized intelligences.
    (E) the students' scores on the PAT will be positively correlated to their final grades in Mrs. Coburn's class.

309. Dr. Hammer developed an assessment to measure bias in the perception of women in STEM fields. He divided the assessment so that half of his subjects took the even-numbered items and the rest took the odd. He then looked at the correlation between the groups' scores. Dr. Hammer used this approach to determine if his scale

    (A) was standardized.
    (B) produced normally distributed scores.
    (C) accurately measured g.
    (D) had predictive validity.
    (E) was reliable.

310. Robert has been a bus driver for 30 years. Since he has been driving the same route for a good part of his career, he knows the streets and those who regularly take his bus very well. Over time, Robert has developed many skills that have made him successful in his career. Raymond Cattell would suggest that Robert demonstrates a high level of

    (A) fluid intelligence.
    (B) heritability.
    (C) naturalistic intelligence.
    (D) crystallized intelligence.
    (E) analytical intelligence.

311. It is suspected that 17-year-old Madelyn may have some learning disabilities. She is meeting with the school psychologist to take an intelligence test. This test measures not only her general intelligence but also assesses her verbal and performance abilities across 15 different subtests, including vocabulary and picture completion. Which of the following is Madelyn most likely taking?

    (A) The Stanford-Binet
    (B) The Myers-Briggs Type Indicator (MBTI)
    (C) The Wechsler Adult Intelligence Scale (WAIS)
    (D) The Binet-Simon intelligence scale
    (E) The Minnesota Multiphasic Personality Inventory (MMPI)

312. Leslie is intellectually disabled and blind, but he has a natural affinity for music. One evening, he listened to a song on a television program. In the morning, 14-year-old Leslie played Tchaikovsky's Piano Concerto No. 1 flawlessly, from memory. Since that time, Leslie only has to hear a piece and he can recreate it perfectly. Which of the following theories best explains savant syndrome?

    (A) Spearman's concept of g
    (B) Gardner's multiple intelligences
    (C) Emotional intelligence
    (D) Cattell's fluid intelligence
    (E) Binet's mental age

313. Which of the following statements reflects a fixed mindset rather than a growth mindset?

    (A) "This may take some time and effort."
    (B) "I can always improve, so I'll keep trying."
    (C) "Mistakes help me learn better."
    (D) "I am going to figure out how she does it."
    (E) "I just can't learn this."

NAMES

314. Who is known for introducing the concept of mental age?

    (A) Alfred Binet
    (B) Lewis Terman
    (C) Francis Galton
    (D) Charles Spearman
    (E) L. L. Thurstone

315. Who developed the Stanford-Binet test that has been widely used to measure intelligence?

    (A) Alfred Binet
    (B) Francis Galton
    (C) Lewis Terman
    (D) Charles Spearman
    (E) David Wechsler

316. Which of the following theorists would most likely agree that intelligence is fixed and determined solely by one's genetic inheritance?

    (A) Francis Galton
    (B) Carol Dweck
    (C) Howard Gardner
    (D) Raymond Cattell
    (E) Alfred Binet

317. Which of the following theorists differentiated between his belief in multiple intelligences and the myth of learning styles?

    (A) Howard Gardner
    (B) Robert Sternberg
    (C) Albert Bandura
    (D) Raymond Cattell
    (E) L. L. Thurstone

RESEARCH METHODS

318. If researchers discovered a positive correlation between students' college entrance exam scores and their freshman grade point averages, the researchers might conclude that the college entrance exam

    (A) is reliable.
    (B) has high content validity.
    (C) is biased.
    (D) has high predictive validity.
    (E) has been standardized.

319. A researcher developed a measure of happiness. She administered the measure to a group of 40 individuals and collected scores. Then the researcher waited for 3 months and administered it again. The researcher found that there was a +.80 correlation coefficient between scores on the measure. What might the researcher be able to conclude?

 (A) As scores on the first test increased, scores on the second test decreased.
 (B) The measure has high test-retest reliability.
 (C) The measure has high predictive validity.
 (D) The differences in scores are statistically significant.
 (E) The measure has high content validity.

320. In 1921, Lewis Terman began studying children with IQ scores over 135. He followed these children into adulthood, repeatedly administering intelligence tests and recording other measures, such as education level. Terman's method of study is considered

 (A) a double-blind procedure.
 (B) cross-sectional.
 (C) a naturalistic observation.
 (D) experimental.
 (E) longitudinal.

Use the following scenario to answer questions 321–323.

Researchers randomly assigned black students and white students to one of three different groups. Students in the first group were given a test and told it would assess their intellectual ability. Students in the second group were given the same test but were told that it was a simple problem-solving task and had nothing to do with intellectual ability. Students in the third group were also given the same test. They were told it had nothing to do with intellectual ability but that the test was challenging. Researchers found that black subjects in the first group performed worse on the test than did the white students. The researchers concluded that when we believe that others view us through the lens of a negative label, performance decreases.

321. What research method did these investigators use to study the impact of belief on performance?

 (A) A correlational study
 (B) A survey
 (C) A naturalistic observation
 (D) An experiment
 (E) A case study

322. Which group(s) acted as the control?

    (A) There was no need for a control group.
    (B) Group 1 was the control group.
    (C) Group 2 was the control group.
    (D) Group 3 was the control group.
    (E) Groups 2 and 3 were the control groups.

323. These researchers demonstrated that there is a decrease in performance when individuals believe that others will judge them according to a negative stereotype associated with their group membership. This is called

    (A) fundamental attribution error.
    (B) fixation.
    (C) belief perseverance.
    (D) framing.
    (E) stereotype threat.

PERSPECTIVES

324. Which of the following would be most interested in using twin studies to understand better the roles of nature and nurture on intelligence?

    (A) Psychoanalysts
    (B) Humanists
    (C) Behavior geneticists
    (D) Sociocultural psychologists
    (E) Behaviorists

Developmental Psychology

Answers for Chapter 9 are on pages 272–284.

STIMULUS

325. Which of the following best summarizes the information presented in the chart?

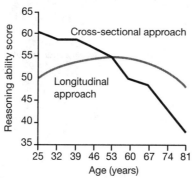

Cross-Sectional and Longitudinal Comparisons of Intellectual Change

(A) As individuals age, their scores on tests of reasoning ability decrease.

(B) Cross-sectional studies reveal that intelligence test scores remain fairly stable over time, while longitudinal studies demonstrate a steady decline in intelligence test scores.

(C) As individuals grow older, scores of reasoning ability increase.

(D) There is no correlation between age and intelligence test scores.

(E) The results of longitudinal studies suggest that intelligence is stable over the life span, while cross-sectional studies predict a decline.

DEFINITIONS

326. Which of the following best represents the nature position in the historical debate between the forces of nature and nurture on development?

   (A) Albert Bandura's research revealed that children learn aggression through observation and imitation.
   (B) Diana Baumrind suggested that different parenting styles impact the social and emotional development of children.
   (C) Konrad Lorenz demonstrated that attachment was innate in young ducklings.
   (D) B. F. Skinner believed that children acquire language through the principles of reinforcement as they begin associating words with specific meanings.
   (E) John Locke believed that all children are born as a "blank slate," where experience determines knowledge.

327. At conception, the egg and sperm fuse together to form a single cell called a

   (A) gene.
   (B) ovum.
   (C) zygote.
   (D) teratogen.
   (E) blastocyst.

328. Nine weeks after conception, the developing human organism is called a(n)

   (A) zygote.
   (B) neonate.
   (C) fetus.
   (D) gamete.
   (E) embryo.

329. Phenytoin is medication used to control seizures associated with epilepsy. If taken during the first trimester of pregnancy, there is a 10% chance that the baby will be born with birth defects, such as heart malformations. Phenytoin is

   (A) a monocular cue.
   (B) a glial cell.
   (C) dizygotic.
   (D) a teratogen.
   (E) heritable.

330. Typically, 4-month-old infants can lift their heads off the floor while lying on their stomachs. By 8 months, most can sit independently. This ordered sequence of motor development is a result of which of the following?

    (A) Assimilation
    (B) Scaffolding
    (C) Imprinting
    (D) Maturation
    (E) Accommodation

331. Research has demonstrated that children have very few, if any, conscious memories of events before age 4. Which of the following is most likely immature and therefore responsible for this infantile amnesia?

    (A) Reticular formation
    (B) Medulla
    (C) Hippocampus
    (D) Somatosensory cortex
    (E) Pituitary gland

332. Of the following children, who is demonstrating object permanence?

    (A) Three-year-old Amanda is upset when her pancake is cut into 5 pieces and her brother's identical pancake is cut into 10 pieces because "He gets more!"
    (B) When asked by her mother if she can "See her mommy" when 2-year-old Whitney has her own eyes covered, Whitney responds, "No!"
    (C) Ten-year-old Curtis understands that when 8 ounces of juice are poured from a short, wide glass into a tall, thin glass, the amount of juice remains the same.
    (D) Eight-month-old Brackstyn searches for his bunny toy when it is covered with his blanket.
    (E) Four-year-old Beau believes that his teddy bear gets cold if not covered with a blanket at night.

333. Which of the following represents the correct order of Piaget's stages of cognitive development?

    (A) Sensorimotor, concrete operational, preoperational, formal operational
    (B) Preoperational, sensorimotor, concrete operational, formal operational
    (C) Sensorimotor, preoperational, formal operational, concrete operational
    (D) Concrete operational, preoperational, formal operational, sensorimotor
    (E) Sensorimotor, preoperational, concrete operational, formal operational

334. Twelve-year-old Devin was asked, "If you were given a third eye, where would you put it?" Devin responded that he would put the eye onto his hand so he could see around corners. Devin's 10-year-old brother Brad said he would put a third eye "onto my forehead." According to Piaget, Devin's response demonstrates which stage of cognitive development?

    (A) Preoperational
    (B) Concrete operational
    (C) Conventional
    (D) Formal operational
    (E) Sensorimotor

335. Konrad Lorenz found that ducklings imprinted to the first moving object they see right after hatching. If ducklings saw Lorenz during this time, they followed him wherever he went and could not unlearn this behavior. Imprinting must occur during

    (A) the sensorimotor stage.
    (B) a critical period.
    (C) the identity stage of psychosocial development.
    (D) a zone of proximal development.
    (E) the preconventional stage.

336. Shawna is a very demanding parent. She is strict and expects her orders to be obeyed without question. If her children disobey, she withholds her affection from them. Shawna's parenting style is most likely

    (A) authoritative.
    (B) responsive.
    (C) authoritarian.
    (D) permissive.
    (E) neglecting.

337. Dr. Martin Luther King Jr. was arrested 30 times for demonstrating and participating in nonviolent protests against segregation. He felt that the laws at the time were unjust and that he had to break the law to bring attention to injustice in American society. Dr. King's reasoning would be characterized by Lawrence Kohlberg as

   (A) formal operational.
   (B) preconventional.
   (C) preoperational.
   (D) conventional.
   (E) postconventional.

338. Ryan is 20 years old and doesn't really feel like an adolescent anymore, but he doesn't feel like an adult either. He has changed jobs several times in the past few years while he has been going to school and living with his parents. Ryan feels unsure about his college major. However, he feels like he still has time to figure out what he wants his life to be like. Ryan's experiences best reflect which of the following?

   (A) Piaget's concrete operational stage of cognitive development
   (B) Erikson's psychosocial stage of initiative versus guilt
   (C) Freud's psychosexual stage of latency
   (D) Arnett's emerging adulthood
   (E) Kohlberg's preconventional morality

339. Regina is in her mid-30s and wants to find a romantic partner but is afraid of being rejected. She is not sure she could handle the pain of a breakup, so she tends to avoid getting into long-term relationships even though she is lonely. Erik Erikson would suggest that Regina is experiencing the psychosocial crises of

   (A) identity versus role confusion.
   (B) trust versus mistrust.
   (C) autonomy versus shame and doubt.
   (D) integrity versus despair.
   (E) intimacy versus isolation.

340. During childhood, connections between neurons increase. However, in adolescence, neurons that are underutilized are removed. This process is called

   (A) the all-or-none response.
   (B) a refractory period.
   (C) pruning.
   (D) habituation.
   (E) sensory adaptation.

341. LaMar is 85 years old and has difficulty remembering to take his daily heart medication. The type of memory that involves remembering something that we must do later and that commonly declines in older adulthood is called

 (A) flashbulb memory.
 (B) implicit memory.
 (C) iconic memory.
 (D) mood congruent memory.
 (E) prospective memory.

342. Which of the following is a common early symptom of Alzheimer's disease?

 (A) Failing to recognize a close family member
 (B) Forgetting events from many years past
 (C) Telling the same stories repeatedly
 (D) The inability to communicate with others
 (E) Difficulty learning new tasks

343. Research has found that regular exercise can slow the aging process by maintaining the DNA on either end of the chromosomes. These endings are called

 (A) telomeres.
 (B) agonists.
 (C) the myelin sheath.
 (D) synapses.
 (E) glial cells.

344. Which of the following refers to the biological differences between males and females, including differences in genitalia and genetics?

 (A) Sexual orientation
 (B) Sex
 (C) Androgyny
 (D) Gender
 (E) Identity

345. What is gender identity?

 (A) The cultural expectations for the behavior of men and women
 (B) The blending of masculine and feminine personality characteristics
 (C) Learning one's gender through modeling and imitation
 (D) One's internal sense of being male, female, or a blending of the two
 (E) The biological category we are assigned to based on our chromosomes and genitalia

SCENARIOS

346. Gerald is a fussy baby who does not like to be held, startles easily, and cries often. Gerald's characteristic pattern of behaving is referred to as

(A) habituation.
(B) object permanence.
(C) animism.
(D) androgyny.
(E) temperament.

347. Risa was raised in the United States and is familiar with fruit-flavored hard candies. In psychology class, she tastes a musk-flavored candy from Australia. Risa can't accept musk as a flavor because she associates it only with the scent of cologne. Apparently, Risa is struggling with which of the following?

(A) Assimilation
(B) Egocentrism
(C) Conservation
(D) Artificialism
(E) Habituation

348. A researcher shows a child a box of crayons and asks, "What do you think is in this box?" The child replies, "Crayons." The researcher then opens the box to reveal candles. The researcher closes the box and shows the child a stuffed dog toy that has been under the table. The researcher says, "This dog hasn't heard what we've said or seen what's inside the box. What do you think the dog will think is in the box?" If the child replies "Candles," this reflects that she most likely lacks

(A) conservation.
(B) a theory of mind.
(C) artificialism.
(D) object permanence.
(E) basic trust.

349. Pam took her 8 month old, Lisa, to see the pediatrician. When the doctor reached to take the child for her examination, Lisa began to cry and cling to her mother. Lisa is showing the signs of

(A) imprinting.
(B) habituation.
(C) conservation.
(D) animism.
(E) stranger anxiety.

350. Three-year-old Bergen is shown two equal-sized balls of clay and is asked, "Is there the same amount of clay in each ball?" The researcher then takes one of the balls and smashes it flat. Then he asks Bergen, "Now does each piece have the same amount of clay, or does one have more?" Bergen responds, "The smashed one has more." Bergen's response indicates that she in which stage of Piaget's theory of cognitive development?

    (A) Preoperational
    (B) Sensorimotor
    (C) Formal operational
    (D) Postformal thought
    (E) Concrete operational

351. When 2-year-old Andi has some bright red color dabbed on her nose, she immediately touches her nose when shown her face in the mirror. It appears that Andi has developed

    (A) object permanence.
    (B) self-concept.
    (C) basic trust.
    (D) secure attachment.
    (E) concrete operational thought.

352. Katie will not speed while driving to school because she's afraid of getting a ticket. Katie's reasoning best reflects which of Kohlberg's stages of moral development?

    (A) Preoperational
    (B) Preconventional
    (C) Conventional
    (D) Concrete operational
    (E) Postconventional

353. Lillie is 81 years old, is widowed, and lives alone. As she thinks about her long life, Lillie is comfortable with the choices she made and has come to terms with the thought that her time yet to live is short. Erik Erikson would suggest that Lillie has achieved a sense of

    (A) trust.
    (B) identity.
    (C) generativity.
    (D) integrity.
    (E) competence.

354. Every morning, 6-year-old Jackie watches her mother clean the house and take care of her baby sister. When Jackie plays, she often plays house and takes care of her dolls. When she does, Jackie's mother praises her and tells her that she is "just like Mommy." Which theory explains how Jackie is acquiring her sense of gender?

    (A) Gender schema
    (B) Social learning
    (C) Psychodynamic
    (D) Biological
    (E) Evolutionary

355. To test a child's cognitive development, Jean Piaget presented a three-dimensional model of 3 mountains. The mountains were of different sizes, colors, and features. For example, one had a house on it. Another mountain had snow on it. The child was allowed to look at the model and then was introduced to a doll that was able to see the mountains from a perspective different from the child's. When asked what the doll could see, that child might report that the doll could see exactly what the child could see, describing features that would be impossible for the doll to see. According to Piaget, this child is demonstrating

    (A) conservation.
    (B) preconventional reasoning.
    (C) insecure avoidant attachment.
    (D) generativity.
    (E) egocentrism.

356. Pablo is 17 years old and has recently begun questioning his beliefs. He has engaged in heated debates with his parents over differences in their political and religious ideals. Jean Piaget would suggest that Pablo is

    (A) entering the postconventional stage.
    (B) becoming formal operational.
    (C) struggling with the conflict of identity versus role confusion.
    (D) having an insecure attachment with his parents.
    (E) dealing with an unresolved Oedipal conflict.

357. Chandler and Alex's youngest child just graduated from high school and is moving to a different state for college. If they experience depression, stress, and loneliness as a result, some might suggest Chandler and Alex are experiencing

    (A) a midlife crisis.
    (B) identity versus role confusion.
    (C) stranger anxiety.
    (D) empty-nest syndrome.
    (E) insecure attachment.

358. Chuck is 45 years old and unmarried, lives with his parents, and is a freshman in college. Chuck's current state is atypical for someone his age. The expectations to marry, establish a home, and go to college by a certain time are determined by

    (A) the zone of proximal development.
    (B) heritability.
    (C) a critical period.
    (D) theory of mind.
    (E) the social clock.

NAMES

359. Harry Harlow studied infant monkeys raised with surrogate mothers. One mother was covered in soft cloth, while the other was made of wire. The wire mother provided nourishment, while the cloth mother was warm and able to rock. Based on Harlow's findings, what did he believe was the key factor in developing a strong attachment between a mother and her infant?

    (A) If the infant had developed a theory of mind
    (B) The development of object permanence
    (C) The warmth associated with close body contact
    (D) Receiving nourishment from the mother
    (E) The temperament of the infant

360. For his seventh birthday, Crew receives a new bicycle. He has never tried riding a two-wheeled bicycle without training wheels before. Crew's dad takes him out to a deserted parking lot. The dad helps by holding the bicycle and steadying Crew until Crew can balance and pedal on his own. This time period from beginner to expert that requires the help of an adult is referred to by Lev Vygotsky as

    (A) a period of assimilation.
    (B) the theory of mind.
    (C) formal operational thinking.
    (D) a zone of proximal development.
    (E) the conflict of autonomy versus shame and doubt.

361. What was the key feature in the parenting style of those tested in Mary Ainsworth's strange situation procedure that led to a secure attachment between the toddlers and their mothers?

    (A) Postconventional reasoning
    (B) Demands for obedience
    (C) Little use of punishment
    (D) Responsiveness to a child's needs
    (E) Extroverted personality

362. Two-month-old infants were shown a toy lion before it was hidden by a screen. When the lion reappeared, it was in a different location than the infants expected. Researchers found that these young infants stared longer at this impossible event, demonstrating surprise. The ability of these young infants challenges the conclusions of which of the following theorists?

    (A) Erik Erikson
    (B) Jean Piaget
    (C) Lawrence Kohlberg
    (D) Lev Vygotsky
    (E) Mary Ainsworth

363. What was Carol Gilligan's main criticism of Lawrence Kohlberg's stages of moral development?

   (A) What individuals say in response to the fictional Heinz dilemma would not be predictive of how they would behave in real life.
   (B) Kohlberg shouldn't have used a cross-sectional design because a longitudinal design would be a more accurate reflection of changes in moral development over the life span.
   (C) Kohlberg's theories favored individualistic cultures that emphasize personal rights over collectivist cultures that focus on the well-being of the group.
   (D) Kohlberg's scoring system was unreliable as coding certain responses as being exclusively in one specific stage of development was difficult.
   (E) Kohlberg's all-male sample was biased and reflected a male focus on justice in deciding moral questions while discounting female values, such as compassion.

RESEARCH METHODS

364. Correlational studies have linked parenting styles to specific outcomes in children. For example, children with authoritative parents tend to have higher levels of social competence. What is the primary reason we must be cautious before suggesting that a causal relationship exists?

   (A) Correlational studies do not show the relationship between two variables.
   (B) The situation might be artificial, and you can't generalize the results to the real world.
   (C) A third variable might be producing the relationship between the two variables.
   (D) Researchers may not have followed all ethical guidelines in the treatment of participants.
   (E) It must be determined if a double-blind procedure was used to reduce experimenter bias.

365. Researchers were interested in how reasoning ability may change across the life span. Researchers tested 5,000 individuals at 7-year intervals beginning in 1956. This research technique is called a(n)

   (A) case study.
   (B) longitudinal study.
   (C) experiment.
   (D) cross-sectional study.
   (E) naturalistic observation.

366. Which of the following depicts the use of habituation to investigate child development?

 (A) Measure the amount of time that infants stare when repeatedly shown a red circle and then compare it to the amount of time they stare when the shape becomes a green square.

 (B) Observe infants' reactions when shown a favorite toy and then when the toy is covered by a blanket.

 (C) Test infants for whether or not they can stand on their own and then compare those results to those for same-aged children.

 (D) Watch how a baby responds when separated from his or her mother and then when the baby is reunited with the mother.

 (E) Dab rouge onto a baby's nose, and then hold him or her up to a mirror to see if the baby will touch his or her nose.

367. In the 1960s, Walter Mischel tested children's ability to delay gratification by offering them one marshmallow they could eat immediately or two if they could wait. Later he found that those able to delay gratification had higher SAT scores. In 2018, researchers repeated Mischel's study and found the mother's educational level determined whether a child could delay gratification or had academic success. This case is an example of the importance of which of the following to science?

 (A) Using random sampling
 (B) Employing a double-blind technique
 (C) Replication
 (D) Determining statistical significance
 (E) Controlling for the placebo effect

368. Harry Harlow isolated newborn infant monkeys from other monkeys for a year. He demonstrated that those who were not part of a social group when young exhibited dysfunctional behavior when older, such as difficulty mating. Why has Harlow's study been criticized?

 (A) Harlow did not obtain informed consent before conducting his research.

 (B) Harlow deprived social animals of contact and caused excessive distress, which is inhumane.

 (C) Harlow did not clearly demonstrate that his research would increase knowledge of the processes underlying development.

 (D) Deception was used in Harlow's research, and participants were not adequately debriefed.

 (E) Confidentiality was not maintained to protect the welfare of the subjects.

PERSPECTIVES

369. Erik Erikson believed that the ego develops over a lifetime through a series of psychosocial crises. He suggested that social and environmental factors in a person's life exert a powerful influence over how the ego develops. Erikson's focus on the ego suggests that he identified as a

    (A) humanistic psychologist.
    (B) cognitive psychologist.
    (C) psychodynamic psychologist.
    (D) sociocultural psychologist.
    (E) biological psychologist.

370. John Bowlby suggested that infants were biologically preprogrammed to form attachments with others because doing so helps infants survive. Bowlby's beliefs best illustrate which of the following perspectives in psychology?

    (A) Behavioral
    (B) Cognitive
    (C) Humanistic
    (D) Sociocultural
    (E) Evolutionary

371. Albert Bandura believed that children learn to be aggressive by observing and imitating an adult modeling such behaviors. Bandura would most likely be associated with which of the following perspectives?

    (A) Psychodynamic
    (B) Humanistic
    (C) Biological
    (D) Evolutionary
    (E) Social-cognitive

372. Which of the following explanations for the development of moral reasoning reflects the biological perspective?

    (A) Moral reasoning develops as we are challenged by moral problems and must think through our positions of right and wrong.
    (B) Authority figures, such as parents and teachers, model appropriate moral behaviors in teaching children what is right and wrong.
    (C) A higher level of moral reasoning is associated with increased activity in the brain's reward system.
    (D) The superego develops as a result of conflict in the Oedipal stage of psychosexual development.
    (E) Cultural rules and expectations establish what is considered moral in any society.

Motivation and Emotion

Answers for Chapter 10 are on pages 284–295.

CHAPTER

10

STIMULUS

Use the following fictional example to answer questions 373–376.

The observation notes below were used as part of a naturalistic observation study of a group of middle school students. All names are pseudonyms.

Context:

- During the 10 minutes of this observation, this group of four middle school students worked to complete a project assigned by their English teacher.

- The four students were seated around a table, which was covered with construction paper, scissors, glue sticks, and their open textbooks.

- The students' task was to make a creative display that communicates their feelings about the end of the school year.

- All observation entries are time stamped, student comments are in quotation marks, and student actions are in brackets.

Student	Time	Quotation
Carter	12:06	"I hope you all don't screw around like last time. I want to get a good grade on this thing."
Ava	12:06	"Fine, Carter, got it. You always just want to get a good grade. Sheesh."
(The group works in silence for about 4 minutes.)		
Guy	12:10	"Ava, that looks pretty cool. Nice."
Ava	12:11	"Thanks. Yeah, it's turning out OK. I really like this kind of project. I just want it to look nice and turn out good."
Guy	12:11	"Way better than mine [sighs]. I keep screwing this thing up; I think I'm too nervous. I do OK sometimes when I'm just a bit nervous, but I'm way too stressed right now, so I don't think I can do this right."
Danny	12:12	"We are totally getting this done! Good job, everybody. I feel like I'm getting this now. By the time we're done with this thing, I feel like I'll have this DOWN. I will be the master of construction paper and glue!"

373. Look at the information from the naturalistic observation notes about Carter. What kind of motivation does Carter seem to be influenced by, based solely on the information you find in these observation notes?

    (A) Achievement motivation
    (B) Extrinsic motivation
    (C) Mastery motivation
    (D) Intrinsic motivation
    (E) Instrumental motivation

374. Look at the information from the naturalistic observation notes about Ava. What kind of motivation does Ava seem to be influenced by, based solely on the information you find in these observation notes?

    (A) Achievement motivation
    (B) Extrinsic motivation
    (C) Mastery motivation
    (D) Intrinsic motivation
    (E) Instrumental motivation

375. Look at the information from the naturalistic observation notes about Danny. What kind of motivation does Danny seem to be influenced by, based solely on the information you find in these observation notes?

    (A) Achievement motivation
    (B) Extrinsic motivation
    (C) Mastery motivation
    (D) Intrinsic motivation
    (E) Instrumental motivation

376. Look at the information from the naturalistic observation notes about Guy. Which of the following motivation principles seems to fit Guy's experience best, based solely on the information you find in these observation notes?

    (A) Achievement motivation
    (B) Extrinsic motivation
    (C) Yerkes-Dodson law
    (D) Intrinsic motivation
    (E) Law of effect

DEFINITIONS

377. Which of the following is the most correct definition of the term *instinct*?

(A) An internal motivation shared by all organisms in the same species
(B) A basic drive related to the survival needs of hunger, shelter, and reproduction
(C) A behavior motivated solely by biological preconditions that evolved over time to ensure the survival of the species
(D) An impulse to seek reinforcements and avoid punishments
(E) An unlearned, complex behavior common throughout a species and that follows a fixed pattern

378. Which term refers to an unlearned, complex behavior common throughout a species and that follows a fixed pattern?

(A) Drive
(B) Instinct
(C) Autonomic
(D) Homeostasis
(E) Basal

379. Which of the following concepts describes how performance can increase or decrease in effectiveness based on either stress or arousal?

(A) Achievement motivation
(B) Extrinsic motivation
(C) Homeostasis
(D) Yerkes-Dodson law
(E) Performance anxiety

380. What type of question can the Yerkes-Dodson law help answer?

(A) Why are some organisms motivated to help others even if there are significant costs to themselves?
(B) What are the different impacts of internal and external motivations?
(C) If a person is very anxious about performing a task, will that help or hurt the person's performance?
(D) Are there specific biological reactions associated with different kinds of emotions?
(E) Why are some people more highly motivated to achieve than others?

381. When working with people you do not know well, what motivations are most effective at changing behaviors quickly, for at least a short amount of time?

    (A) Achievement motivation
    (B) Extrinsic motivation
    (C) Two-factor motivation
    (D) Intrinsic motivation
    (E) Autonomic motivation

382. If your goal is to motivate long-term changes that persist even when people are unobserved, what kind of motivation is most useful?

    (A) Achievement motivation
    (B) Extrinsic motivation
    (C) Two-factor motivation
    (D) Intrinsic motivation
    (E) Autonomic motivation

383. Which motivation theory describes how physiological needs create impulses to lessen those needs in order to regain a balanced internal state?

    (A) Drive reduction theory
    (B) Instinct theory
    (C) Maslow's hierarchy of needs
    (D) Homeostasis motivation
    (E) Limbic system

384. Which of the following is an accurate description of drive reduction theory?

    (A) Humans are driven to achieve mastery of their environments and to reduce their feelings of stress and anxiety through motivated behaviors.
    (B) Organisms are born with unlearned, complex behaviors that follow a fixed pattern.
    (C) Our needs are prioritized from least to most important, and this ranked list motivates our behaviors.
    (D) In order to reduce unconscious stress, we are driven to satisfy needs created earlier in life.
    (E) Physiological needs create impulses to lessen those needs in order to regain a balanced internal state.

385. According to drive reduction theory, humans are motivated to reduce drives in order to regain a balanced state. What is this state called?

   (A) Autonomic
   (B) Hypothalamus
   (C) Homeostasis
   (D) Refractory period
   (E) Self-actualization

386. In drive reduction theory, what does homeostasis refer to?

   (A) Impulses transmitted across the synaptic gap in the limbic system that reduce physiological drives
   (B) The drive to achieve the state of confident mastery over the environment
   (C) The stage just below self-actualization, which is achievable by most adults
   (D) A balanced internal state, free of drives produced by physiological deficits
   (E) The balance between internal and external motivations that result in productive, mature behaviors

387. What is the premise behind Maslow's hierarchy of needs theory?

   (A) Some needs are more important in some cultures, which causes the behavioral differences we see in different countries.
   (B) People are motivated to satisfy needs in a specific order, starting with physiological needs.
   (C) Everyone is motivated to achieve mastery over his or her environment, which is the highest-ranking need in the hierarchy.
   (D) Biological needs evolved in a specific order in humans, which impacts behaviors in predictable ways.
   (E) Each person internalizes a hierarchy of needs over time, based on past experiences.

388. What is the correct order of the levels in Maslow's hierarchy of needs?

   (A) Intrinsic needs, extrinsic needs, achievement needs, homeostasis, self-actualization
   (B) Physiological needs, safety needs, love and belongingness, self-esteem, self-actualization
   (C) Instinct, drive, drive reduction, intrinsic motivation, extrinsic motivation, achievement motivation
   (D) Sensorimotor, preoperational, concrete operational, formal operations
   (E) Biological, cognitive, emotional, connectedness, spiritual

389. Which of the following brain structures is most involved in eating motivation?

    (A) Hypothalamus
    (B) Amygdala
    (C) Thalamus
    (D) Pons
    (E) Sensorimotor cortex

390. What is one of the most important ways that the hypothalamus influences human motivation?

    (A) Intrinsically motivated actions begin in the hypothalamus.
    (B) Our memories of important, motivating events are stored in the hypothalamus.
    (C) Maslow believed that the order of the hierarchy of needs is determined by the hypothalamus.
    (D) The hypothalamus controls addiction behaviors.
    (E) The hypothalamus influences whether we feel hungry or full.

391. Damage to the lateral hypothalamus would result in what change in motivation?

    (A) Achievement motivations would be drastically decreased.
    (B) Since this is where instincts are stored in the brain, survival may be affected.
    (C) The person would probably not feel hungry, even after a long period of not eating.
    (D) The refractory period would be significantly shorter, impacting sexual motivations and behaviors.
    (E) Extrinsic motivations would be more likely effective than would intrinsic motivations.

392. Damage to the ventromedial hypothalamus would result in what change in motivation?

    (A) It may impact the order of motivations in Maslow's hierarchy of needs.
    (B) The impulse to achieve mastery over skills may be dramatically lessened.
    (C) Since the hypothalamus is the link between emotions and the rest of the brain, flat affect may occur.
    (D) The person would probably never feel full, even after eating a large meal.
    (E) The person may react to intrinsic motivations but not to extrinsic motivations.

393. **Why might a person want to influence or change his or her set point?**

    (A) The set point refers to the weight our body wants to maintain, which influences our hunger and satiation feelings.
    (B) This is the point at which our balance of intrinsic and extrinsic motivators is set, which determines which motivations we react most strongly to.
    (C) In achievement motivation theory, humans have a set point of achievement they are motivated to achieve.
    (D) Drive reduction theory is based on the set point at which our drives motivate us to reduce them rather than resisting or ignoring them.
    (E) According to two-factor theory, each motivation involves at least two factors, and the balance point between them is the set point.

394. **Which of the following is the most important difference between anorexia and bulimia?**

    (A) Craving
    (B) Purging
    (C) Hypothalamus
    (D) Pathway
    (E) Etiology

395. **The James-Lange and Cannon-Bard theories both focus on which of the following questions?**

    (A) Which kind of motivation is most effective at changing behavior over the long term: intrinsic, extrinsic, or achievement motivation?
    (B) Why do some people choose to sacrifice their own safety needs in order to help others, which contradicts the predictions of Maslow's hierarchy of needs theory?
    (C) How do physiological changes (like a racing heart, increased respiration, and so on) change how we interpret the actions of others?
    (D) What is the basic set of human instincts (called drives), and how do humans seek to reduce these drives in order to attain or reestablish our natural state of homeostasis?
    (E) Are we aware of an emotion first and then experience physiological changes, or do we experience physiological changes and then become aware of the emotion?

396. Humans experience similar physiological changes as we feel different emotions. Our heart rate goes up in response to both fearful and exciting situations. This fact supports which of the following theories?

    (A) James-Lange theory
    (B) Yerkes-Dodson theory
    (C) Two-factor theory
    (D) Drive reduction theory
    (E) Self-actualization theory

SCENARIOS

397. Molly's new baby, Levi, turns his head and makes sucking motions with his lips when Molly strokes his cheek. Molly's pediatrician explains that all humans do this because it helps the baby find the mother's nipple and get milk. Levi's behavior is an example of which of the following?

    (A) Yerkes-Dodson law
    (B) Instinct
    (C) Operant conditioning
    (D) Conditioned response
    (E) Reciprocal determinism

398. Franz is working hard to finish a draft of his short story. He's been working all day. By 5:00, though, he is so hungry that he must stop working and find something to eat. After he eats a sandwich, he goes back to work and finishes the draft of the story. Which motivation theory is most applicable to this situation?

    (A) Instinct theory
    (B) Yerkes-Dodson law
    (C) Self-actualization theory
    (D) Drive reduction theory
    (E) Satiation theory

399. Jim is about to participate in the finals of a speech competition. He's understandably nervous, but he has participated in many of these events before. This time, he feels like he's "just nervous enough" that he will give the best performance of the year. Jim wins the competition. Which of the following principles might explain why Jim does well in the finals?

    (A) Drive reduction theory
    (B) Yerkes-Dodson law
    (C) Autonomic nervous system
    (D) Performance anxiety
    (E) Naturalistic observation theory

400. Daniel is excited to volunteer at the library this summer. He's looking forward to talking with other people who like to read as much as he does. His grandmother decides to give him $5 every time he volunteers. He decides to tell her she doesn't need to give him money; he wants to volunteer just for fun! Daniel's grandmother is confused about the impact of what kinds of motivation?

    (A) Extrinsic and intrinsic motivations
    (B) Instincts and drives
    (C) Operant and classically conditioned responses
    (D) Preoperational and concrete operational cognitions
    (E) Retroactive and proactive thoughts

401. The day before you are to leave for college, you open the letter your grandmother sent you. In the letter, she says, "Remember, sweetie, to listen to your body: eat when you're hungry, sleep when you're tired, and stay warm. There is wisdom in your body. It wants to keep you in balance, and it will tell you how to regain that balance." What psychological principle is most like the advice your grandmother is giving in her letter?

    (A) Self-actualization
    (B) Reciprocal determinism
    (C) Social facilitation
    (D) Transduction
    (E) Homeostasis

402. Your college roommate confides in you that he is struggling with his weight. He says, "No matter what I do, I just keep putting on the pounds. I'm not vain or anything, but it really bothers me, and I have no idea what to do. I've heard about this all cabbage soup diet. Do you think I should try it? You're majoring in psychology. What should I do?" Which of the following terms might be most useful to include in your advice to your roommate?

    (A) Instinct
    (B) Id
    (C) Set point
    (D) Refractory period
    (E) Amygdala

403. You are asked to consult with a group of doctors as they try to diagnose patient "CMOT," who presents with an unusual cluster of symptoms.

    • He never seems to be hungry, even after a long period without food.
    • His anxiety seems constant. Hospital staff have to keep careful watch or he will try to run out of the hospital. When restrained, he will sometimes fight staff.
    • He often fights inappropriately with hospital staff or visitors.

    If one of the following was not functioning properly with CMOT, it might explain all these behaviors. Which one of the following could be malfunctioning?

    (A) Brainstem
    (B) Amygdala
    (C) Fungiform papillae
    (D) Hypothalamus
    (E) Transduction

404. A group of developmental psychologists start a longitudinal study involving 120 school-age children. They plan to follow these children from kindergarten through their senior year of high school and attempt to measure several variables. The researchers want to correlate those variables with the later success (or lack of success) of the students. Which of the following variables would be most important to choose for this study and would be the most difficult to define operationally?

(A) Grade point average
(B) Achievement motivation
(C) Extrinsic motivation
(D) Attitude toward school
(E) Psychosocial maturational stage

405. Otto starts taking a new medication for his low blood pressure, but he's having trouble adjusting to some of the side effects. The medication causes his heart rate, blood pressure, and respiration to elevate quickly whenever he is startled or feels excited. Otto also reports to his doctor that he "feels" things more deeply. He says, "It's hard to explain, but when I'm in a happy situation, I think I feel happier, and when something stressful happens, it feels more like an emergency than it did before." Which of the following theories might help explain Otto's new emotional experiences?

(A) Two-factor theory
(B) James-Lange theory
(C) Drive reduction theory
(D) Cannon-Bard theory
(E) Yerkes-Dodson theory

406. In May 2018, Mamoudou Gassama saw a child hanging from a fourth-floor balcony in Paris. The child seemed about to fall, and no adult was nearby to help. Mr. Gassama proceeded to climb and leap up the outside of the building from balcony to balcony, eventually reaching the child and possibly saving the child's life. Which of the following motivation theories would have the most difficulty explaining why Mr. Gassama chose to complete this heroic act?

(A) Intrinsic motivation
(B) Achievement motivation
(C) Extrinsic motivation
(D) Altruism
(E) Maslow's hierarchy of needs

NAMES

407. Which researcher would be interested in investigating why some people are motivated to look for their "purpose" in life, seeking meaning for their lives beyond materialistic concerns?

    (A) Carl Lange
    (B) Alfred Kinsey
    (C) Abraham Maslow
    (D) William James
    (E) Walter Cannon

408. Two researchers independently developed a very original idea about how humans experience emotions—that our bodies change before we are consciously aware of what emotion we are experiencing. Since each researcher developed the theory separately around the same time, the theory shares both their names. Which two researchers developed this theory?

    (A) Carl Lange and William James
    (B) Virginia Johnson and William Masters
    (C) Philip Bard and Walter Cannon
    (D) Henry Murray and Abraham Maslow
    (E) B. F. Skinner and John Watson

409. Which researcher attempted to uncover the sexual behaviors of Americans by carefully surveying a representative, nationwide sample?

    (A) Carl Lange
    (B) Alfred Kinsey
    (C) Abraham Maslow
    (D) William James
    (E) Walter Cannon

410. Stanley Schachter and Jerome Singer uncovered a potential resolution to the principal disagreement between the James-Lange and Cannon-Bard theories of emotion. What was this resolution?

    (A) Emotional experiences turn out to be more meaningful and memorable than experiences that are primarily cognitive.
    (B) Men are more emotional than women, but cultural norms cause men to underestimate their emotional experiences.
    (C) Humans experience physiological reactions before our conscious experience of an emotion.
    (D) Our cognitive interpretation of a physiological response produces the experience we interpret as emotion.
    (E) Physiological reactions result from past conditioning experiences based on emotional experiences.

411. Which researcher established that some emotional responses do not involve any cognitive interpretation?

    (A) Philip Bard
    (B) Albert Bandura
    (C) Robert Zajonc
    (D) Daniel Kahneman
    (E) Robert Garcia

RESEARCH METHODS

412. Researchers are interested in designing an experiment to determine what variables are most effective at establishing homeostasis. Which of the following is a likely operational definition for the dependent variable in their experiment?

    (A) A personality test based on trait theory
    (B) Reaction time instruments, specifically hand-eye coordination devices
    (C) Self-report instruments designed to assess either intrinsic or extrinsic motivations
    (D) Scans from an fMRI that can detect whether physiological responses occur before emotions or vice versa
    (E) Physiological instruments (such as blood pressure and respiration sensors)

413. Which of the following research methods would be most useful if a researcher wanted to investigate which intrinsic motivations are most common among elementary school teachers?

(A) Experiment
(B) Self-report (survey)
(C) Correlation
(D) Naturalistic observation
(E) Empirical (data based)

414. A researcher is testing the hypothesis "People who have high achievement motivation are more productive at work." Why might the researcher NOT use random assignment?

(A) Random assignment cannot be used because people with high achievement motivation will be assigned to one group and those with low achievement motivation will be assigned to the other group.
(B) It is more important to use the double-blind technique than random assignment in this study because there is a greater risk for experimenter bias than for subject bias.
(C) Random assignment is used in quasi-experiments. True experiments require random sampling, not random assignment.
(D) The statistical techniques required for random assignment cannot be used with a subjective variable like achievement motivation because greater quantitative precision is required.
(E) Random assignment requires that every member of a population has an equal chance of being chosen as a participant.

415. A university's Ethics Review Board denies a researcher permission for a study investigating the lower levels of Maslow's hierarchy of needs. What is the most likely reason for this denial?

(A) The researchers were probably guilty of coercing participants because Maslow's hierarchy of needs is such a popular motivation theory.
(B) The Ethics Review Board probably objected to the researcher using an outdated motivation theory.
(C) One of the ethical requirements for research is that participants need to be fully informed about the nature of the research, and that would not be possible with this study.
(D) The lower levels of the hierarchy of needs involve basic needs and safety, and the proposed research may have involved too much risk.
(E) Nonhuman animals are typically used for this type of research, and the ethical considerations for research with nonhuman animals are complex.

416. Professor Worblehat wants to research how stress impacts the refractory period in young adults. Which of the following research methods is Professor Worblehat least likely to use?

    (A) Focus group
    (B) Interview
    (C) Naturalistic observation
    (D) Survey
    (E) Qualitative analysis

PERSPECTIVES

417. Explanations for the overjustification effect involve which psychological perspective and which term from motivation theory?

    (A) Cognitive perspective and instinct
    (B) Sociocultural perspective and set point
    (C) Humanism and two-factor theory
    (D) Structuralism and achievement motivation
    (E) Behaviorism and intrinsic motivation

418. Researchers from which psychological perspective might be most interested in research indicating that drive reduction theory predicts human behaviors better than a cognition-based theory, like achievement motivation?

    (A) Sociocultural perspective
    (B) Behaviorism perspective
    (C) Evolutionary perspective
    (D) Biological perspective
    (E) Behavioral-genetics perspective

419. Motivation researchers investigating hunger include the following statement in the conclusion section of a journal article:

   "Hunger results almost exclusively from impulses originating in different areas in the hypothalamus, which determine an individual's set point. Efforts to exert conscious control over this process are not likely to succeed."

   Which of the following statements accurately summarizes this statement?

   (A) The article disproves homeostasis theory, which predicts that our cognitions about food impact hunger significantly.
   (B) The article emphasizes the primacy of biology and the reduced role of cognitive psychology.
   (C) These researchers believe that humanistic theory, like Maslow's hierarchy of needs, best explains hunger motivation.
   (D) The research from this journal article must prove that the hypothalamus contradicts set-point theory.
   (E) Data in the article most likely comes from an fMRI machine, which measures cognitions rather than just brain impulses.

420. Which theory of emotion argues that human emotional experiences are inevitably the product of a combination of the cognitive and biological perspectives?

   (A) Display rules
   (B) Yerkes-Dodson law
   (C) Two-factor theory
   (D) Top-down processing
   (E) Drive reduction theory

Personality

Answers for Chapter 11 are on pages 295–305.

STIMULUS

One of your friends on social media shares with you the personality test shown here. Use the image to answer questions 421–424.

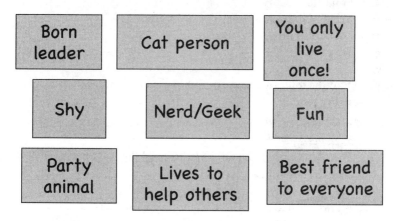

What describes you best?

Born leader

Cat person

You only live once!

Shy

Nerd/Geek

Fun

Party animal

Lives to help others

Best friend to everyone

421. **How would you check to see whether this personality test is reliable?**

    (A) Check the results of this test against a separate, reliable personality test.

    (B) Have many people take the test repeatedly to see if they choose the same box each time.

    (C) Ask a random sample of people to take the test to see if it's statistically significant.

    (D) After volunteers take the test, interview them to see how accurate the test is.

    (E) If the test is reliable, people should get different results each time based on their changing moods.

422. **How would you check to see whether this personality test is valid?**

    (A) Examine a large number of results from volunteers and use inferential statistics to check test validity.
    (B) After many people take the test, check to see if they get the same results each time.
    (C) Perform a factor analysis.
    (D) Correlate results of this test with a different personality test that is known to be valid.
    (E) Check to make sure the personality theory that the test is based on is valid.

423. **This personality test is probably based on which personality theory?**

    (A) Psychodynamic theory
    (B) Projection theory
    (C) Reciprocal determinism
    (D) Locus of control
    (E) Trait theory

424. **Which of the following is the most accurate evaluation of this personality test?**

    (A) It is a projective test that may reveal unconscious stressors or anxieties.
    (B) The test is likely to be valid, but its reliability would have to be checked carefully.
    (C) This personality test is likely to be reliable but not valid.
    (D) All tests shared through social media are unreliable and invalid.
    (E) Valid personality tests necessarily involve scenarios and more elaborate questions.

DEFINITIONS

425. **Which personality theory traces personality characteristics to unconscious influences?**

    (A) Psychoanalytic
    (B) Trait
    (C) Cognitive
    (D) Psychosexual
    (E) Reciprocal determinism

426. Psychoanalysts would be most likely to use which of the following terms in their work?

    (A) Extroversion, conscientiousness, neuroticism
    (B) Reliability, validity, factor analysis
    (C) MMPI, MBTI, IQ
    (D) Id, unconscious, ego, defense mechanisms
    (E) Learned helplessness, reciprocal determinism, collectivism

427. Which part of the unconscious mind did Freud think was most responsible for our most basic impulses, such as greed or sex?

    (A) Id
    (B) Oedipal
    (C) Ego
    (D) Psychosexual
    (E) Superego

428. Which part of the unconscious mind did Freud think was most responsible for "moral thinking," referred to as conscience?

    (A) Id
    (B) Postconventional
    (C) Ego
    (D) Formal operational
    (E) Superego

429. Which part of the unconscious mind did Freud think was most responsible for negotiating compromises between our animalistic impulses and our "higher self" that wants to act morally?

    (A) Id
    (B) Working memory
    (C) Ego
    (D) Medulla
    (E) Superego

430. **What is the most important difference between psychoanalysis and psychotherapy?**

    (A) Psychotherapy is performed by psychiatrists. Psychoanalysis is performed by any trained clinical psychologist.
    (B) Psychotherapists often use a variety of therapeutic approaches. Psychoanalysts primarily use the psychodynamic perspective.
    (C) Psychoanalysis is usually more effective for anxiety and mood disorders. Psychotherapy is more effective for dissociative and schizophrenic disorders.
    (D) Psychoanalysis is the overall category. Psychotherapy is a specific kind of psychoanalysis.
    (E) Therapy that involves psychoactive medication is called psychotherapy. Therapy that does not involve medication is called psychoanalysis.

431. **What is the primary difference between projective and trait theory personality tests?**

    (A) Projective tests tend to be more reliable and valid than trait theory personality tests.
    (B) Projective tests are developed based on research of different categories of personality types. Trait theory tests are empirically derived.
    (C) Both types of tests try to measure personality. Trait theory tests are based on qualitative analysis, and projective tests use quantitative analysis.
    (D) Projective tests try to reveal unconscious influences. Trait theory tests try to measure specific personality characteristics.
    (E) Trait tests rely on self-report measures. Projective tests do not.

432. **A personality test asks respondents to look at a series of ambiguous visual images and explain what the image reminds the respondent of or what the respondent sees. What personality test is probably being administered?**

    (A) Myers-Briggs Type Indicator (MBTI)
    (B) Intelligence Quotient (IQ)
    (C) Minnesota Multiphasic Personality Inventory (MMPI)
    (D) Big five trait theory test
    (E) Thematic Apperception Test (TAT)

433. What would a researcher conclude about a personality test that returns different results each time a specific person takes the test?

(A) The test is not reliable and not valid.
(B) The test is not reliable but may be valid.
(C) The test is not valid but may be reliable.
(D) The test is not reliable, and more evidence is needed to determine validity.
(E) The test is not valid, and more evidence is needed to determine reliability.

434. Which of the following statements is true about the relationship between reliability and validity?

(A) Validity is a necessary but not sufficient condition for reliability.
(B) Reliability is subjective, but validity is objective and empirically measurable.
(C) A personality test must be reliable in order to be considered valid.
(D) The theoretical basis for a test establishes its validity, while the results may establish reliability.
(E) In order to be considered reliable, a test must be valid.

435. Which of the following phrases is the best explanation of this statement? "Reliability is a necessary condition but is not a sufficient condition for validity."

(A) Conditions for reliability depend on a statistical analysis of validity.
(B) If a test is not valid, its reliability, or consistency of results, must be examined. However, if a test is valid, its reliability can be assumed.
(C) An analysis of reliability is predicated on assumptions about validity.
(D) If a test does not deliver consistent results, the test is not valid. Just because a test is reliable does not mean that it is valid.
(E) The relationship between reliability and validity is reciprocal. An increase in validity causes an increase in reliability and vice versa.

436. Which of the following personality tests is considered to be most valid?

(A) Myers-Briggs Type Indicator (MBTI)
(B) Kohlberg theory test
(C) Minnesota Multiphasic Personality Inventory (MMPI)
(D) Rorschach theory test
(E) Thematic Apperception Test (TAT)

437. **Which of the following options lists the most agreed upon, and research supported, set of personality traits?**

   (A) Introversion/extroversion, sensing/intuition, thinking/feeling, judging/perceiving
   (B) Extroversion, agreeableness, conscientiousness, neuroticism, openness
   (C) Id, ego, superego
   (D) Internal locus of control, external locus of control, individualism, collectivism
   (E) Personal factors, the environment, behavior

438. **Which of the following is the underlying assumption behind the trait theory of personality?**

   (A) Personality traits are revealed by Jung's work on the collective unconscious, which accurately described the different elements of personality through opposing dichotomies.
   (B) Human thinking and behavior are influenced by past experiences and stresses that we may repress out of our conscious mind but that still affect our current choices and actions.
   (C) Our consistent patterns of thinking and feeling are highly individualistic, and personality trait categories vary between cultures and across time.
   (D) Trait theory tests reveal an underlying aptitude and mental capacity that are related to problem solving and neural speed.
   (E) Human personalities can be categorized into useful groups of characteristics, which are descriptions of ways of thinking/feeling that are consistent across contexts.

439. **Which personality theory predicts that our characteristic patterns of feeling and behaving result from the interactions among what we learned from past experiences, our internal thoughts/feelings, and environmental influences?**

   (A) Reciprocal determinism
   (B) Person-environment interaction
   (C) Behavior genetics
   (D) Sociocultural dynamics
   (E) Collective unconscious

440. If you wanted to determine whether a trait personality test was valid, which statistical technique would be most useful?

    (A) Measures of central tendency
    (B) Inferential statistics
    (C) Factor analysis
    (D) Qualitative analysis
    (E) Double-blind technique

SCENARIOS

441. You are nervous about your job interview with the Discworld Company because you really want this job. You receive an e-mail asking you to report to the human resources department to participate in a personality test to determine if you are a good match for the company. During the test, you are asked to look at a series of ambiguous visual images and explain what you see or what the image reminds you of. What personality test did you probably participate in, and was it appropriate for the company to require this test?

    (A) MBTI. Yes, it was appropriate because the MBTI can reveal leadership skills.
    (B) IQ. No, it was not appropriate because intelligence testing is not allowed by most human resources departments.
    (C) MMPI. Yes, it was appropriate because the MMPI is an empirically validated test.
    (D) Big Five. Yes, it was appropriate because the Big Five personality traits have been established by many research studies.
    (E) TAT. No, it was not appropriate because the hiring process is not a valid use of a projective test.

442. Professor Bleedwell gathers the following data from participants who take the same personality test twice.

Participant Number	Test Result Day 1	Test Result Day 2
P1	Extrovert/agreeable/open	Introvert/agreeable/closed
P2	Introvert/not agreeable/closed	Introvert/agreeable/open
P3	Extrovert/not agreeable/open	Introvert/agreeable/closed
P4	Introvert/agreeable/open	Introvert/agreeable/closed
P5	Introvert/not agreeable/closed	Extrovert/not agreeable/open

What can you conclude about this personality test based on these data?

(A) The test may be valid but is not consistent.
(B) Professor Bleedwell used a projective test in this research.
(C) These participants have highly variable personalities.
(D) The data indicate that the test isn't highly reliable.
(E) Professor Bleedwell should use a factor analysis to confirm these results.

443. Dr. Bleakly is treating her client Rupert for a dissociative disorder. Dr. Bleakly encourages Rupert to say the first things that come to his mind and not censor himself. Dr. Bleakly reads a list of words, and Rupert tries to say the first thing that comes to mind. What technique is Dr. Bleakly using?

(A) Reciprocal determinism
(B) Free association
(C) Introspection
(D) Internal locus
(E) Functionalism

444. W. M. Arthur, a famous poet, has trouble controlling his temper. Often, he will get very angry while at the coffee house because he is frustrated with his writing. When he gets home, he will yell at his family. Which of the following is most relevant to this scenario?

(A) Displacement
(B) Regression
(C) Denial
(D) Dissociation
(E) Reaction formation

445. Ms. Humpeding is feeling extreme stress because her solo choral performance occurs in three days. One night, the stress starts to overwhelm her. She tucks herself into bed with the blanket she used as a child and sucks her thumb to try to calm down. Which of the following is most relevant to this scenario?

    (A) Projection
    (B) Regression
    (C) Denial
    (D) Dissociation
    (E) Reaction formation

446. Your roommate rushes back into your dorm room after a psychology lecture and says, "I knew it! Freud and all the neo-Freudians are full of it! There's no current empirical evidence that supports any of their claims about the supposed unconscious mind!" Which of the following areas of research might change your roommate's opinion?

    (A) Free association
    (B) Trait theory
    (C) Priming
    (D) Dream analysis
    (E) Reliability

447. Your artist friend Frida asks you, "Is there anything in all that psychology research that might help me with my art? Maybe anything about symbols I could use in my paintings that a lot of different people might react to?" Which of the following concepts would you choose to share with Frida?

    (A) The big five
    (B) Reciprocal determinism
    (C) Structuralism
    (D) Social facilitation
    (E) Collective unconscious

448. The Dorfl Corporation contracted with a psychometric consultant to develop a test for job applicants. The test is supposed to predict which employees will be the most productive. The president of the Dorfl Corporation proposes that the company give the new test to current employees who are known to be very productive. What psychological principle of the test does the president want to investigate?

    (A) Reliability
    (B) Accuracy
    (C) Correlation
    (D) Validity
    (E) Generalization

449. Agnes has lived all over the world and speaks multiple languages. She finds a personality test that has been translated into three of the languages she speaks and takes the test in each of those languages. Agnes gets different results each time she takes the test in a different language. What psychological principle is most relevant to Agnes's experience?

    (A) Reliability
    (B) Trait theory
    (C) Validity
    (D) Inferential statistics
    (E) Descriptive statistics

450. You are studying psychology in college. During one of your phone calls home, your father says, "Don't take those psychologists too seriously! They think our whole personality can be described by numbers instead of actually talking to the person and figuring out what makes them tick!" Which personality theory should you tell your father about in order to change his mind?

    (A) Collective unconscious
    (B) Trait theory
    (C) Behaviorism
    (D) Reciprocal determinism
    (E) Psychosexual stages

451. Professor Magpyr is excited because his team's journal article was accepted for publication. The article describes how the team developed the Magpyr Personality Test by field testing hundreds of statements about identity until they had accurate statistics that indicated which items successfully measure several personality traits. What can you conclude about the Magpyr Personality Test?

    (A) It is a projective test.
    (B) Professor Magpyr is a humanistic researcher.
    (C) It was empirically derived.
    (D) The research team used correlational techniques.
    (E) It measures the big five personality traits.

452. You attend a lecture about literary theory in the 1900s. The speaker argues that authors of this era were obsessed with "internal competing forces" within their characters. The speaker claims that symbols in the novels reveal how each character deals with inner voices representing selfishness, moral conscience, and compromise. Which list of personality vocabulary is most relevant to the speaker's argument?

    (A) Past experiences, internal feelings, cognitive interpretations
    (B) Id, ego, superego
    (C) Big five traits
    (D) Reliability, validity, factor analysis
    (E) Internal, external, inherent locus of control

NAMES

453. Which psychological perspective grew out of the personality theories of Sigmund Freud?

    (A) Trait theory
    (B) Humanistic perspective
    (C) Reciprocal determinism
    (D) Collectivism and individualism theory
    (E) Psychodynamic perspective

454. Which personality researcher is the most likely source for a quote like this: "Behavior, interpersonal factors, and environmental influences all combine in reciprocal relationships to produce our personalities"?

    (A) Albert Bandura
    (B) Abraham Maslow
    (C) Gordon Allport
    (D) Carl Jung
    (E) Karen Horney

455. Which researcher would be most interested in research that grouped all the words in a dictionary associated with personality into five or ten large, unique categories?

    (A) Albert Bandura
    (B) Alfred Adler
    (C) Gordon Allport
    (D) Carl Jung
    (E) Sigmund Freud

456. Carl Rogers might be most interested in a personality test that assesses which of the following?

    (A) The big five personality traits
    (B) Repressed conflicts in the unconscious through projection
    (C) Characteristic patterns of thinking and behavior that persist across contexts
    (D) Differences between the ideal self and the actual self
    (E) Clusters of personality traits based on factor analysis

RESEARCH METHODS

457. A researcher is interested in validating her new trait theory personality test by comparing results from 100 randomly chosen test takers with results on the big five personality test from the same participants. The researcher finds that results from her test predict results on the big five personality test. What analytic technique did this researcher most likely use?

    (A) Experiment
    (B) Correlation
    (C) Inferential statistics
    (D) Descriptive statistics
    (E) Factor analysis

458. Consider this hypothesis: "Results on personality tests are impacted by sleep deprivation." Which of the following would be the most useful tool to define the dependent variable operationally when researching this hypothesis?

(A) A trait theory personality test
(B) Data on the sleep habits of participants
(C) Self-report data indicating that tiredness impacts how we react
(D) A group of participants who are sleep deprived
(E) A random sample of college students who are willing to participate in the study

459. Which of the following hypotheses uses one of the big five personality traits as the independent variable?

(A) Men are more likely to have high levels of neuroticism than are women.
(B) Openness scores are highly correlated with extraversion scores.
(C) Social skills development training can significantly impact extraversion scores on personality tests.
(D) Rural individuals score higher on conscientiousness than do urban individuals.
(E) The level of extraversion in individuals impacts the number of friends they have at age 50.

PERSPECTIVES

460. Which psychological perspectives are most related to Bandura's reciprocal determinism personality theory?

(A) Cognitive, psychodynamic, sociocultural
(B) Structuralism, functionalism, empiricism
(C) Behaviorism, humanism, positive psychology
(D) Behavior genetics, evolutionary, biological
(E) Biological, cognitive, behaviorism

461. Which of the following terms would a psychodynamic personality theorist most likely use?

    (A) Openness, extroversion, neuroticism
    (B) Reliability, validity, empirical data
    (C) Factor analysis, standard deviation, inferential statistics
    (D) Unconscious, superego, defense mechanisms
    (E) Reciprocal determinism, internal locus of control, external locus of control

462. Which of the following perspectives would be most interested in whether the big five personality traits are correlated with recall of stories, based on mood congruent memory?

    (A) Sociocultural
    (B) Cognitive
    (C) Behaviorism
    (D) Psychodynamic
    (E) Humanism

Abnormal Psychology

Answers for Chapter 12 are on pages 305–314.

STIMULUS

Use the fictionalized advertisement below to answer questions 463–465.

SPEAKER SERIES:
THE TRUTH ABOUT INSANITY THAT
"THEY" DON'T WANT YOU TO KNOW!!!

Come to the lively presentation by Dr. Ron Xenu—one of the leading authorities worldwide in the human thinking potentiality movement—tonight, February 29th, at the community center at 7:30. Dr. Xenu will discuss many of the facts he has discovered about so-called psychological disorders, including:

- Efforts by so-called psychiatrists to keep adding disorders for every behavior and never eliminating any diagnosis
- Facts the medical conglomerate suppress about ineffectiveness of psychological drugs
- Environmental origins of all psychological disorders
- The impact of creating labels for almost every behavior, even common, nonharmful behaviors
- The sinister origins of psychology and psychiatry

At the end of the talk, Dr. Xenu will sell his 17-part DVD series that will help you clear your mind and spirit. Credit cards are gladly accepted.

---

463. Which of the following research findings might be most challenging for Dr. Xenu to explain?

    (A) Different parenting styles are correlated with different life outcomes and personality temperaments.
    (B) IQ scores are highly predictive of multiple variables later in life, including college graduation and career choices, indicating that environmental influences have less influence on adult outcomes.
    (C) The DSM-5 is based primarily on case study research and generally does not include empirical research findings.
    (D) If one identical twin develops symptoms of schizophrenia, the other twin has a 50% chance of also manifesting schizophrenic symptoms, no matter the environmental influences.
    (E) Stress is a major contributing factor when people exhibit symptoms of psychological disorders.

464. Consider the criteria used to determine whether or not behaviors should be labeled as "psychologically disordered." Which answer below summarizes the criteria that might contradict Dr. Xenu's claims?

    (A) Causal, predictive, associative
    (B) Atypical, maladaptive, disturbing
    (C) Mood, anxiety, dissociative
    (D) Internal locus of control, external locus of control, disconnected locus of control
    (E) Socially facilitated, identity facilitated, environmentally facilitated

465. According to the flyer, Dr. Xenu claims that disorders keep accumulating and none are ever eliminated. Which of the following statements is most true about how the number and categories of psychological disorder diagnoses have changed over time?

    (A) In the first edition of the DSM, psychiatrists decided that no more than 10 new diagnoses could be added in each future edition of the DSM.
    (B) The number of psychological diagnoses remains stable over time, with old diagnoses being removed as new diagnoses are added.
    (C) Many diagnoses in earlier versions of the DSM have been removed, and the categories have changed significantly among different editions of the DSM.
    (D) Many fewer psychological disorders are listed in the DSM now than in earlier editions because many disorders have been cured by new developments in psychoactive drugs.
    (E) The DSM doesn't technically list any labels for psychological disorders; it primarily describes behaviors and does not include labels used by the medical community.

DEFINITIONS

466. When psychologists use the term *maladaptive* in the context of psychological disorders, what do they mean?

    (A) Behaviors that do not conform to the current cultural environment
    (B) Individuals who cannot adapt to new, stressful situations
    (C) Behaviors that interfere with or get in the way of a person's daily life
    (D) Behaviors that, statistically, are extremely unusual in their environment
    (E) Individuals who believe they have developed a malady or disease that will eventually incapacitate them

467. Which of the following statements is true regarding how homosexuality was treated by the psychological community in the past?

    (A) Homosexuality was never listed as a psychological disorder since it does not meet the criteria of being maladaptive.
    (B) Some psychiatrists argued that homosexuality should be included in the DSM, but research psychologists prevented it from being included.
    (C) Throughout its history, the psychological community considered homosexuality part of a person's identity rather than a disorder.
    (D) The term *homosexuality* has been included as part of the description of psychological disorders in every edition of the DSM.
    (E) Homosexuality was considered a psychological disorder for about two decades, from the 1950s through the early 1970s.

468. Which of the following terms are associated with the medical model of psychological disorders?

    (A) Diagnosis, symptoms, treatment
    (B) Atypical, disturbing, maladaptive
    (C) Biopsychological, behavior genetics
    (D) Epigenetics, diathesis-stress model
    (E) Anxiety, mood, dissociative

469. Which of the following terms are associated with the biopsychosocial model of psychological disorders?

    (A) Anxiety, mood, dissociative
    (B) Epigenetics, diathesis-stress model
    (C) Internal locus of control, external locus of control
    (D) Biopsychological, behavior genetics
    (E) Physiological drives, psychological motivations

470. A therapist who uses terms like *cure, diagnosis,* and *symptoms* is most likely using which of the following?

    (A) Biopsychosocial model
    (B) Classical model
    (C) Psychodynamic model
    (D) Medical model
    (E) Treatment model

471. Therapists interested in epigenetics research and the influence of the diathesis-stress model on the development of psychological disorders are most likely using which model of psychological disorders?

    (A) Biopsychosocial model
    (B) Behavior genetics model
    (C) Humanistic model
    (D) Medical model
    (E) Cognitive-behavioral model

472. Which of the following statements best describes the purpose of the *Diagnostic and Statistical Manual of Mental Disorders* (DSM-5)?

    (A) It describes the history of treatments that have been used for different mental illnesses and the relative effectiveness of the different treatments.
    (B) It is an overall guidebook for statistics related to psychological research, including guidelines for which statistics to use for different kinds of research questions.
    (C) It is used by researchers to report which physical and mental medical diagnoses are most common and which are no longer used.
    (D) It is used by mental health care professionals to decide which diagnostic labels should be used to describe psychological disorders.
    (E) It is the fifth edition of the most commonly used APA textbook for college-level classes about psychological disorders.

473. What is the primary difference between the terms *insanity* and *psychological disorder*?

    (A) Psychological disorders are specific types of insanities.
    (B) Clinical psychologists treat psychological disorders, but insanity must be treated by psychiatrists.
    (C) Insanity is a legal term and is used in the context of the court system.
    (D) Psychological disorders are caused by environmental influences, while insanity is caused by genetic predispositions.
    (E) Insanities are specific kinds of psychological disorders and are more related to medical conditions than are psychological issues.

474. **Which of the following issues is an important area of research related to the DSM?**

(A) Correlations between labels and categories
(B) Reliability of diagnoses among practitioners
(C) Statistically significant differences between diagnoses
(D) Operational definitions of dependent variables
(E) Historical accuracy of terminology

475. **Which of the following statements describes a technique used to assess the reliability of the DSM?**

(A) Comparing outcome research about treatment effectiveness based on past research
(B) Including a false diagnostic label at random within each edition of the DSM in order to detect which practitioners may be misusing the manual
(C) Assigning different editions of the DSM to different parts of the world and measuring which edition provides the most consistent diagnoses
(D) Using the double-blind method to authenticate the validity of the inferential tests used in the DSM
(E) Measuring how often different practitioners choose the same diagnostic label from the DSM for the same description of behaviors

476. **Which of the following statements is most true about the relationship between psychological disorders and violent crime?**

(A) Individuals diagnosed with anxiety disorders are statistically more likely than those with mood disorders to be involved in violent crimes.
(B) Psychological disorders that are treated with psychoactive drugs are likely to be associated with violence.
(C) The term *insanity* is used in the context of the legal system, but lawyers do not use it to refer to psychological disorders that are associated with violence.
(D) Mental health issues are not involved in most violent crimes, and most people diagnosed with psychological disorders do not commit violent crimes.
(E) When socioeconomic class is included as a variable in studies about violent crime and mental health, researchers find that families with more wealth experience more issues.

477. **Which of the following kinds of psychological disorders are most commonly diagnosed?**

    (A) Social anxiety disorders
    (B) Post-traumatic stress disorder
    (C) Depressive disorders
    (D) Antisocial personality disorder
    (E) Bipolar disorder

478. **When do the first symptoms of psychological disorders typically occur?**

    (A) Symptoms usually first occur in late adolescence or early adulthood (before about age 25).
    (B) Some symptoms are usually evident in subtle ways soon after birth.
    (C) The symptoms typically appear after a person begins his or her career and assumes adult responsibilities.
    (D) The first symptoms typically occur after psychoactive drug use.
    (E) Symptoms almost always start later in life as hormonal influences lessen.

479. **The terms *generalized* and *free floating* are most likely to be used by clinical psychologists in which context?**

    (A) Depressive disorders
    (B) Anxiety disorders
    (C) Dissociative disorders
    (D) Schizophrenia
    (E) Phobias

480. **Which of the following are two of the most commonly diagnosed mood disorders?**

    (A) Major depressive disorder and bipolar disorder
    (B) Phobias and obsessive-compulsive disorder
    (C) Post-traumatic stress disorder and reactive disorder
    (D) Somatic disorder and conversion disorder
    (E) Dissociative disorder and antisocial personality disorder

481. **Which of the following elements is shared by all the somatic disorders?**

    (A) Neurological issues involving the soma, myelin sheath, and other neural structures

    (B) Symptoms expressed as physical issues, such as physical pain or disabilities

    (C) A combination of mood- and anxiety-related symptoms, usually instigated by high stress situations

    (D) Persistent feelings of being dissociated from one's body and physical self

    (E) Episodes of agnosia and synesthesia caused by deficiencies in neurotransmitter levels

482. **Depressive disorders are often associated with imbalances with which of the following neurotransmitters?**

    (A) Acetylcholine

    (B) Glutamate

    (C) Serotonin

    (D) Gamma-aminobutyric acid (GABA)

    (E) Selective serotonin reuptake inhibitor (SSRI)

483. **Which of the following is the most accurate statement about the relationship between environmental stresses and depressive disorders?**

    (A) Psychological disorders are influenced much more by genetics than by environmental stresses.

    (B) Environmental stresses alter the genetic predisposition toward depressive episodes.

    (C) Depressive disorders, unlike other psychological disorders, are caused by environmental stresses.

    (D) Stresses related to life events often come before major depressive episodes.

    (E) Genetic factors predetermine which individuals will develop symptoms of depressive disorders.

484. **Which of the following is a common negative symptom experienced by people diagnosed with schizophrenia?**

    (A) Threatening, negative hallucinations

    (B) Disorganized, meaningless speech

    (C) Inappropriate, embarrassing emotional reactions

    (D) Delusions of persecution

    (E) A flat affect or lack of emotions

485. **How does the DSM categorize psychological disorders?**

    (A) By similar symptoms and impacts on behaviors
    (B) According to when the disorder was first diagnosed historically
    (C) By which kind of treatment (cognitive, biological, and so on) is most recommended
    (D) During an annual national mental health conference of people diagnosed with that disorder
    (E) By the type of neurotransmitter causing the disorder

SCENARIOS

486. **Two psychiatrists, Dr. Kellison and Dr. Bower, are discussing recent changes in the DSM. They wonder if the diagnostic criteria for a new disorder listed in this new edition are specific enough. They decide that they will each read the same set of published case studies and independently choose the diagnosis they think best fits each case study. Then Dr. Kellison and Dr. Bower will compare their choices to see if they match. What are Dr. Kellison and Dr. Bower trying to test about the DSM?**

    (A) Validity
    (B) Accuracy
    (C) Reliability
    (D) Authenticity
    (E) Consistency

487. **Mr. Oleron's family reports that he is missing. A week later, Mr. Oleron is found is a neighboring town. He has no memory of how he got there, does not respond to his name, and seems generally confused and dazed. What category of disorder seems to fit Mr. Oleron's behaviors best?**

    (A) Depressive
    (B) Dissociative
    (C) Anxiety
    (D) Schizophrenic
    (E) Somatic

488. Mr. Vimes has suffered from being sad for years. He was passed over for a promotion at work because of his drinking. He lost touch with his friends and family because he was reluctant to leave the house. Recently, Mr. Vimes started spending large amounts of money on clothes and gambling recklessly. He is now far more excited about life, but he hasn't been able to reconnect with his family or friends. What psychological disorder seems to fit Mr. Vimes's behaviors best?

    (A) Major depression
    (B) Somatic depression
    (C) Bipolar disorder
    (D) Antisocial personality disorder
    (E) Post-traumatic stress disorder

489. Walter Plinge talks with his counselor about his recent emotional difficulties. "I just feel really frustrated all the time, and that's never going to change. I used to just get frustrated about work, but now it's all the time, and it affects everything I do in my life. I know I should just be able to snap out of it, but I can't. I think it's a part of my personality." Which list below describes the kinds of self-defeating cognitions Mr. Plinge is expressing?

    (A) Anxious, dissociated, depressed
    (B) Extroversion, neurotic, openness
    (C) Alarm, resistance, exhaustion
    (D) Stable, global, internal
    (E) Intimacy, passion, commitment

490. "I was sure I was going to die," Mr. Lipwig told his doctor. "My heart was racing, I felt a huge weight on my chest, and I wondered if I was having a heart attack. But you're telling me there's nothing wrong with me?" What psychological disorder most closely matches Mr. Lipwig's experience?

    (A) Specific phobia
    (B) Generalized anxiety disorder
    (C) Post-traumatic stress disorder
    (D) Somatic symptom disorder
    (E) Panic disorder

491. Some of Ms. Dinwiddie's friends referred her to the company's human resources department because they are worried about her. They noticed that Ms. Dinwiddie constantly checks the location of everything on her desk and moves any item that is "out of line." She gets very upset when anyone bumps her desk or even gets too close. Which of the following disorders might the company counselor talk about with Ms. Dinwiddie?

    (A) Obsessive-compulsive disorder
    (B) Panic disorder
    (C) Generalized anxiety disorder
    (D) Social anxiety disorder
    (E) Bipolar disorder

492. Agnes's therapist reports that Agnes sometimes blacks out during therapy sessions and wakes up claiming to be "Perdita," not Agnes. When this occurs, "Perdita" speaks with a different voice and claims to be a different person than Agnes. Which psychological disorder do you think Agnes's therapist may consider diagnosing Agnes with?

    (A) Somatoform disorder
    (B) Dissociative identity disorder
    (C) Schizophrenia
    (D) Schizotypal personality disorder
    (E) Dissociative amnesia with fugue

493. You read a newspaper article about a local therapist who is being accused of misconduct. He is accused of improper therapy techniques with a client who eventually expressed different personalities during therapy. A review board examined notes and video of therapy sessions and concluded that this therapist used improper, leading questions and other techniques that led the client to manufacture personalities. What psychological diagnosis was the client probably diagnosed with?

    (A) Schizophrenia
    (B) Social anxiety disorder
    (C) Obsessive-compulsive disorder
    (D) Dissociative identity disorder
    (E) Antisocial personality disorder

494. A client named Jonathan Tetime is referred to a counselor by the court system for evaluation. Mr. Tetime started getting in trouble with law enforcement officials early in life. He is described in reports as having a "lack of remorse and no conscience." He compulsively lies and often steals small items from stores. As Mr. Tetime got older, he started to pick on younger children, tormenting them both physically and emotionally. Which psychological disorder do you think the counselor may consider diagnosing Mr. Tetime with?

    (A) Post-traumatic stress disorder
    (B) Dissociative identity disorder
    (C) Antisocial personality disorder
    (D) Bipolar disorder
    (E) Schizophrenia

495. Myria's friends are worried about her because they feel she is too skinny. When they are eating together, sometimes Myria refuses to eat because she's "just not hungry." At other times, she eats a huge amount of food in one sitting. Myria often declines social invitations because she won't miss or alter her exercise regimen. She works out at least two hours a day, and her friends think that she may be exercising often more than that. Which psychological disorder might Myria's behaviors fit best?

    (A) Anorexia nervosa
    (B) Binge-eating disorder
    (C) Obsessive-compulsive disorder
    (D) Fugue disorder
    (E) Bulimia nervosa

496. Professor Keith is researching differences among how often different psychological diagnoses are used in different cultures. Which of the following diagnostic labels do you predict might vary the most among different countries?

    (A) Schizophrenia
    (B) Anorexia nervosa
    (C) Major depressive disorder
    (D) Bipolar disorder
    (E) Alzheimer's disease

497. Marco Soto was referred to a psychiatrist because he started reporting partial blindness after he witnessed a horrible traffic accident that involved some of his family members. Doctors can't find any physical cause for the blindness. Which of the following diagnoses do you predict the psychiatrist might investigate based on Marco's symptoms?

 (A) Conversion disorder
 (B) Illness anxiety disorder
 (C) Schizotypal personality disorder
 (D) Dissociative disorder
 (E) Catatonic schizophrenia

498. Researchers at a neuroscience lab announce that they uncovered a strong link between dopamine and the symptoms of a serious psychological disorder. This link was already known in the psychiatric community, but data from the neuroscience lab confirmed the connection. Which psychological disorder is the lab probably researching?

 (A) Generalized anxiety disorder
 (B) Schizophrenia
 (C) Conversion disorder
 (D) dissociative amnesia
 (E) Anorexia nervosa

NAMES

499. Which of the following best describes Sigmund Freud's perspective on psychological disorders?

 (A) Psychological disorders are caused by a combination of genetic predisposition and environmental stresses.
 (B) The symptoms of psychological disorders are largely controlled by brain chemistry, but cultural influences determine how the disorders are expressed.
 (C) Most psychological disorders are caused by traumatic life events.
 (D) Behaviors associated with disorders result from unresolved unconscious conflicts and anxieties.
 (E) Freud viewed disorders using the medical model, using the traditional symptom and diagnosis model.

500. Which researcher investigated the influence of psychological labels on the ways people are treated, including psychiatric treatments?

   (A) Carl Jung
   (B) Sigmund Freud
   (C) David Rosenhan
   (D) Philippe Pinel
   (E) Aaron Beck

501. Which of the following individuals argued early in the history of clinical psychology that individuals suffering from psychological disorders should be treated humanely rather than just be incarcerated and locked away?

   (A) Albert Ellis
   (B) Sigmund Freud
   (C) David Rosenhan
   (D) Philippe Pinel
   (E) John Watson

RESEARCH METHODS

502. Which of the following is the best description of the independent variable in Rosenhan's thud study, which investigated the influence of psychological labels on the ways people are treated?

   (A) The independent variable was the different ways the participants were treated after they faked their way into the mental health care hospitals.
   (B) There was no independent variable because the Rosenhan study was correlational research, examining how well a psychological diagnosis predicted the later treatment of patients.
   (C) Rosenhan's independent variable was the prediction that medical staff would continue to treat patients as if they were mentally ill even after their symptoms stopped.
   (D) The independent variable was identical to the dependent variable: the symptoms the participants faked in order to be admitted to the hospitals.
   (E) Rosenhan thought that psychological labels caused caregivers to react to people differently, so the independent variable in the study was the psychological labels.

503. **Which of the following research descriptions might be useful to help investigate the reliability of diagnostic labels in the DSM?**

    (A) Using a random sample of psychiatrists, providing the same descriptions of symptoms, and checking the labels each psychiatrist applies to the descriptions
    (B) A longitudinal study of individuals diagnosed with a specific disorder in order to determine if the label predicts the individual's long-term behavior
    (C) Gathering multiple points of data about individuals' behaviors in order to determine whether or not the label correlates with all the data points appropriate for the context
    (D) Using factor analysis in order to determine if the various factors are intercorrelated to acceptable levels
    (E) Using operational definitions to establish a true independent variable carefully in order to measure precisely the impact on the dependent variable

504. **A researcher wants to determine whether the symptoms of major depression are alleviated by depriving individuals of sleep. Which of the following describes how the researcher might use random assignment in this study?**

    (A) Randomly assign the dependent variable to at least half the sample group in order to determine whether or not the independent variable is effective.
    (B) Flip a coin to determine which individuals in the sample will participate in the sleep deprivation group and which will be in the other group.
    (C) Gather a list of individuals diagnosed with major depression, and use a random number table to determine who will participate in the study.
    (D) Operationally define half the group using a truly random procedure, such as a computer program.
    (E) Measure sleep deprivation at random intervals throughout the day and night across the entire sample.

505. A group of researchers carefully analyze video footage from a mental hospital that specializes in treating individuals with schizophrenia. The researchers gather data about these individuals' behaviors, tracking time stamps and sequences of behaviors carefully. Which of the following is being used in this study?

    (A) Case study
    (B) Experiment
    (C) Inferential statistics
    (D) Naturalistic observation
    (E) Correlation

506. If a researcher wanted to ensure that her research on a psychiatric drug is double blind, what should the researcher do?

    (A) She should make sure that the participants are not aware of the hypothesis or to which group they have been assigned.
    (B) The population should be blind as to whether they might be selected for the sample, and the sample should be blind as to whether or not they were chosen from the population.
    (C) Neither the researcher nor the participants should know who is assigned to which group in the experiment.
    (D) When data from the study are analyzed, they need to be analyzed by impartial observers who are "double blind" to the purpose of the study and the data analysis details.
    (E) Participants in both the experimental group and the control group must be blind, or unaware of the independent variable in the study.

PERSPECTIVES

507. Research in which psychological perspective is most likely to produce useful results for individuals who are diagnosed with schizophrenia?

    (A) Humanism
    (B) Cognitive
    (C) Behaviorism
    (D) Biological
    (E) Sociocultural

508. A therapist who treats people with specific phobias by rewarding them each time they are around the object of their phobia is using which psychological perspective?

    (A) Sociocultural
    (B) Humanism
    (C) Cognitive
    (D) Biological
    (E) Behaviorism

509. A therapist using the cognitive perspective might be most likely to treat clients with which of the following psychological disorders?

    (A) Schizophrenia
    (B) Major depression
    (C) Antisocial personality disorder
    (D) Dissociative identity disorder
    (E) Bipolar disorder

510. Which of the following perspectives might be most interested in research regarding international case studies of bulimia?

    (A) Behaviorism
    (B) Cognitive
    (C) Humanism
    (D) Biological
    (E) Sociocultural

Treatment of Psychological Disorders

CHAPTER 13

Answers for Chapter 13 are on pages 314–324.

STIMULUS

511. **Which of the following therapy techniques is best represented in the dialogue presented below?**

   Therapist: Where would you like to begin?

   Patient: I have difficulty getting on subways. I am afraid of them.

   Therapist: What are you telling yourself?

   Patient: That I am in danger.

   Therapist: What's the danger? I travel on subways all the time, and I've never been hurt.

   Patient: I think the danger is in my head. If someone looks at me, I think they want to hurt me.

   Therapist: You are inventing the danger. What can you tell yourself when you are afraid on the subway?

   Patient: I can tell myself that my fear is irrational. There is lots of evidence that subways are very safe. If something happened, I would most likely be safe.

   Therapist: What can you tell yourself so you won't panic?

   Patient: That I am overreacting and being irrational. My thoughts are wrong.

   Therapist: Right. It's your belief. You can always change your beliefs.

   (A) Active listening
   (B) Free association
   (C) Rational emotive behavior therapy (REBT)
   (D) Counterconditioning
   (E) Eye movement desensitization and reprocessing (EMDR)

DEFINITIONS

512. Which of the following individuals best demonstrates using an eclectic approach to therapy?

   (A) Emily: while expecting resistance during a session, she uses free association to bring insight to her patients' memories they have repressed since childhood.
   (B) Shannon: her use of active listening provides clients with an environment conducive to growth.
   (C) Jake: he uses systematic desensitization to help those with specific phobias.
   (D) Jill: she uses cognitive restructuring to alter illogical thinking patterns associated with depression.
   (E) Megan: she provides unconditional positive regard while focusing on changing illogical thinking and role playing more adaptive ways of behaving.

513. When traumatic experiences are pushed into the unconscious mind to protect the individual from experiencing anxiety, what has occurred?

   (A) Resistance
   (B) Free association
   (C) Active listening
   (D) Repression
   (E) Transference

514. Which of the following is the therapeutic technique most associated with Sigmund Freud?

   (A) Aversive conditioning
   (B) Active listening
   (C) Cognitive restructuring
   (D) Psychoanalysis
   (E) Flooding

515. Which of the following reflects the technique of free association?

   (A) The therapist listens carefully and paraphrases what he or she has heard.
   (B) The patient is asked to relax and then imagines a fear-evoking stimulus.
   (C) Antidepressant medications are prescribed to help balance depressed moods.
   (D) The therapist asks direct questions challenging illogical beliefs.
   (E) The patient is asked to relax and say aloud whatever comes to mind.

516. When an individual unconsciously redirects his or her emotions from one person, often an individual from the patient's childhood, it is called

    (A) a token economy.
    (B) transference.
    (C) client-centered therapy.
    (D) resistance.
    (E) exposure therapy.

517. Providing acceptance and support of another person regardless of what that individual says or does is central to which therapeutic approach?

    (A) Client-centered therapy
    (B) Psychoanalysis
    (C) Aversive conditioning
    (D) Rational emotive behavior therapy (REBT)
    (E) Flooding

518. Which of the following demonstrates systematic desensitization?

    (A) Lorianne paints her fingernails with polish that tastes terrible if she chews her nails.
    (B) Bryan tries to maintain his relaxed state while being exposed to increasingly fearful stimuli.
    (C) When she feels anxious, Parvene thinks to herself, "Everything is OK. This feeling will pass."
    (D) Brenda keeps a diary and shares her dreams with her therapist who helps interpret their meaning.
    (E) While sedated, Alex is given a dose of electrical current that triggers a seizure.

519. While considered upsetting, harmful, ineffective, and unethical today, at one time researchers attempted to change people's homosexual feelings by showing them erotic pictures and then applying a shock when they became aroused. This approach is called

    (A) aversive conditioning.
    (B) systematic desensitization.
    (C) transference.
    (D) flooding.
    (E) rational emotive behavioral therapy (REBT).

520. Which of the following benefits is unique to group therapy?

(A) It provides hope that change is possible.
(B) It allows individuals to see that they are not alone and that others face similar challenges.
(C) It provides an explanation as to why a person feels like he or she does.
(D) An individual can develop a trusting relationship with a therapist.
(E) An individual learns to take on more personal responsibility for his or her thoughts and feelings.

521. Antipsychotic drugs are close enough in chemical structure to dopamine that they can occupy dopamine's receptor sites and block its activity. These chemicals are called

(A) hallucinogens.
(B) depressants.
(C) agonists.
(D) stimulants.
(E) antagonists.

522. Selective serotonin reuptake inhibitors (SSRIs) are most effective in treating the primary symptoms of

(A) schizophrenia.
(B) depression.
(C) dissociative identity disorder (DID).
(D) specific phobias.
(E) borderline personality disorder.

523. Which of the following is commonly used to reduce the severity and frequency of the manic phase in the bipolar cycle?

(A) Antipsychotics
(B) Antidepressants
(C) Lithium
(D) Antianxiety drugs
(E) Electroconvulsive therapy (ECT)

524. Which of the following treatments may lead to memory loss?

(A) Repetitive transcranial magnetic stimulation (rTMS)
(B) Electroconvulsive therapy (ECT)
(C) Lithium
(D) Deep brain stimulation
(E) Selective serotonin reuptake inhibitors (SSRIs)

SCENARIOS

525. During free association, Jean notices that her patient changes the subject whenever she asks a probing question about the patient's relationship with her mother. Psychoanalysts call this experience

    (A) transference.
    (B) counterconditioning.
    (C) resistance.
    (D) cognitive restructuring.
    (E) meta-analysis.

526. When Lark said, "No one really understands what I've gone through and no one really cares," her therapist responded, "What I'm hearing is that you are frustrated by how others have treated you." Her therapist is using which of the following techniques?

    (A) Free association
    (B) Counterconditioning
    (C) Cognitive restructuring
    (D) Aversive conditioning
    (E) Active listening

527. After Rik misbehaved, his parent said, "What you did was wrong, and I don't want you to do it again. While your behavior was bad, you are not bad, and I will always love you." This statement reflects

    (A) resistance.
    (B) unconditional positive regard.
    (C) transference.
    (D) cognitive restructuring.
    (E) aversive conditioning.

528. As a child, Alan developed a fear of spiders after being surprised by one floating in a swimming pool. As an adult, Alan's therapist encourages him to relax while picturing a spider. The goal is to replace Alan's fear with a new response. This approach to therapy is called

    (A) psychoanalysis.
    (B) client-centered therapy.
    (C) a token economy.
    (D) cognitive restructuring.
    (E) counterconditioning.

529. As a part of Darcy's treatment for depression, her therapist asked her to be mindful of when she thought, "I can never do anything right." Whenever Darcy had that thought, she was to make a list of evidence that either supported or disproved this illogical thinking. Then she was to practice thinking, "I've made some mistakes, but most of the time I make good choices." Darcy's therapist is using which of the following techniques?

    (A) Resistance
    (B) Active listening
    (C) Counterconditioning
    (D) Cognitive restructuring
    (E) Aversive conditioning

530. Greg believes that others are plotting against him and often hears voices telling him that he is worthless. Which of the following would be most effective in helping decrease Greg's symptoms?

    (A) Antidepressants
    (B) Antianxiety drugs
    (C) Electroconvulsive therapy (ECT)
    (D) Antipsychotics
    (E) Stimulants

531. Which of the following best describes the use of electroconvulsive therapy (ECT)?

    (A) A coil is placed near the skull, and then a magnetic field is directed to a specific area of the cortex.
    (B) Implanted electrodes are placed into specific brain regions and send electrical impulses to specific areas in the brain.
    (C) While using an orbitoclast, a doctor severs the connections to the frontal lobe.
    (D) Patients are exposed to intense artificial light for prescribed periods of time.
    (E) A doctor administers anesthesia and a muscle relaxant and then delivers an electrical current to the brain to produce a seizure.

532. **Antidepressant drugs would be most effective in treating which of the following?**

(A) Arnold's thoughts are grandiose and disorganized as he strings together words that don't seem to make sense together.

(B) For many months Mary has been experiencing profound sadness, difficulty concentrating, difficulty sleeping, and suicidal thoughts.

(C) On the surface Don is charming, but he is a manipulative and accomplished liar who shows no remorse when he hurts others.

(D) Jessica is so terrified of spiders that she won't walk barefoot in her own home or go into her basement.

(E) Vivian worries that her headache signals that she is seriously ill even though she has no physical evidence of a disease.

533. **Vickie was depressed. Her therapist first helped Vickie identify self-defeating thoughts, such as, "I am a failure at everything I do." Her therapist then helped Vickie restructure her thinking and schedule one pleasant activity a day that she wouldn't normally do but that would allow Vickie to feel successful. The therapist's approach to Vickie best illustrates**

(A) psychoanalysis.

(B) a token economy.

(C) systematic desensitization.

(D) active listening.

(E) cognitive-behavioral therapy (CBT).

534. **As a freshman in high school, Kai felt stressed and started to do poorly. His parents suggested he visit with a therapist. The therapist taught Kai more about his body's response to stress and helped Kai isolate what he was telling himself. So, instead of thinking, "This class is too difficult; I will fail," Kai practiced thinking, "I studied hard. I am willing to give it my best." This approach to therapy is called**

(A) exposure therapy

(B) stress inoculation training

(C) a token economy

(D) active listening

(E) free association

NAMES

535. Who would be most likely to say the following?

"When a person realizes he has been deeply heard, his eyes moisten. I think in some real sense he is weeping for joy. It is as though he were saying, 'Thank God, somebody heard me. Someone knows what it's like to be me.'"

(A) Sigmund Freud
(B) Aaron Beck
(C) Carl Rogers
(D) B. F. Skinner
(E) Albert Ellis

536. Mary Cover Jones worked with Peter, a child terrified of rabbits. While Peter was calmly eating a snack, she would introduce a rabbit in a cage. Over time, she moved the cage closer and closer to Peter. After 2 months, Peter was able to hold the rabbit in his arms. Which of the following techniques is Mary Cover Jones known for developing?

(A) Free association
(B) Electroconvulsive therapy
(C) Active listening
(D) Rational emotive behavior therapy
(E) Counterconditioning

537. In treating depression, which of the following psychologists would use gentle questioning techniques aimed at helping the patient become more aware of his or her illogical thinking and restructuring such thought patterns?

(A) Sigmund Freud
(B) Carl Rogers
(C) Abraham Maslow
(D) Aaron Beck
(E) Joseph Wolpe

538. Behavior modification therapies strive to change the way individuals respond to environmental stimuli using both positive and negative reinforcement. Which of the following provided the bases for this approach to treatment?

(A) Aaron Beck
(B) B. F. Skinner
(C) Albert Ellis
(D) Carl Rogers
(E) Joseph Wolpe

RESEARCH METHODS

539. Sigmund Freud believed that repressed traumatic events could contribute to a person's present-day problems. Freud based his beliefs on the many interviews he conducted with individuals who presented unique problems. Freud's approach to developing his core beliefs stems from which of the following methods?

(A) Surveys
(B) Experiments
(C) Case studies
(D) Correlational studies
(E) Naturalistic observations

Use the following scenario to answer questions 540 and 541.

Dr. Pozniak was interested in the effectiveness of a new antianxiety medication. Three hundred patients were randomly assigned to two groups. Group A received the new medication, while Group B received a pill that had no active ingredients. After 6 months, Dr. Pozniak measured anxiety-related symptoms as reported by the participants.

540. It is important for Dr. Pozniak to have two groups because sometimes just believing in a cure can lead to an improvement. By having Group B, Dr. Pozniak is helping to control for

(A) ethical concerns.
(B) subject bias.
(C) perceptual adaptation.
(D) the placebo effect.
(E) sampling bias.

541. Based on Dr. Pozniak's experiment, what is the dependent variable?

    (A) The antianxiety medication
    (B) The number of patients
    (C) The method used to divide subjects into groups
    (D) The anxiety-related symptoms
    (E) The 6-month time period after first receiving the medication

PERSPECTIVES

542. Dr. Thomas listens carefully to what her patients say. She pays special attention to their dreams and what happened in their early childhood. She encourages her patients to identify what they are feeling and helps them understand the unconscious factors that drive their behavior. What psychological perspective does Dr. Thomas most likely identify with?

    (A) Cognitive
    (B) Behavioral
    (C) Psychodynamic
    (D) Evolutionary
    (E) Sociocultural

543. In the 1970s, hospitalized patients with schizophrenia earned small tokens for doing specific target behaviors, such as brushing their teeth or making their beds. Such tokens could be exchanged for other reinforcers, such as ice cream, puzzle books, or other desirable items. Which of the following perspectives provides the basis for this approach?

    (A) Cognitive
    (B) Biological
    (C) Humanistic
    (D) Behavioral
    (E) Psychodynamic

544. The electrical activity in the brain is altered in depressed patients undergoing repetitive transcranial magnetic stimulation (rTMS). In this procedure, a coil is held close to the scalp that focuses a magnetic field onto a specific area of the cortex. This approach to treating depression reflects which of the following perspectives?

    (A) Cognitive
    (B) Evolutionary
    (C) Biological
    (D) Behavioral
    (E) Psychodynamic

545. Maya was terrified of flying. Her therapist suggested that she try virtual reality exposure therapy in which she would be immersed in a computer-generated, three-dimensional world and guided through the experience of flying. Which type of therapist would be most likely to use this approach to treating specific phobias?

    (A) Behavioral
    (B) Biological
    (C) Psychodynamic
    (D) Humanistic
    (E) Evolutionary

546. Dr. Rao, whose treatment techniques focus on an individual's decision making, was ineffective in helping a Chinese client with a collectivist approach to problem solving. Which perspective focuses on the impact of a client's life experiences and values when approaching therapy?

    (A) Psychodynamic
    (B) Biological
    (C) Sociocultural
    (D) Humanistic
    (E) Evolutionary

Social Psychology

Answers for Chapter 14 are on pages 325–336.

STIMULUS

Use the newspaper classified advertisement below to answer questions 547–550.

547. Which of the following best describes an important difference between the study described in the newspaper clipping and the Zimbardo prison study?

  (A) The Zimbardo prison study took place at an actual prison, while this study seems to take place on a college campus.

  (B) In this study, this researcher highlights the IRB procedures followed and that participants can leave any time. Zimbardo has been criticized for potentially violating ethical requirements.

  (C) Zimbardo's study focused on obedience to the prison guards. The study described in the newspaper article seems to focus on authority rather than on obedience.

  (D) The research described in the newspaper article is most likely an experiment, while the Zimbardo prison study was a correlational study.

  (E) Zimbardo's prison study was concentrated over the course of 2 days, while the study described in the newspaper article will take place over a longer period of time.

548. **Which of the following best describes an important difference between the study described in the newspaper clipping and Asch's social psychology study?**

    (A) Asch's study focused on in-group and out-group bias rather than on the responses to authority as described in the newspaper clipping.
    (B) Both studies research perceptions of authority. However, Asch's participants were children while the study in the newspaper clipping uses college students.
    (C) The study described in the newspaper article is most likely a case study of the college students who respond to the ad. The Asch study was a true experiment with both experimental and control groups.
    (D) Asch's study investigated influences on conformity. The goal of the study in the newspaper clipping is to research influences on authority and obedience.
    (E) The researcher who posted the ad in the newspaper is most likely studying who responds to the newspaper article. Asch investigated responses to personal letters.

549. **Which of the following best describes an important difference between the study described in the newspaper clipping and Milgram's obedience study?**

    (A) The independent variable in Milgram's study was age, while the independent variable in the study described in the newspaper clipping is most likely year in school (college).
    (B) Milgram was a social psychologist, and the researcher described in the newspaper clipping is most likely a behaviorist.
    (C) The researcher in the newspaper clipping reveals that deception and confederates will be used in the study, while Milgram kept the use of confederates secret.
    (D) Milgram's obedience study was a qualitative study, while the study in the newspaper clipping is probably a quantitative study.
    (E) The research in the newspaper article includes deception, and Milgram's study did not.

550. **Which of the following is the most likely independent variable in the study described in the newspaper clipping?**

    (A) Perception of authority
    (B) Conformity
    (C) Perception of behavior
    (D) Response to authority
    (E) Age

DEFINITIONS

551. Which of the following theories explores how we explain the behaviors of other people by combining both situational and personality factors?
   (A) Trait theory
   (B) Attribution theory
   (C) Drive reduction theory
   (D) Fundamental attribution error
   (E) Locus of control theory

552. What concept can best explain why we are more likely to judge the behaviors of strangers harshly but give ourselves the benefit of the doubt?
   (A) Similarity
   (B) Attribution theory
   (C) Social facilitation
   (D) Fundamental attribution error
   (E) Social loafing

553. Which of the following statements is the most accurate summary of the fundamental attribution error?
   (A) We are more likely to attribute human behaviors to environmental factors, like stress, than to temporary biological factors, like genetics or brain chemistry.
   (B) Nonexperts are more likely to attribute successful performances to luck or chance, while experts are more likely to attribute success correctly to hard work and practice.
   (C) Behavioral attributions are more likely to be correct if they are based on long-term empirical data.
   (D) Inaccurate cognitive schemata are likely to cause incorrect attributions of others' behaviors.
   (E) We tend to attribute the behaviors of strangers to their character or personality but to attribute our own behavior to situational factors.

554. An advertisement that uses emotional language and attention-grabbing visuals in order to try to convince you to make a specific choice is using which persuasive method?
   (A) Norm of reciprocity
   (B) Central route to persuasion
   (C) Peripheral route to persuasion
   (D) The foot-in-the-door phenomenon
   (E) External locus of control

555. An advertisement uses compelling statistics and other relevant factual evidence to try to influence viewers' decisions. Which persuasion method is this advertisement using?

    (A) Norm of reciprocity
    (B) Central route to persuasion
    (C) Peripheral route to persuasion
    (D) The foot-in-the-door phenomenon
    (E) External locus of control

556. Which persuasion technique involves starting with a small request and then gradually increasing the request slightly until you eventually reach your final target request?

    (A) The door-in-the-face phenomenon
    (B) Central route to persuasion
    (C) Peripheral route to persuasion
    (D) The foot-in-the-door phenomenon
    (E) Norm of reciprocity

557. Which term describes the discomfort people feel when their actions aren't consistent with their thinking or internal attitudes?

    (A) Cognitive dissonance
    (B) Role playing
    (C) Self-serving bias
    (D) Ethnocentrism
    (E) Mere exposure effect

558. Which of the following factors most influences whether or not a person's behavior is influenced by conformity?

    (A) Genetic factors that are either activated or inhibited by environmental factors
    (B) Internal personality characteristics, such as extroversion or neuroticism
    (C) Past operant conditioning experiences, such as positive reinforcements for conforming
    (D) The presence of a strong, respected authority figure who is giving clear, forceful directions
    (E) Being surrounded by a unanimous group who are all making the same decision

559. Which of the following factors most influences whether or not a person's behavior is influenced by obedience?

    (A) Genetic factors that are either activated or inhibited by environmental factors
    (B) Internal personality characteristics, such as extroversion or neuroticism
    (C) Past operant conditioning experiences, such as positive reinforcements for conforming
    (D) The presence of a strong, respected authority figure who is giving clear, forceful directions
    (E) Being surrounded by a unanimous group who are all making the same decision

560. Which term describes enhanced performance that occurs in front of a group of people?

    (A) Group polarization
    (B) Social facilitation
    (C) Groupthink
    (D) Yerkes-Dodson law
    (E) Social loafing

561. Which term best describes the decreased effort a person is likely to give when the person knows that he or she is acting as part of a group?

    (A) Group polarization
    (B) Social facilitation
    (C) Groupthink
    (D) Yerkes-Dodson law
    (E) Social loafing

562. Many psychological concepts help us gain insight into our sense of self—our inner attitudes, beliefs, and ways of thinking. Which psychological concept could be said to involve the loss of self?

    (A) Self-actualization
    (B) Group polarization
    (C) Deindividuation
    (D) Self-fulfilling prophecy
    (E) Egocentrism

563. Which term might be most helpful in predicting the influence of a series of discussion groups on controversial topics?

(A) Obedience
(B) Group polarization
(C) Deindividuation
(D) Social facilitation
(E) Social loafing

564. Which of the following group discussion rules might help prevent groupthink?

(A) Requiring that every group include at least one person who disagrees with the other members of the group about the issue being discussed
(B) Making sure that no one individual in each group discussion is perceived as an authority figure or an expert
(C) Ensuring that every person in the group discussion has an equal amount of speaking time and that no one interrupts others during the discussion
(D) Establishing clear and understandable group norms, which are rules for behavior during the discussion
(E) Measuring the anxiety of group members both before and after the group discussion in order to determine whether or not stress played a role in the group's decisions

565. What is the most important difference between the definitions of prejudice and discrimination?

(A) Discrimination is a cognitive psychology concept, and prejudice is a social psychology concept.
(B) Prejudice occurs among groups, while discrimination occurs within a group.
(C) Discrimination occurs among "low-power" groups, while prejudice occurs between a "high-power" and a "low-power" group.
(D) Prejudices are attitudes, and discrimination involves behaviors.
(E) Discrimination is a historical term, and prejudice is a modern term.

566. Which of the following concepts could help explain why we tend to like places and people that are more familiar to us because of repeated contact?

(A) Similarity
(B) Companionate love
(C) Social facilitation
(D) Locus of control
(E) Mere exposure effect

567. Which social psychology principle is most closely related to the saying "You scratch my back, I'll scratch yours."

(A) Foot-in-the-door strategy
(B) Groupthink
(C) Norm of reciprocity
(D) Social facilitation
(E) Altruism

568. Which of the following concepts can best help explain the increase in crime that occurs as temperatures rise?

(A) Social scripts
(B) Frustration-aggression principle
(C) Operant conditioning
(D) Fundamental attribution error
(E) Observational learning

569. Which concept might help explain why we are more likely to appreciate social media posts by people whom we agree with and are similar to than posts by people who don't meet these criteria?

(A) Ingroup bias
(B) Similarity theory
(C) Groupthink
(D) Self-fulfilling prophecy
(E) Discrimination

570. Children's literature and stories often end with a satisfying moral conclusion: the evil characters are punished, and the good characters are rewarded. This storytelling pattern may be satisfying to young people because of which of the following?

    (A) Positive reinforcement
    (B) Feel-good, do-good phenomenon
    (C) Ingroup bias
    (D) Just-world phenomenon
    (E) Preconventional morality

571. Social psychology researchers find that superordinate goals help reduce which of the following?

    (A) Ingroup bias
    (B) Generalization
    (C) Frustration-aggression principle
    (D) Confounding variables
    (E) Selection bias

SCENARIOS

572. Lorenzo is excited about buying a motorcycle. He researches what brand to buy. During his research, though, he reads about the number of brain injuries caused by motorcycle accidents. After completing this research, Lorenzo decides to not buy a motorcycle after all. This change of heart is an example of which social psychology process?

    (A) Attitudes affecting actions
    (B) Conformity
    (C) Obedience
    (D) Actions affecting attitudes
    (E) Social facilitation

573. Lance and Carter are hanging out with their friends Guy and Sam. Guy and Sam talk Lance and Carter into playing basketball, even though Lance and Carter really don't like basketball. Later that week, the P.E. teacher asks them how they feel about basketball, and Lance and Carter say, "Oh, it's OK. I don't love it, but I don't hate it." This change may be an example of what social psychology process?

    (A) Attitudes affecting actions
    (B) Conformity
    (C) Obedience
    (D) Actions affecting attitudes
    (E) Social facilitation

574. On his first day at a new school, Wolfgang wears his Nebraska Huskers cap pulled down tightly on his head all day. His classmates conclude that Wolfgang is a big football fan. However, the only reason Wolfgang wore his hat that day was that he woke up with horrible bed head. Wolfgang's classmates are guilty of which of the following?

    (A) Stereotyping
    (B) Concept formation
    (C) Ingroup bias
    (D) Fundamental attribution error
    (E) Selection bias

575. Which of the following is an example of the central route to persuasion?

    (A) A television commercial that uses a well-liked actor to endorse life insurance
    (B) A vitamin ad that explains the health benefits and side effects of a vitamin pill
    (C) A case study that describes in detail a woman who is forced to give up her daughter for adoption
    (D) A nonfiction book with a cover designed by a famous graphic artist
    (E) An online TED Talk with over one million likes and over a thousand comments

576. Which of the following is an example of the peripheral route to persuasion?

   (A) A television commercial that uses a well-liked actor to endorse life insurance
   (B) A vitamin ad that explains the health benefits and side effects of a vitamin pill
   (C) A research paper that uses inferential statistics to determine whether or not a result is significant
   (D) Survey results that indicate whether or not a politician is gaining popularity
   (E) A YouTube woodworking instructional video with an advertisement for a power saw

577. Swedish Ambassador Felmet met with the delegation from Norway to discuss fishing rights in disputed waters between their countries. Which of the following psychological concepts might be most useful during these negotiations?

   (A) Self-serving bias
   (B) Bystander effect
   (C) Foot-in-the-door phenomenon
   (D) Self-disclosure
   (E) Just-world phenomenon

578. Mr. Miller's classmates in high school remember his disturbing opinions about women and ethnic minorities. Later in life, the company that Mr. Miller works for is acquired by a different corporation, and Mr. Miller now works for a female boss. Over the next few months, Mr. Miller's friends notice that he becomes less misogynistic and more open-minded. Which psychological principle might be the cause of Mr. Miller's attitude change?

   (A) Ingroup bias
   (B) Collectivism
   (C) Superordinate goals
   (D) Just-noticeable difference
   (E) Cognitive dissonance

579. Which of the following concepts might be one of the most powerful forces that leads people to join and stay in religious cults?
    (A) Absolute threshold
    (B) Conformity
    (C) Variable-interval schedules
    (D) Selective attention
    (E) Attribution

580. Ms. Band, a third-grade teacher, likes to talk with new teachers at her school about "the look"—a way of looking at an individual student as a discipline technique. Which type of psychological research might be most interesting to Ms. Band?
    (A) Binocular disparity
    (B) Visual capture
    (C) Conformity research
    (D) Obedience research
    (E) Norms of reciprocity research

581. Dr. Wolfe declares that he is going to start using social facilitation to help improve student performance in class. Students will be randomly chosen to write a response to a free-response question (FRQ) and project it onto the screen at the front of the room. If Dr. Wolfe wants this technique to help performance, which of the following is a key factor according to social facilitation theory?
    (A) Social facilitation predicts that the ingroup (the group that is perceived as more skilled) in the class will perform better in this social situation.
    (B) The class will perceive this challenge as a superordinate goal and will socially facilitate classmates' answers in order to maintain group cohesion.
    (C) The FRQ tasks must be fairly easy for the students so that the social situation enhances, rather than hurts, their performance.
    (D) This high-pressure social situation will inhibit students' performance on cognitive tasks, such as writing an FRQ.
    (E) Writing in front of other students is likely to increase selective attention and self-efficacy, enhancing student performance.

582. Professor Herting decides to require her introductory psychology students to organize themselves into groups and ask each group to complete an independent research project. Which of the following concepts might interfere most when Professor Herting assigns grades to individual students in each group?

    (A) Social loafing
    (B) Operational definition
    (C) Group polarization
    (D) Availability heuristic
    (E) Confidence interval

583. Which social psychology concept might explain why so many people are attracted to the following social situations that all involve large crowds behaving in unison: a soccer game, a pop music concert, a religious revival meeting, and a dance/rave?

    (A) Debriefing
    (B) Obedience
    (C) Attribution
    (D) Groupthink
    (E) Deindividuation

584. A group of social psychologists wants to organize political discussion groups in order to reduce hostilities and misunderstandings in their community. The psychologists decide to make sure each discussion group includes people with different opinions about the discussion topic. Which psychological concept may have convinced them to organize the discussion groups in this way?

    (A) Group polarization
    (B) Obedience
    (C) Social facilitation
    (D) Groupthink
    (E) Deindividuation

585. A small town is surprised when a young man wins its mayoral election. The young man appoints several people he admires from the local community college to serve as his consultation cabinet. The individuals in the cabinet all respect each other and want to be sure to maintain group harmony. Together, they decide to revitalize the town by investing a significant amount of money in a winter sports complex to attract tourists. They call the complex Ice Town. It quickly fails, nearly bankrupting the town. Which psychological concept might help explain why the mayor and the consultation cabinet made such a poor decision?

(A) Fundamental attribution error
(B) Groupthink
(C) Cognitive dissonance
(D) Fluid intelligence
(E) Long-term potentiation

NAMES

586. Participants in a research study are convinced to perform a boring task, and then their attitudes about that task are measured. The study finds that people change their attitudes about how boring the task is based on whether they are rewarded for performing the task. Which psychological researcher might be most interested in this research study?

(A) Solomon Asch
(B) Stanley Milgram
(C) Leon Festinger
(D) Philip Zimbardo
(E) Bibb Latane

587. Which of the following questions would Solomon Asch's research help answer?

(A) What determines whether a person will cause harm to another person?
(B) Why are some people more likely to perform altruistic acts, while others refuse to help even in obvious emergency situations?
(C) Are we more influenced by our inner morals and character or by the social roles and influences we encounter daily?
(D) Why do some people dress the same as their friends and social group, while others take risks with their fashion choices?
(E) Are our actions influenced by cultural stereotypes we are not consciously aware of?

588. In the future, some individuals involved in atrocities committed during the ongoing war in Syria might be brought to trial for war crimes. Research from which of the following psychologists might be most relevant during these trials?

    (A) Solomon Asch
    (B) Stanley Milgram
    (C) Leon Festinger
    (D) Hermann Ebbinghaus
    (E) Bibb Latane

589. Which psychologist's research has been criticized based on its methodological flaws, such as the lack of a true control group and ethical violations?

    (A) Solomon Asch
    (B) Elliott Aronson
    (C) Leon Festinger
    (D) Philip Zimbardo
    (E) Bibb Latane

590. Which of the following researchers are most associated with bystander intervention research?

    (A) Watson and Skinner
    (B) Asch and Milgram
    (C) Festinger and Carlsmith
    (D) Darley and Latane
    (E) Myers and Dewall

RESEARCH METHODS

591. Which of the following is the closest description of an independent variable in the Zimbardo Stanford prison study?

    (A) The instructions given to the guards about how to treat the prisoners
    (B) Manipulating prisoners' conditions over the course of the experiment
    (C) Films and experimenter notes about the behaviors of the guards and the prisoners
    (D) Students who responded to the newspaper advertisement asking for participants in the study
    (E) Whether a participant was randomly assigned to the guard role or to the prisoner role

592. **How was the dependent variable in the Milgram obedience study operationally defined?**

  (A) The level of shock the teacher administered
  (B) Whether the participant was assigned the teacher role or the learner role
  (C) Measures of the verbal and nonverbal behaviors of the teachers
  (D) Learner performance on the tasks
  (E) Whether or not the teachers obeyed the orders of the authority figure

593. **Which of the following statements accurately describes the role of confederates in the Zimbardo, Asch, and Milgram studies?**

  (A) Asch used confederates to research conformity. No confederates were used in either the Milgram or the Zimbardo study.
  (B) The Milgram obedience study depended on the use of confederates since deception was used. Neither the Asch nor the Zimbardo study required confederates.
  (C) Confederates were used in the Asch (conformity) and Milgram (obedience) studies but not in the Zimbardo prison study.
  (D) Confederates add power to the inferential power of the experimental method. So, all three researchers used confederates in order to best measure social influences.
  (E) Confederates and deception were essential in the Zimbardo prison and in the Asch conformity studies. In contrast, the Milgram obedience study used a true control group.

594. **What was the dependent variable in Sherif's Robbers Cave study?**

  (A) Superordinate goals
  (B) Random assignment to experimental and control conditions
  (C) Careful observations of the participants' behaviors toward each other
  (D) Evidence of ingroup/outgroup bias
  (E) A physical description of the supposed thief based on eyewitness testimony

595. Which of the following is one possible independent variable that Asch may have tested in his conformity study?

(A) The proximity of the authority figure to the participants
(B) Varying how many confederates gave the wrong answer to the key question
(C) Whether or not confederates were used
(D) Determining whether participants conformed to the incorrect answer given by the confederates
(E) The number of times participants gave the same answer to the key question as did the confederates

596. Which elements of the experimental method are used more often in social psychology research than in other kinds of psychology research?

(A) Random sampling and assignment
(B) Independent variables
(C) Dependent variables
(D) Double-blind technique
(E) Deception and confederates

PERSPECTIVES

597. A psychology researcher hypothesizes that participants in Asch's conformity study conformed to the incorrect answer because of their schemata about how adults should behave politely in groups. Which psychological perspective does this hypothesis represent?

(A) Humanistic psychology
(B) Sociocultural psychology
(C) Cognitive psychology
(D) Behaviorism
(E) Biological

598. A social psychology study finds that no matter what kind of social situation participants are placed in, the hierarchy of needs usually predicts the participants' behaviors well. For example, participants act to reduce physiological needs if needed before other kinds of needs. This research most supports which psychological perspective?

    (A) Humanistic psychology
    (B) Sociocultural psychology
    (C) Cognitive psychology
    (D) Behaviorism
    (E) Biological

599. Professor Brunsman discovers that positive reinforcements cause specific kinds of reactions to social cues. These reactions are consistent no matter which individuals receive the positive reinforcements. These reactions are also consistent across social contexts. Professor Brunsman is exploring the interaction between which of the following?

    (A) Humanistic and positive psychology
    (B) Sociocultural and social psychology
    (C) Cognitive and humanistic psychology
    (D) Behaviorism and social psychology
    (E) Biological and behavioral psychology

600. Researchers discover that a recently discovered neurotransmitter is involved in several important aspects of human behavior. They found that when this neurotransmitter is blocked by an antagonist, we are far less likely to commit the fundamental attribution error. This research could be used to argue that which psychological perspective might explain many social psychology findings?

    (A) Humanistic psychology
    (B) Sociocultural psychology
    (C) Cognitive psychology
    (D) Behaviorism
    (E) Biological

ANSWERS

CHAPTER 1: HISTORY AND APPROACHES

Stimulus

1. **(B)** Wilhelm Wundt and other professors in Germany are credited with starting the science of psychology because they used the scientific method and laboratory experiments to carefully investigate human perception. Choices A and D are not mentioned in the excerpt. Choice C is not an accurate statement about the history of psychology. Choice E is inaccurate because Freud did not begin psychology and did not investigate sensation. (Skill 1c)

2. **(D)** Biopsychology is an important and current psychological perspective. However, this perspective (the influence of genetics and brain chemistry on thinking and behavior) is not mentioned in the excerpt. Evolutionary theory, choice A, is not mentioned in the excerpt. Choices B and C are both historical psychological perspectives but not contemporary ones. Choice E is another an important psychological perspective. However, it is referenced when the excerpt states, "another group decides that we shouldn't even talk about 'thinking' anymore because that can't be measured, and we should only describe behaviors." (Skill 1c)

3. **(E)** The excerpt clearly describes the behaviorist perspective ("another group decides that we shouldn't even talk about 'thinking' anymore because that can't be measured, and we should only describe behaviors") and cognitive psychology ("a different group decides that thinking might just be important after all"). Choice A does not list conflicting perspectives. Instead, these two perspectives align in their view of the biological causes of thinking and behavior. Choice B mixes a personality measure (trait theory) and a psychological perspective. Choice C lists two competing explanations of hypnosis. The terms in choice D both describe talk therapies. (Skill 1c)

Definitions

4. **(D)** Applied research tries to find solutions to specific problems, as in increasing volunteerism. Choice A focuses on increasing our knowledge of basic psychological phenomena. Choice B is a method where a subject provides a subjective report of his or her experiences. Choice C is a statistical technique used to identify trends in large amounts of data. Choice E is a way of determining which genes are involved in the expression of a trait by examining the DNA of family members who show that trait and those who do not. (Skill 1a)

5. **(E)** Cognitive psychologists research how our mental interpretations of the world (how we think about what happens to us) influence our

actions. Choice E refers to students' mental interpretations of the world and the impact of these interpretations on anxiety. Choice A refers to conditioning (learning theory). Choice B references biological influences (biological perspective). Psychoanalytic theory references the unconscious mind (choice C). Sociocultural psychologists emphasize the importance of cultural rules and conventions (choice D). (Skill 1a)

6. **(B)** Behaviorists research conditioned and unconditioned relationships among stimuli and responses. Choices A, C, and D are psychological perspectives. However, they are not specifically interested in stimuli and automatic physiological responses. Choice E isn't a psychological perspective. Developmental psychology is a psychological research subfield. However, developmental psychologists may use any of the psychological perspectives in their work. (Skill 1a)

7. **(C)** Cognitive psychologists investigate our cognitive (thinking) interpretations of events and how the actions of others influence our behavior. Behavioral psychologists research the influence of rewards and punishments. The perspectives listed in choice A do not focus specifically on rewards/punishments or on cognitions. Choices B and E mix psychological perspectives (sociocultural and evolutionary) and historical psychological perspectives. Choice D lists two perspectives focused on the physiological causes of behavior, not on how we think about events or rewards/punishments. (Skill 1a)

8. **(E)** The researchers who started the positive psychology movement were interested in investigating the "positive" end of the human experience—how we use our strengths and virtues to improve lives. Choices A and B are factually incorrect. Many clinical psychologists are interested in and use positive psychology (choice C). However, positive psychology is not used exclusively by clinical psychologists. Psychology is the science of human thinking and behavior, so choice D is incorrect. (Skill 1a)

9. **(C)** Clinical psychologists treat psychological disorders or other cognitive/emotional issues. Choice A would be most relevant to developmental psychologists or to psychological historians. Choice B is a concept from learning/behavioral psychology. The experimental method (choice D) is used by all psychological researchers. Statistical principles might be interesting to experimental methodologists but probably not to clinical psychologists. Clinical psychologists often work with clients on personality-related issues (choice E). However, the reliability and validity issues of personality testing are not the main focus of clinical psychology. (Skill 1a)

10. **(A)** Psychoanalysis, beginning with Sigmund Freud, was revolutionary because it involved talking with patients about mental issues. In many ways, the advent of psychoanalysis marks the beginning of clinical

psychology. Practitioners of psychoanalysis primarily used case study methodology rather than experiments (choice B). They were interested primarily in internal states like emotion (choice C). In the early history of psychoanalysis, no attempts were made to investigate across cultures as referred to in choice D. Choice E refers to positive psychology, not psychoanalysis. (Skill 1a)

11. **(B)** The early behaviorists wrote a manifesto declaring that for psychology to be a science, it needed to focus exclusively on what can be measured, which is behavior, rather than on internal cognitive states that can't be observed. The other psychological movements referred to in choices A, C, D, and E would not have agreed with this statement. These other movements were all interested in internal cognitive states to greater or lesser degrees. (Skill 1a)

Scenarios

12. **(C)** Evolutionary psychologists believe that certain behavioral predispositions, including fears, have been passed down through generations because these traits increase our chance of survival. Choice A focuses on observable behaviors learned from the environment. Choice B looks at human potential for growth and focuses on the role of free will in our behavior. Choice D supposes that our thoughts influence our behavior. Choice E considers the role of unconscious forces in shaping behavior. (Skill 1c)

13. **(D)** Psychometricians research how best to measure psychological constructs, such as reading achievement. Choice A is relevant to how we learn to read as young people, but developmental psychologists are not likely to be interested in specific issues related to this kind of testing. Choices B, C, and E do not specifically focus on measurement issues and are therefore not relevant to the scenario. (Skill 1c)

14. **(A)** Sociocultural psychologists (also known as cross-cultural psychologists) research how psychological principles do or do not influence human behavior in different countries and cultures. Choice B, behaviorism, matches Dr. Keith's early research career. Cognitive psychologists, choice C, research how the ways we think and remember information influence our behaviors. Humanism and functionalism, choices D and E, are not relevant to this scenario. Neither one focuses on examining how psychological research applies across cultures. In addition, choice E refers to a historical perspective, not to a modern perspective. (Skill 1c)

15. **(D)** Researchers from the humanist perspective, like Abraham Maslow, were interested in how people could become their "best selves." Maslow

used examples of "self-actualized" individuals throughout history (like Gandhi) to show how people progressed through different stages of needs as they grew into self-actualized individuals. Researchers specializing in the perspectives mentioned in choices A, B, and C might be interested in specific aspects of the topic Steve mentions. However, they don't focus specifically on self-actualization. Choice E, Gestalt psychology, focuses on how people put individual elements into a "whole" perception, investigating the influence of details like grouping, similarity, and other factors. (Skill 1c)

Names

16. **(B)** Freud believed that our conscious mind represses unacceptable impulses, anxieties, and fears. These repressed thoughts form our unconscious mind, which ultimately controls much of our thinking and behavior. Choice A refers to our tendency to conform to (agree with) the opinion of the majority of a group. Choice C is a direct observation of humans or other animals in their natural environments. Choice D refers to the negative impact of rewards on behaviors that are intrinsically motivated. Choice E involves the manipulation of an independent variable under controlled conditions and its effect on the dependent variable. (Skill 1a)

17. **(E)** Wundt used the method of introspection. He asked subjects to examine their own thoughts carefully and to report their conscious experiences in order to investigate mental experiences. Choice A refers to an experimental technique where subjects are assigned by chance to either an experimental or a control condition. Choice B describes a method used by psychoanalysts to gain insight into unconscious processes. Choice C is a skill used by humanistic therapists that involves mirroring back feelings communicated by a client. Choice D is an operant conditioning method used to teach new behaviors. (Skill 1b)

Perspectives

18. **(D)** Dr. Leary is interested in examining the relationship between biological processes (the impact of oxytocin) and behavior (drug use), which is the focus of the biological perspective. Choice A concentrates on the conditions that lead to growth. Choice B aims at explaining how observable behaviors are learned from the environment. Choice C centers on applying Darwin's theory of evolution to behavioral traits. Choice E investigates the impact of unconscious processes on behavior. (Skill 1c)

CHAPTER 2: METHODS

Stimulus

19. **(A)** The data chart indicates that as school absences increase, grade point averages decrease. This is a negative correlation. This relationship is correctly depicted in choice A. Choice B depicts a positive correlation, where as one variable increases so does the other variable. Since the data points are without pattern in choice C, this scatter plot shows that there is no relationship between the two variables. Choice D illustrates a curvilinear relationship. That relationship occurs when one variable increases, so does the second variable, but only up to a certain point. Then, as one variable continues to increase, the other decreases. Choice E illustrates no relationship between the two variables. (Skill 2)

20. **(C)** The data in the chart shows a negative relationship. As student absenteeism increases, grade point averages decrease. Choice A, a positive correlation, means that as the number of student absences increases, grade point averages also increase. A perfect relationship, choice B, means that the relationship between the two variables is either positive or negative 100% of the time. This is not indicated in the data provided in the chart. If there were no relationship between the two variables (choice D), researchers could not predict the presence of one variable from the presence of the other. This is not the relationship suggested by the data provided. Significance, choice E, refers to the likelihood that differences between groups are likely due to chance. The data provided do not allow for such an inference to be made. (Skill 2)

21. **(D)** Choice D illustrates the correct negative correlation between absenteeism and grades. It also uses appropriate correlational language. Choices A, B, and C use causal language. Since this is a correlational study, using language that suggests cause and effect would be inappropriate. In addition, choice B suggests a positive correlation between the two variables. Choice E suggests that no relationship was found between student absenteeism and grades, which was not suggested by the data. (Skill 2)

Definitions

22. **(E)** If a sample is drawn randomly from a population, that sample is more likely to be representative. Replication, choice A, is an important step in validating research findings, but it doesn't specifically relate to generalizing results from a sample to a population. Choice B allows researchers to be sure that individual characteristics are distributed more evenly between the experimental and control groups so that differences between

the groups are more likely due to the manipulation of the independent variable. Choice C allows researchers to control for experimenter bias and participant expectations. Choice D lets researchers control for the belief that a treatment will be effective. (Skill 1a)

23. **(E)** Theories attempt to explain events by proposing ideas that organize and integrate what has been observed about a particular phenomenon. Choice A describes an operational definition. Choice B focuses on the individual differences of those in a sample drawn from a population. Choice C concerns how participants in an experiment are randomly assigned to either an experimental or a control condition. Choice D relates to the ethical guidelines that direct the treatment of participants, including informed consent and debriefing, in research studies. (Skill 1a)

24. **(D)** The hypothesis is central to research. It identifies what outcomes support or invalidate the theory from which the hypothesis was generated. Choice A, correlation, looks at the relationship between two variables. Choice B, meta-analysis, refers to a statistical technique that combines the results of numerous research studies. A theory, choice C, is an attempt to explain a particular phenomenon. A theory is the source for a hypothesis. Choice E, independent variable, is the factor manipulated across different conditions in an experiment. (Skill 1a)

25. **(A)** The key component of an operational definition is measurement. Researchers must specify how the variables will be measured. Choice A clearly outlines that the researcher will collect grade point averages to measure the impact of listening to music in class. Choice B does not provide a specific measurement for judgment. Choice C also does not provide a specific method for measuring happiness in college students. Choice D lacks detail about how the researchers would measure "empty nest syndrome." Choice E does not explain what constitutes aggressive behavior and how that behavior will be measured. (Skill 1b)

26. **(B)** When a researcher operationally defines his or her procedures, it assists others in repeating the earlier study. Random sampling, choice A, helps ensure that the sample is representative of the population. Random assignment, choice C, helps minimize the differences between those in the experimental group and those in the control group. The double-blind procedure, choice D, allows researchers to control for experimental bias and participant expectations. Choice E, the debriefing of participants at the end of a research study, is ethically required in an experiment. (Skill 1a)

27. **(A)** Since a case study focuses either on one person or on a group of individuals who share a common unusual characteristic, generalizability to the population is a drawback of its use. Such atypical cases can lead

researchers to draw conclusions that cannot be applied to all people. Choice B, which describes wording effects, is more of an issue when a researcher conducts a survey. Survey questions can be phrased in a way that impacts the results. Choice C describes the use of the double-blind technique to reduce experimental bias in an experiment. Choice D is not accurate in describing case studies as they tend to take a long time to complete. Choice E is more relevant to experimentation, which is the only method that involves the manipulation of variables. (Skill 1a)

28. **(E)** Naturalistic observation allows researchers to observe and record the behavior of organisms in their natural environment. Choice A describes an advantage of using an experiment. Choice B describes the use of a case study in research. Choice C is a description of a survey. Choice D refers to the use of a correlational study. (Skill 1a)

29. **(D)** Random sampling helps a researcher obtain a group of participants that is representative of the population. From a sample that is representative, a researcher has greater confidence in generalizing the results to the population. Random assignment, choice A, is used in an experiment to minimize differences among representatives in the experimental and control conditions. The double-blind technique, choice B, allows a researcher to control for bias in an experiment. Operationally defining procedures, choice C, allows other researchers to replicate research studies. Informed consent, choice E, is required by the current ethical guidelines to ensure participants understand the nature of the study before agreeing to participate. (Skill 1a)

30. **(C)** Correlational studies involve using a statistical measure, called a correlation coefficient, to determine how closely two variables are related. If a correlation exists between two variables, the presence of one variable can predict the presence of the other. Random assignment, choice A, is used to ensure that the subject variables in both the experimental and control groups are equalized. Case studies, choice B, allow researchers to study an unusual instance in detail. Surveys, choice D, provide researchers with self-reporting data on an individual's attitudes. Statistical significance, choice E, indicates how likely chance is operating in differences found among groups in an experiment. (Skill 1a)

31. **(E)** A scatter plot contains an x-axis (horizontal), a y-axis (vertical), and a series of dots. Each dot signifies the values of the x- and y-variables in a data set. The points reveal the direction and strength of the relationship between the variables. A normal curve, choice A, is a visual representation of data. It is distributed in a symmetrical, bell-shaped curve with most scores near the mean and fewer scores near the extremes. Factor analysis,

choice B, is a statistical technique that allows researchers to reduce large amounts of data by identifying clusters of related factors. A histogram, choice C, is a bar graph of a frequency distribution. Statistical significance, choice D, suggests how likely the differences between groups are due to chance. (Skill 1a)

32. **(D)** A positive correlation indicates that as one variable increases, the other variable also increases. Choice A is incorrect because a positive correlation means the variables have a direct relationship, not an indirect relationship. Choice B is incorrect because a correlation of .70 suggests a strong relationship between the two variables. A finding that is statistically significant, choice C, indicates that differences between groups are probably not due to chance. Statistical significance is not reported by a correlation coefficient. Whether or not the data are normally distributed, choice E, cannot be inferred by a correlation coefficient. (Skill 2)

33. **(B)** A correlation coefficient ranges from −1 to +1. The weaker the relationship is, the closer the number is to 0. In this case, +.20 is closest to zero and reflects the weakest relationship of the choices given. Choice A, −1.00, reflects a perfect negative relationship between two variables. Choices C, D, and E are closer to either +1 or −1 and suggest a stronger relationship between two variables. (Skill 2)

34. **(E)** Because there is no manipulation of a variable across carefully controlled conditions, correlational studies can only suggest possible cause-and-effect relationships. A possible third variable cannot be ruled out that may be leading to the perceived relationship. Choice A is defining a cross-sectional study. Choice B refers to doing a meta-analysis. Choice C describes a standard deviation. Choice D explains statistical significance. (Skill 1a)

35. **(C)** Since individuals tend to grow taller as they get older, you could predict that a positive correlation would be found. A positive correlation indicates that as one variable increases, the other variable also increases. A negative correlation, choice A, would indicate that as one variable increases, the other decreases. A perfect correlation, choice B, can either be positive (+1) or negative (−1). If a perfect correlation exists, knowing the value of one variable allows you to predict the value of the other variable exactly. An illusory correlation, choice D, exists when you perceive a relationship between variables that does not really exist. Significance, choice E, refers to the likelihood that differences in the collected data from either an experimental or a control group are likely due to chance. (Skill 3)

36. **(A)** When a person perceives a relationship that doesn't really exist, it is an illusory correlation. In this example, the football player sees a relationship

between wearing his lucky socks and winning games. Choice B is an example of a color afterimage. Choice C illustrates the process of cognitive dissonance. Choice D is an example of parallel processing. Choice E reflects the ability to conserve, which is an ability first present in those who are concrete operational. (Skill 1b)

37. **(E)** Since an experiment is conducted under controlled conditions and with at least two randomly assigned groups, it is the only research method listed that allows a researcher to determine if there is a cause-and-effect relationship between variables. Since correlational studies (choice A), case studies (choice B), naturalistic observations (choice C), and surveys (choice D) lack controlled conditions, a researcher cannot use these methods to specify cause and effect. (Skill 1a)

38. **(D)** Random assignment is unique to experimental design because in an experiment, researchers manipulate an independent variable while holding constant other variables across experimental and control groups. In order to minimize the differences among individuals in different groups, researchers use random assignment. Random sampling, choice A, is not used only in experiments but also when a researcher does a survey to ensure that the sample is representative of the population. Positive correlations, choice B, are obtained only in correlational studies. It is important to define operationally the variables and procedures used in psychological research, not only in experiments. Therefore, choice C is incorrect. Descriptive statistics, choice E, are used to represent data collected from a number of research designs and are not unique to experiments. (Skill 1a)

39. **(C)** If a study uses the double-blind technique, neither the researcher nor the subject knows what condition the subject has been assigned to. This helps control for the expectations that the subject and researcher might have that could bias the results. Random assignment, choice A, helps to minimize any preexisting differences among members of the experimental and control conditions. Inferential statistics, choice B, help researchers know if their findings are likely to be due to random chance or to the effect of the intervention (independent variable). Split-half reliability, choice D, helps researchers determine if a test yields consistent results. Researchers first divide the test in half, into odds and evens. Then they administer the odd questions to half of the sample and the even questions to the other half. Random sampling, choice E, helps to ensure that the sample is representative of the population. (Skill 1a)

40. **(D)** The mean is the arithmetic average. It is determined by adding all of the scores and dividing by the number of scores. Thus, extreme scores, called outliers, are more likely to impact this measure. The median,

choice A, is the score at the 50th percentile. It is not impacted by extremes, which makes it a more accurate measure of data that includes outliers. The mode, choice C, is the most frequently occurring score in a distribution. It is not heavily impacted by outliers. The range and the standard deviation, choices B and E, are measures of variation, not of central tendency. (Skill 1a)

41. **(E)** Statistical significance refers to the likelihood of chance operating in the differences between two tested groups. However, finding statistical significance does not, as suggested in choice A, mean that the findings are important. Statistical significance also does not focus on whether the distributions of scores are normally distributed (choice B) or if outliers have skewed the distribution (choice C). The key is whether the averages from the two groups are reliable and if the difference is relatively large. If those conditions are present, it is likely that the results are statistically significant. Choice D, which concerns a possible positive correlation, is not the issue. Whether or not a result is unlikely to happen by chance is central in establishing cause and effect from data collected. Correlational studies indicate if there is an association between variables. However, finding an association is not the same as finding causation, even if the findings are statistically significant. (Skill 1a)

Scenarios

42. **(E)** Since the participants were randomly assigned to two conditions where some are given the drug and the other a placebo, this research method is an experiment. Choice A is typically used to collect self-report data to assess attitudes. Choice B is an in-depth analysis of one person. Choice C is a careful observation done in one's natural environment. Choice D looks for the relationship between two variables but does not include the manipulation of an independent variable as in an experiment. (Skill 3)

43. **(A)** The independent variable (IV) is the variable that is manipulated between the experimental and control conditions. In this case, the IV is administration of the supplement to one group and the placebo to the other. Choice B is the dependent variable, which is the results of the manipulation of the IV. Choice C refers to the subjects in the study. Choice D refers to the control group that received the fake treatment. Choice E was not manipulated; thus, it is not the IV. (Skill 3)

44. **(A)** Random assignment balances the experimental group and the control group in terms of various subject variables, such as personality characteristics. As a result, researchers have more confidence that differences

in the results are due to manipulation of the independent variable, not due to the characteristics of the people in the groups. Choice B refers to the importance of operationally defining variables. Choice C refers to the need to use a double-blind study to control for experimenter bias. Choice D refers to the need for gaining informed consent from the participants before conducting research. Choice E describes the need for replication to increase confidence in the experimental results. (Skill 3)

45. **(C)** Those who received the treatment were members of the experimental group. In this case, those who received hot chocolate in orange cups were exposed to the treatment. The group that received the white cups were acting as a control group to give researchers a basis for comparison. Thus, choice A is incorrect. Choice B is incorrect because the dependent variable is the outcome of the manipulation of the independent variable and cannot be given to a group. Choice D is incorrect because participants were not randomly sampled into different conditions. Instead, they were randomly assigned into different groups. Based on the description of this experiment, a placebo group was not used. Therefore, choice E is incorrect. (Skill 3)

46. **(A)** The use of media was the factor manipulated in the experiment and therefore is the independent variable. Choice B, recall accuracy of the event, was the dependent variable because it was the outcome measured in the experiment. Choice C, the number of subjects, is a concern of experimental design. However, it was not manipulated across the groups. Choice D may be a confounding variable, but it was not the independent variable outlined by the researchers. Choice E could possibly be measured by the experimenters but was not manipulated across the groups. (Skill 3)

47. **(C)** The dependent variable is the outcome that is measured in the experiment. In this case, it is the number of words recalled by the participants. Choices A, B, and D are important to the design of the experiment. However, none are the outcomes measured after manipulating the independent variable. Choice E is the independent variable, which is the factor manipulated across the experimental and control groups. (Skill 3)

48. **(C)** A positive correlation indicates that as one variable increases (how close to the front of the room the students sit), so does the other (higher grades). An inverse relationship, choice A, suggests that as one variable increases, the other decreases. If a result is statistically significant, choice B, chance was not likely the cause of group differences in an experiment. Negatively skewed results, choice D, demonstrates that in a distribution of scores, there are fewer low values than high values. The placebo effect, choice E, refers to the influence of belief on the effectiveness of a treatment. (Skill 1b)

49. **(B)** Because researchers randomly assigned participants to different experimental conditions, the researchers can have more confidence that the differences between the groups are due to the manipulation of the independent variable. Participants are randomly assigned only in an experiment. Thus, choice A is incorrect because experimentation is not a descriptive research method. Choice C is also incorrect because the study is an experiment and not a correlational study. Choice D focuses on only the results of the study, which is not enough to conclude that a cause-and-effect relationship exists. Operationally defining the dependent variable happens in any study that collects data; thus, choice E is incorrect. (Skill 3)

50. **(D)** According to the current ethical guidelines, personal information from individual participants must remain confidential. Subjects in the described study were not deceived; thus, choice A is incorrect. Although it is important that researchers are aware of how their personal values may impact how they interpret research findings, this is not against current ethical guidelines. So, choice B is incorrect. For an experiment to be conducted, an independent variable must be manipulated across the experimental and control groups. Thus, choice C is incorrect. Choice E is also incorrect as items from the SAT exam could be used to measure academic performance. (Skill 3)

51. **(D)** To determine the mean, you must add the scores and divide the sum by the number of scores. The sum for this distribution of scores is 5 + 10 + 10 + 10 + 15 + 25 + 25 + 30 = 130. Therefore, the mean is 130 ÷ 8 = 16.25. Choice A, 10 minutes, is the mode, which is the most frequently occurring score in the distribution. Choice B, 12.5 minutes, is the median score. Since there is an even number of scores in this distribution, the median is found by obtaining the average of the two middle scores when the scores are aligned in either ascending or descending order: 10 + 15 = 25 and 25 ÷ 2 = 12.5. Choice C is incorrect. Choice E reflects the range, which is a measure of variation. The range is found by subtracting the lowest score from the highest score: 30 − 5 = 25. (Skill 2)

52. **(C)** The standard deviation would be the preferred statistical measurement for variation because it considers every score in the distribution. The mode, choice A, is the most frequently occurring score in a distribution. Choice B, the mean, is a measure of central tendency, not of variation. A correlation coefficient, choice D, is an indication of the relationship between two variables. A p value, choice E, is used to determine statistical significance. (Skill 2)

53. **(C)** If the scores are normally distributed, approximately 50% of the scores fall between 70 and 100, where a score of 100 is 3 standard

deviations above the mean. An additional 34% of the scores fall between the mean and 1 standard deviation below the mean, which is 60. So 34% of scores fall between 60 and 70. Thus, the percentage of students with scores between 60 and 100 is 50% + 34% = 84%. Choice A reflects the percentage of scores 1 standard deviation above *or* below the mean. Choice B is the total number of scores 1 standard deviation above *and* below the mean. Choice D reflects the percentage of scores 2 standard deviations above and below the mean. Choice E represents the percentage of scores 3 standard deviations above and below the mean. (Skill 2)

54. **(D)** If the results are statistically significant, the differences between groups are not likely to have occurred by chance. Choice A reflects the acceptable *p* value when stating that the results are statistically significant. However, it does not define what statistical significance means in the context of this study. Choice B is incorrect because it lacks a statement of probability, such as "The difference between groups is *likely due* to the manipulation of the independent variable." Just because the results of a study are statistically significant does not mean that the results have practical importance. Thus, choice C is incorrect. Choice E is incorrect because correlation coefficients illuminate the association between two variables. Finding an association is not the same as establishing cause and effect, even if the findings are statistically significant. (Skill 3)

Names

55. **(B)** A case study is an in-depth study of one individual. Choice A gathers self-report data from large groups using questionnaires. Choice C is a direct observation of humans or other animals in their natural environments. Choice D analyzes a possible relationship between two variables. Choice E involves the manipulation of an independent variable and its effect on the dependent variable under controlled conditions. (Skill 3)

56. **(D)** At the conclusion of a study, participants must have information about the research explained to them, including any deception. Choices A, B, and E are all ethical requirements but do not pertain directly to the deception that took place in the Milgram study. Choice C concerns the committee that reviews research proposals to ensure that all ethical guidelines have been considered. (Skill 3)

57. **(B)** The study of H. M. was a case study. Researchers were examining one person in depth and hoped to learn more about the inner workings of the brain. H. M.'s case was unique. It was not a repeat of earlier studies, as suggested in choice A. The retention curve, choice C, was first studied by Hermann Ebbinghaus (1850–1909). A correlation coefficient, choice D,

is a measure of the relationship between two variables and does not accurately describe the studies on H. M. In an experiment, participants are divided into different conditions. In order to control for bias, participants are kept blind about their assigned condition. This safeguard was not a part of the H. M. studies (choice E). (Skill 3)

58. **(E)** The independent variable is the one manipulated in an experiment. Since all participants viewed the same films of traffic accidents, these films are not a variable. Therefore, choice A is incorrect. The age of the participants (choice B) and the number of participants (choice D) were not manipulated. So, neither one is the independent variable. The speed reported by the participants, choice C, is the dependent variable. (Skill 3)

Research Methods

59. **(C)** A negative correlation means that higher values for one variable (more time on social media) are associated with lower values for the other variable (lower overall grades). Choice A would signify that higher values for one variable would be associated with higher values for the other variable. Choice B is not possible because in a correlational study, there is no random assignment to groups with the manipulation of an independent variable. Thus, a correlational study cannot determine a cause-and-effect relationship. Choice D indicates that the results of the study are unlikely to have been due to chance. This can be determined only using inferential statistics. Choice E focuses on whether or not test scores are stable over time. (Skill 1b)

60. **(B)** A hypothesis is a prediction that can be tested by researchers under controlled conditions. Choice A, naturalistic observation, is a method where researchers carefully watch and record the behavior of organisms in their natural conditions. Choice C, an illusory correlation, occurs when a relationship is perceived between two variables even though no relationship actually exists. A random sample, choice D, refers to a subset of the population, chosen by chance, that participates in a research study. A theory, choice E, is an integrated set of explanations for psychological phenomena. A good theory can lead to the creation of hypotheses. (Skill 1b)

61. **(D)** A theory helps organize and integrate observable phenomena as well as make predictions about future behavior. A hypothesis, choice A, is more specific than a theory. Hypotheses are generated from a theory and are testable. Choice B refers to the method used to measure a variable, not the overall theory referred to in this question. Choice C, replication, refers to a researcher repeating an earlier study to see if the results can be reproduced. Choice E is a specific research method that allows a

researcher to do an in-depth study of a single person or group of people who share a common characteristic. (Skill 1b)

62. **(D)** When a researcher cannot randomly assign participants to an experimental or a control condition, a correlational study is appropriate and necessary. For example, if a researcher is investigating the impact of illegal drug use on depression, the researcher obviously can't assign one group of people to take illegal drugs. The researcher will instead likely look for correlations between drug use and depression rates in people who already use illegal drugs. Choice A argues for the use of experimentation, not correlation, as cause and effect can be established only under the controls of an experiment. The focus of choice B is the ability to generalize from a small sample to a population. However, it is not the primary reason to use a correlational study over an experiment. Concern about the impact of the placebo effect in an experiment, the focus of choice C, may lead a researcher to use a placebo group as a control. The results of a correlational study, as suggested in choice E, do not establish whether or not the findings are statistically significant. (Skill 1a)

63. **(C)** Because of the small sample size, the study is unlikely to be representative of the population. Since the procedures were defined, other researchers would be able to replicate this study. So, choice A is incorrect. An illusory correlation, choice B, happens when a relationship between two variables is perceived but does not actually exist. Heritability, choice D, refers to the impact of genetics on the differences in a trait within a population. Choice E, ethics, refers primarily to the treatment of participants. This is not related to the sample size, which is the focus of this question. (Skill 3)

64. **(B)** Validity means that the experiment is testing what it is supposed to test. Framing, choice A, refers to how questions are posed or how information is presented that may impact an individual's decisions. Reliability, choice C, focuses on whether or not the experiment can be repeated. Statistical significance, choice D, refers to the likelihood that chance factors led to the differences in the tested groups. Heritability, choice E, is related to the impact of genetics on differences in a trait within a population. (Skill 3)

Perspectives

65. **(C)** Craik and Tulving are interested in how we process and store information. This directly relates to the cognitive perspective. The psychodynamic perspective, choice A, focuses on the role of the unconscious in influencing behavior. Choice B, the behavioral approach, looks to explain

how we learn observable behaviors from the environment. Neuroscience, choice D, stresses the role of the nervous and other physiological systems in influencing behavior. The social-cultural perspective, choice E, addresses the impact of our culture on our behavior. (Skill 1c)

66. **(D)** Modern psychology focuses on careful observation of behavior and the careful collection of empirical data. Freud's ideas lack hypotheses that can be tested empirically. Choice A is incorrect as it is not a major criticism. Furthermore, the data do suggest a link between these variables. Choice B is incorrect as Freud did not use experimentation to test his ideas. So, statistical significance cannot be determined. In choice C, the focus is on Freud's use of case studies. This method is still considered a useful tool in psychological science. Although Freud's research may lack a direct tie to the brain, it is not a major criticism of his work. So, choice E is incorrect. (Skill 3)

CHAPTER 3: BIOLOGICAL BASES OF BEHAVIOR

Stimulus

67. **(B)** The image of the flower projected to the left visual field is processed by the right side of the retina in both eyes. Then the message travels via the optic nerve to the left visual cortex in the occipital lobe. Because the person's language centers are in the left hemisphere, the person would be able to say, "I saw a basket." Choice A is incorrect because the left hand is controlled by the right hemisphere. The image of the basket would not be seen by the right hemisphere. Choice C is incorrect since the right hand, which is controlled by the left hemisphere, did not see the image of the flower, so the person would be unable to select a flower from an array of objects. Choice D is incorrect because, although the corpus callosum is severed in the brain of a split-brain patient, the optic nerve is not damaged. Choice E is incorrect since the person does not have language abilities in the right hemisphere. He or she would not be able to say, "I saw a flower." (Skill 1b)

Definitions

68. **(A)** Dendrites receive the neurotransmitters from other neurons. The neurotransmitters bind with the receptor cells located in the dendrites. The myelin sheath, choice B, covers the axon and helps speed neural transmission. In the axon, choice C, is where an action potential is generated. Terminal branches, choice D, are the endings of the axon where the neural messages are passed from one neuron to the next. The vesicles, choice E,

are located inside the buttons at the end of the terminal branches and contain the neurotransmitters. (Skill 1a)

69. **(D)** The axon conducts the electrical impulses from the soma down the length of the neuron. Choice A, the dendrite, is the part of the neuron that receives neurotransmitters from other neural cells. Choice B, the terminal branch, is one of the endings of the axon. The information will be sent to adjacent neurons from the terminal branch. Choice C, the vesicle, is a structure that houses the neurotransmitters in the terminal branches buttons. Glial cells, choice E, provide support and nourishment for neurons. (Skill 1a)

70. **(E)** The myelin sheath is a layer of insulation that forms around the axon. The myelin sheath allows messages to transmit quickly and efficiently along the neuron. Choice A is incorrect because myelin does not nourish the neural cell. Choice B refers to the soma, or cell body, of the neuron. The synapse, choice C, is the junction between the cells. Choice D concerns the function of the vesicles, where excess neurotransmitters are reabsorbed and repackaged to be released again into the synapse. (Skill 1a)

71. **(C)** When the flow of sodium ions into the cell causes it to become positively charged relative to the outside, the neuron is depolarized. When the amount of depolarization is great enough, the neuron will initiate an action potential, which is the electrical charge that travels down the axon. The refractory period, choice A, is a brief period after the neuron fires an action potential when the cell is recharging so it can fire again. A reflex, choice B, is an automatic response generated in the spinal cord. An inhibitory response, choice D, decreases the likelihood that an action potential will be generated. An agonist, choice E, is a chemical that binds to a receptor cell and increases a neurotransmitter's action, for example, by blocking reuptake at the synapse. (Skill 1a)

72. **(D)** Glial cells provide support for cells. They also participate in the transmission of a neural signal. Agonists, choice A, are chemicals that bind to receptor cells and that increase a neurotransmitter's action. GABA, choice B, is a specific neurotransmitter. Interneurons, choice C, are the cells that make up the brain and spinal cord. Receptor sites, choice E, lie along the receiving dendrite and bind with the neurotransmitters. (Skill 1a)

73. **(B)** Once a neuron reaches threshold, it fires in an all-or-none response. This means that the neuron always fires at the same intensity; there is no such thing as a weak or a strong message. The difference threshold, choice A, is the minimum amount of stimulation necessary to detect the difference between two stimuli. The refractory period, choice C, is the time between neural firings when the neuron recharges itself. Reuptake,

choice D, is the process by which excess neurotransmitters in the synapse are reabsorbed by the sending neuron. Weber's law, choice E, states that the stronger a stimulus is, the greater the difference required to tell that a change has occurred. (Skill 1a)

74. **(E)** Neurotransmitters are released from the endings of axon terminals into the synapse in order to communicate with adjacent neurons. Choice A is the soma, which contains the nucleus of the cell that maintains the cell's basic functions. Choice B is pointing to the dendrites. These structures in the neuron contain receptor cells that receive the neurotransmitters. Choice C is the part of the neuron where the action potential is produced. The myelin sheath, choice D, is the outer covering of the axon that insulates the neuron and helps the message travel quickly down the neuron's length. (Skill 1a)

75. **(B)** The synapse is the space between the sending and the receiving neuron. Choice A, myelin sheath, is the outer covering of the axon that helps speed up the neural message. Glial cells, choice C, provide support for the neuron and assist in neural transmission. Antagonists, choice D, are chemicals that block the action of the neurotransmitters at the receptor sites. Vesicles, choice E, are structures that house the neurotransmitters in the endings of the axon terminals. (Skill 1a)

76. **(C)** Neurotransmitters have specific chemical structures and can bind only with particular receptor sites. This is referred to as the lock and key phenomenon. The remaining scenarios (choices A, B, D, and E) do not appropriately illustrate this process. (Skill 1b)

77. **(A)** Excitatory signals increase the likelihood of a neuron firing an action potential. Choice B is referring to chemicals, called antagonists, that occupy receptor sites and block the action of the neurotransmitter. Choice C is focusing on the refractory period, which is a time when a neuron is recharging before it is able to fire again. Choice D is incorrect because a neuron always fires at the same intensity, called the all-or-none response. Choice E is incorrect as it refers to an enzyme that can break down neurotransmitters in the synapse. (Skill 1a)

78. **(E)** The release of endorphins is connected to reducing the experience of pain. Choice A, dopamine, primarily affects sleep, mood, and attention. Serotonin, choice B, is involved in regulating mood. Norepinephrine, choice C, is released when our body is under stress. Norepinephrine is connected to our being alert. Acetylcholine, choice D, is involved in muscle contraction and memory. (Skill 1a)

79. **(A)** The brain and spinal cord make up the central nervous system. The link between the hypothalamus and pituitary gland, choice B, provides

the connections between the brain and endocrine system. Choice C is incorrect since the sensory neurons bring information into the central nervous system, while motor neurons carry messages outward from the central nervous system. The automatic and somatic nervous systems, choice D, are divisions of the peripheral nervous system. Choice E is incorrect as it references the limbic system, which is comprised of the hippocampus, hypothalamus, and amygdala, and the endocrine system, which is our glandular system. (Skill 1a)

80. **(D)** The sympathetic nervous system arouses the body and mobilizes its energy during stressful situations. The parasympathetic nervous system, choice A, calms the body and initiates the rest-and-digest response. Choice B, the endocrine system, refers to the system of glands in our body that may be engaged during fight or flight but does not initiate the response. The hippocampus, choice C, assists in the formation of new long-term memories. The medulla, choice E, regulates autonomic functioning, such as breathing and heart rate. However, it does not initiate the fight or flight response. (Skill 1a)

81. **(B)** PET scans allow researchers to trace the brain's consumption of glucose and produce an image of the brain that depicts its activity in different regions. An EEG, choice A, allows researchers to measure electrical activity on the surface of the brain. An MRI, choice C, allows researchers to generate a detailed picture of the brain. An fMRI, choice D, also allows researchers to create a picture of brain activity. However, an fMRI is based on measuring blood flow as it rushes to specific brain regions. An MEG, choice E, identifies activity in the brain by measuring magnetic fields produced in the brain. (Skill 1a)

82. **(E)** The medulla and pons, along with the midbrain, are located in the brainstem. The hippocampus and amygdala, choice A, are located above the brainstem. The thalamus and hypothalamus, choice B, are located on top of the brainstem. The corpus callosum, choice C, is the band of fibers that connects the left and right hemispheres. The cerebellum, choice D, does share connections with the brainstem but is not considered a part of the brainstem. The cerebellum plays a central role in motor coordination. (Skill 1a)

83. **(E)** The medulla is responsible for regulating autonomic functions, including heart rate and breathing. Choice A, the thalamus, receives the sensory signals that come from the spinal cord and sends them to the appropriate areas in the forebrain. The hippocampus, choice B, is involved in the formation of new long-term memories. The prefrontal cortex, choice C, is primarily responsible for higher-level thinking and problem solving. Choice D, the amygdala, regulates emotional responses. (Skill 1a)

84. **(D)** The thalamus sends all sensory messages, except smell, to the cerebral cortex so they can be processed. The hypothalamus, choice A, is responsible for maintaining homeostasis by regulating such things as hunger and thirst. The pons, choice B, is involved in communicating messages between the cerebral cortex and other areas of the brain. Choice C, the reticular formation, is associated with helping us maintain an alert state. Choice E, the somatosensory cortex, processes incoming sensory messages related to touch sensations. It is located in the parietal lobe. (Skill 1a)

85. **(C)** Although not the only region of the brain associated with reward, the hypothalamus is a part of the reward system. The thalamus, choice A, is primarily responsible for transferring sensory signals to the cerebral cortex. The cerebellum, choice B, helps maintain balance and coordinate muscle movement. The reticular formation, choice D, helps maintain arousal and alertness. The amygdala, choice E, produces automatic emotional responses, such as anger and fear. (Skill 1a)

86. **(E)** The occipital lobe, located at the rear of the brain, contains the primary visual cortex. The frontal lobe, choice A, is associated with decision-making skills and motor abilities. The temporal lobe, choice B, contains the auditory cortex. The optic chiasm, choice C, is formed by the crossing of the optic nerve in the brain. The parietal lobe, choice D, houses the somatosensory cortex. (Skill 1a)

87. **(B)** The association areas of the cortex combine information from the primary sensory areas and integrate that information with stored memory. The corpus callosum, choice A, connects the left and right hemispheres and allows them to communicate. The limbic system, choice C, is a collection of structures that manage memory and emotion and that regulate autonomic functioning in response to threats. The somatosensory cortex, choice D, is located in the parietal lobe. It processes sensory messages such as pain, pressure, and temperature. Wernicke's area, choice E, is primarily involved in language comprehension. (Skill 1a)

88. **(C)** The corpus callosum is a large band of fibers that connects the right and left hemispheres and that allows the halves of the brain to share information. The optic chiasm, choice A, is the spot where the optic nerves cross each other. Broca's area, choice B, is an area in the brain that allows for speech production. The somatosensory cortex, choice D, processes touch sensations and is located in the parietal lobe. The association areas, choice E, are located throughout the cerebral cortex. They integrate information from the primary sensory areas with information previously stored in the cortex. (Skill 1a)

89. **(D)** Plasticity refers to changes in the brain that occur during one's lifetime due to experience. Long-term potentiation, choice A, refers to the

strengthening of synapses between neurons. Choice B, dual processing, refers to the brain's ability to process simultaneously information both consciously and unconsciously. Blind sight, choice C, is a rare phenomenon where a blind individual can experience visual stimuli and respond to it without being consciously aware of the stimuli. Choice E, lesioning, is the destruction of brain cells in a specific location. (Skill 1a)

90. **(D)** The language centers, in individuals who are right-handed, are located almost exclusively in the left hemisphere. Spatial reasoning, choice A, is a specialty of the right hemisphere. Choice B is incorrect because the motor cortex in the right hemisphere is responsible for moving the left side of the body. Reflexes are initiated by the spinal cord. So, choice C is incorrect. The hypothalamus is responsible for instigating the fight or flight response when a person perceives a threat. So, choice E is incorrect. (Skill 1a)

Scenarios

91. **(B)** When acetylcholine is released, it causes the contraction of skeletal muscles that would allow Kaitlyn to swing her tennis racket. Choice A, GABA, is an inhibitory neurotransmitter that would not lead to the initiation of skeletal muscle contraction. Endorphins, choice C, are the body's natural opiates that help control pain. Serotonin, choice D, is primarily involved in mood and arousal. Serotonin release does not cause skeletal muscles to contract. Choice E, norepinephrine, plays a role in helping maintain alertness but is not directly involved in moving muscles. (Skill 1b)

92. **(D)** Antagonists are drugs that block a neurotransmitter's action by blocking it at the receptor site or by decreasing its availability. Agonists, choice A, mimic or increase the actions of a neurotransmitter. Endorphins, choice B, are the body's natural opiates. They influence our perception of pain and pleasure. Reuptake inhibitors, choice C, stop reuptake from happening in the synapse, thus increasing the availability of specific neurotransmitters. Stimulants, choice E, are a category of drugs that increase the activity of the nervous system. (Skill 1b)

93. **(C)** The sympathetic nervous system arouses the body to deal with perceived threats, for example, by increasing the heart rate and raising blood pressure. Choice A, the parasympathetic nervous system, returns the body's physiological state to normal. It does not increase heart rate or sweating. Choice B, the reflex arc, is the pathway taken by neural impulses in a reflex. Choice D, the limbic system, includes regions of the brain involved in memory formation and emotion. Choice E, the central nervous system, includes the brain and spinal cord. (Skill 1b)

94. **(D)** MRI scans allow for a detailed picture of the brain to be made that would reveal the presence of a brain tumor. The triarchic abilities test, choice A, is an assessment based on Robert Sternberg's theory of personality. Choice B, an EEG, measures electrical activity on the surface of the brain. Choice C, lesioning, is a surgical technique where specific brain cells are destroyed to observe the effects. Choice E, TMS, is primarily used to stimulate nerve cells in specific areas of the brain as a method to treat depression. (Skill 1b)

95. **(E)** The cerebellum is responsible for coordinating movement. Either damaging or removing part of the cerebellum would result in the patient having uncoordinated and jerky movements. Choice A refers to the impact of damage to the hippocampus. Choice B might occur if damage occurred in the occipital lobe. Choice C may occur if injury to the sensory cortex or spinal cord occurred. Trouble in recognizing faces related to distress, choice D, is consistent with damage to the amygdala. (Skill 1b)

96. **(D)** The hippocampus assists in storing long-term memory; thus, it was the area damaged in Clive Wearing's brain. The cerebellum, choice A, helps coordinate muscle movement and stores implicit memories. The hypothalamus, choice B, controls metabolic functions, including hunger, thirst, and body temperature. Choice C, the frontal lobe, is the center for decision making and higher-level reasoning. Choice E, the somatosensory cortex, processes touch information such as pain, pressure, and temperature. (Skill 1b)

97. **(C)** The hypothalamus maintains homeostasis, or internal balance, including body temperature. The hippocampus, choice A, is involved in memory formation. Choice B, the amygdala, produces emotions such as anger and fear. The temporal lobe, choice D, contains the primary auditory cortex. The somatosensory cortex, choice E, is located in the parietal lobe and processes messages related to touch sensations. (Skill 1b)

98. **(A)** When the amygdala is stimulated in a specific area, it can cause a docile animal to act violently. The pons, choice B, is primarily engaged during sleep and helps coordinate movement. Choice C, the medulla, is responsible for regulating autonomic functions like breathing and heart rate. Choice D, the cerebellum, helps coordinate movement and stores skill memory. The thalamus, choice E, is a sensory relay center that sends messages to the cortex for processing. (Skill 1b)

99. **(E)** The reticular formation enables arousal and attention. The cerebellum, choice A, coordinates muscles and helps an individual balance. The corpus callosum, choice B, is a band of fibers that connects the left and right hemispheres of the brain. The medulla, choice C, is responsible for

regulating heartbeat and breathing. The hypothalamus, choice D, regulates homeostasis. (Skill 1b)

100. **(D)** The thalamus is a relay center for all sensory information except smell. It receives a sensory input and then transmits the input to the appropriate brain region for processing. Without the thalamus, you would not be able to see your friend. The hypothalamus, choice A, is primarily responsible for maintaining homeostasis so you don't get too hot, too hungry, or too thirsty. The corpus callosum, choice B, is a band of fibers that connects the left and right hemispheres in the brain and allows the two halves to communicate. The spinal cord, choice C, is part of the central nervous system. It connects nearly all parts of the body to the brain. The pons, choice E, is located in the brainstem and is activated during sleep. (Skill 1b)

101. **(B)** The prefrontal cortex is responsible for reasoning and decision making, both needed by Fiona to decide where to attend school. The temporal lobe, choice A, is responsible for processing auditory information. The limbic system, choice C, regulates emotional responses and memory formation. When stimulated, the reticular formation, choice D, increases arousal. The parietal lobe, choice E, contains the somatosensory cortex that processes skin sensations such as pain or pressure. (Skill 1b)

102. **(D)** The somatosensory cortex, located in the parietal lobe, is responsible for processing touch sensations, including pain, temperature, and pressure. Thus, feeling the pressure of your hair touching your face would be the result of the actions of the parietal lobe. Choice A is referring to the processing done by the motor cortex in the frontal lobe. Choice B would result from processing of the auditory cortex in the temporal lobe. Choice C might result from the actions of the medulla that control heart rate or the stimulation of the hypothalamus that initiates the autonomic functions of the sympathetic nervous system. Activation of the reticular formation, responsible for arousal, would cause you to turn toward a sudden noise (choice E). (Skill 1b)

103. **(D)** Plasticity refers to changes in the brain that occur during one's lifetime due to experience. Thus, Jill's experience best exemplifies this concept. Phineas Gage's experience, choice A, provided evidence that the frontal lobe was central to personality. Choice B demonstrates that an implant can be wired to the motor cortex, allowing neural messages to move a prosthesis. Research with split-brain patients, choice C, demonstrates the differences between the left and right hemispheres. Choice E reveals the impact deep-brain stimulation can have on those who suffer with Parkinson's disease. (Skill 1b)

104. **(B)** Red hair is caused by a recessive gene. In order for the red hair to be expressed, both genes in a pair must be recessive. The gene for brown hair is dominant. Thus, even though both of Aidan's parents have brown hair, they each carry a recessive red hair gene that is passed to their offspring. Since Aidan has red hair, he cannot inherit any dominant genes for brown hair. Option D is incorrect for two reasons. First, red hair is a recessive trait (A, C, and D refer to this trait coming from a dominant gene), and, second, it takes two genes (options D and E refer to one gene only). (Skill 1b)

Names

105. **(D)** Broca's area, as it is now called, is located in the left frontal lobe. It is primarily associated with the ability to speak. The corpus callosum, choice A, is a band of fibers that connects the left and right hemispheres of the brain. Choices B and C, the right temporal lobe and the right parietal lobe, are unrelated to speech production. The cerebellum, choice E, is primarily responsible for helping maintain balance and for coordinating motor responses. (Skill 1b)

106. **(E)** Charles Darwin, in *On the Origin of Species,* suggested that an evolutionary process of natural selection led to certain beneficial physical and behavioral traits being passed down through generations. Walter Penfield, choice A, was known for his work in mapping the motor cortex. Wilhelm Wundt, choice B, established the first psychology laboratory in 1879. John Locke, choice C, was a British philosopher who suggested that the environment was exclusively responsible for shaping an individual's traits. Edward Titchener, choice D, established structuralism, which was an early school of psychology. (Skill 1a)

107. **(E)** Sperry and Gazzaniga studied individuals whose hemispheres had been divided by cutting the corpus callosum to reduce seizures caused by epilepsy. By using specialized testing where visual images were presented to either the left or the right visual fields, they were able to establish that the hemispheres were responsible for different functions. For example, when an image was projected to the right visual field, it was processed by the left hemisphere. Patients, when asked to say what they had seen, would verbally report that image because language centers are located in the left hemisphere (in a right-handed individual). When an image was projected to the left visual field, though, the patient would not be able to identify the image verbally. Choice A is referring to the work of Paul Broca, who identified the region in the left hemisphere responsible for speech production. Choice B refers to the mapping of the motor cortex done by Walter Penfield. Phrenology, choice C, is a pseudoscience that

suggests certain traits can be linked to the bumps on the skull. Choice D refers to the work of Santiago Ramón y Cajal who proposed that the neuron was the basic component of the nervous system. (Skill 1a)

108. **(D)** Carl Wernicke first established that if an area in the left temporal region was damaged, the person would have difficulty producing meaningful speech and understanding language. The limbic system, choice A, is comprised of the hypothalamus, hippocampus, and amygdala. These are involved in regulating homeostasis (hypothalamus), forming memory (hippocampus), and specific emotional responses (amygdala). Paul Broca, choice B, first tied an area in the left frontal lobe to speech production. The somatosensory cortex, choice C, is responsible for receiving information from the skin. The thalamus, choice E, is a relay for all sensory information, except smell, to the cerebral cortex. (Skill 1b)

109. **(B)** If identical twins are more similar than fraternal twins in a specific trait, such as intelligence, this is evidence of the impact of genes. Identical twins share twice as many genes in common on average as do fraternal twins. Identical twins reared separately share all of their genes in common but have been raised in different environments. Thus, according to proponents of this research, any similarities between the twins can't be explained by environmental experiences since the twins were not reared in the same environment. Choices A, C, D, and E do not support the proposed hypothesis. (Skill 3)

110. **(B)** Mirror neurons are cells that fire equally when we perform an action and when we watch someone else perform the same action. Synaptic receptors, choice A, are embedded in the postsynaptic membrane and are designed to bind with neurotransmitters. Glial cells, choice C, assist neurotransmitters by helping provide nourishment and stimulate communication between neurons. Interneurons, choice D, are cells found in the brain and spinal cord. Agonists, choice E, are chemicals that mimic the action of a neurotransmitter. (Skill 1b)

Research Methods

111. **(C)** Since the rats were randomly assigned to different conditions, Rosenzweig was conducting an experiment to determine if a cause-and-effect relationship existed. A correlational study, choice A, does not involve the manipulation of an independent variable across different groups. Choice B, a naturalistic observation, is a descriptive method where a researcher systematically observes behavior in real-world settings. Choice D, a longitudinal study, does not involve the manipulation of variables. Instead, it requires repeated observations of the same sample

over a long period of time. A case study, choice E, is a descriptive method where no variables are manipulated. Instead, it is an in-depth study of one person or a small group that share a common characteristic. (Skill 3)

112. **(D)** The independent variable is manipulated across the different groups. In this study, rats were raised in different environments. Choice A, the sex of each rat, was not manipulated. All subjects were male rats. Choice B is the dependent variable because it is the measured outcome of the manipulation. Choice C is incorrect because all rats received adequate amounts of food and water. Choice E is incorrect as the rats were from the same litter and were randomly assigned to different conditions. (Skill 3)

113. **(E)** By keeping the researcher blind as to which condition the rats were raised in, this technique helps control for experimenter bias. Choice A is incorrect because it is the operational definitions of the variables that allows the research to be replicated accurately. To equalize the groups, choice B, random assignment is necessary. To generalize the results from the sample to the population, choice C, the sample should be randomly selected. This technique is not necessary to determine statistical significance. Instead, statistical significance is determined when a p value of .05 or below is obtained. So, choice D is incorrect. (Skill 3)

114. **(C)** Any variable that is not controlled for, such as the handling of the rats, could act as a confounding variable. If so, the researchers would have less confidence that the changes in the cortex were actually due to the differences in the environments in which the rats were raised. A dependent variable, choice A, is the measured result of the manipulation. Internal validity, choice B, refers to the degree that change in the dependent variable is actually due to manipulation of the independent variable. Because handling of the rats was not controlled for, it may actually decrease researcher confidence in the internal validity. Choice D is incorrect because Rosenzweig performed an experiment, not a correlational study. Choice E, a placebo, is a fake treatment used to test whether belief in a treatment is leading to changes in the dependent variable instead of the manipulation of the independent variable. (Skill 3)

115. **(C)** Lesioning is a technique where brain cells are destroyed so that researchers can determine the effects on behavior. Electroconvulsive therapy, choice A, is used primarily to treat severe depression. In this therapy, an electric current is run through the brain, intentionally creating a seizure. A lobotomy, choice B, was an early treatment for mental disorders. It involved destroying the connections to and from the prefrontal cortex. Choice D, split-brain, refers to a surgery that cuts the corpus callosum, which is the band of fibers that connects the left and right hemispheres.

This surgery is used to control epileptic seizures. Neurogenesis, choice E, is the process where new neurons are generated to compensate for damage to the nervous system. (Skill 1b)

116. **(C)** Hemi-inattention occurs when an individual sustains brain damage to the right hemisphere of the brain, causing the person to ignore the stimuli in the left visual field. This patient ignores the left side of the house shown in the model drawing and so does not represent that side in his or her drawing. Since this patient has no damage to the visual system, choice A is incorrect. The reticular formation, choice B, is responsible for arousal. Damage to this area would not lead to the phenomenon shown. The cerebellum, choice D, coordinates physical movement and stores implicit memory. Damage to the cerebellum would not cause the effect seen in the patient's drawing. The limbic system, choice E, is responsible for autonomic responses to initiate the sympathetic nervous system, memory, and emotion. Damage to this system would also not lead to the neglect seen in the patient's drawing. (Skill 1b)

Perspectives

117. **(D)** Biological psychologists study the relationship between behavior and both the brain and nervous system. Such a psychologist would be primarily interested in how an imbalance in neurotransmitters might influence a person's emotional state. An evolutionary psychologist, choice A, would be interested in identifying the beneficial traits that are the result of natural selection. A cognitive psychologist, choice B, primarily focuses on how thoughts impact behaviors. A developmental psychologist, choice C, studies how humans change across the life span cognitively, socially, and physically. A health psychologist, choice E, investigates how psychological, biological, and social factors influence an individual's overall wellness. (Skill 1c)

118. **(C)** A biological psychologist is interested in the relationship between behavior and both the brain and nervous system. When researching happiness, a biological psychologist would be interested in how the neurotransmitter dopamine is involved in a person's experience. Choice A, using a positive explanatory style, would be of interest to a cognitive psychologist. Choice B would be of concern to a positive psychologist. A social psychologist would be interested in both choices D and E as they both concern a person's perception of control and relative deprivation. (Skill 1c)

119. **(D)** Since biological psychologists focus on the connection between physiological processes and behavior, they would be most likely interested

in being able to see what is happening in the brain while it is working. Cognitive psychologists, choice A, are interested in how thought processes impact behavior. Evolutionary psychologists, choice B, are interested in identifying beneficial traits that are the result of natural selection. Behavioral psychologists, choice C, are interested in investigating the principles of learning. Psychodynamic psychologists, choice E, focus on the role of unconsciousness in governing behavior. (Skill 1a)

120. **(E)** Behavior geneticists study the role of genetics in behavior. Evolutionary psychologists, choice A, are interested in identifying beneficial traits that are the result of natural selection. Social-cultural psychologists, choice B, focus on how behavior and cognition change through different social and cultural contexts. Psychiatrists, choice C, are physicians that specialize in treating severe mental illness. Cognitive psychologists, choice D, are primarily interested in understanding how thought processes impact behavior. (Skill 1a)

CHAPTER 4: STATES OF CONSCIOUSNESS

Stimulus

121. **(B)** Based on the figure, after the first cycle of sleep, most older adults spend little time in deep sleep and more time in lighter sleep. This makes choice E incorrect. Younger people at the beginning of a night's sleep experience regular periods of deep sleep. Choices A and C are incorrect because older people apparently wake up more often during a typical night. Choice D is incorrect for both age groups. REM sleep does not come directly after the NREM (non-REM) stage 3 sleep. Stage NREM-2 follows NREM-3, and then comes REM. (Skill 1b)

Definitions

122. **(E)** A circadian rhythm is a biological process that regulates periods of wakefulness and sleep. Choice A refers to hypnagogic experiences, such as feelings of floating, that occur during NREM sleep. Choice B refers to NREM-stage 3 sleep when delta waves are produced. Choice C concerns the sleep spindles produced during NREM-stage 2 sleep. Memory consolidation, choice D, refers to the time during REM sleep when new neural connections are strengthened. (Skill 1a)

123. **(D)** Hypnagogic sensations are vivid hallucinations that occur soon after a person falls asleep. Delusions, choice A, are false beliefs. Apnea, choice B, is a disorder where an individual stops breathing during a night's sleep. The manifest content, choice C, refers to the narrative of a dream. REM

rebound, choice E, occurs when a person is deprived of REM sleep during the night and is then allowed to sleep uninterrupted the next night. The person will go into REM more quickly and spend more time in that stage during the night of uninterrupted sleep. (Skill 1a)

124. **(B)** When light dims, the suprachiasmatic nucleus (SCN), which is located in the hypothalamus, leads the pineal gland to increase the production of the hormone melatonin, making a person sleepy. The medulla, choice A, is located in the brainstem and regulates heart rate and breathing. The cerebellum, choice C, coordinates movement and helps a person maintain balance. The reticular formation, choice D, does help regulate the sleep-wake cycle by helping an individual filter out extraneous external stimuli. The connections in the reticular formation begin in the brain stem and extend out into the cortex. These cells are not light sensitive as are those in the SCN. The somatosensory cortex, choice E, is responsible for processing touch sensations, such as pain, pressure, and temperature on the skin. (Skill 1a)

125. **(D)** Memory consolidation occurs during REM sleep. This is the time when new neural connections are strengthened, thereby helping transfer temporarily stored information to long-term storage. Increased production of human growth hormone, choice A, occurs during NREM sleep. Choice B refers to the activation-synthesis theory, which explains how a person dreams during REM sleep. Choice C refers to an event that occurs when a person is sleep deprived. This increase in ghrelin can lead to weight gain. Choice E refers to REM rebound. (Skill 1a)

126. **(A)** REM is considered paradoxical sleep because the brain is highly active, with beta waves being produced, but motor messages are inhibited in the brainstem. Choice B refers to REM rebound. Choice C is incorrect as delta waves, which indicate deep sleep, are present during NREM-stage 3 sleep. Although choice D does correctly describe the difference between REM sleep in infants and adults, it is not the primary feature of why REM is considered paradoxical. Choice E is incorrect because it does not accurately reflect the paradox. (Skill 1a)

127. **(C)** Tolerance to a drug develops gradually. The more a person takes a drug, the more the person must take to get the same effect. Withdrawal, choice A, occurs when a person is physically addicted to a drug and has negative symptoms when he or she stops using it. Diathesis stress, choice B, is an explanation for why certain disorders occur. It focuses on the interaction of one's biological predispositions and environmental stressors. Choice D, generalization, is when an organism responds to a stimulus similar to the one that was originally learned. Plasticity, choice E, refers to changes in the brain that occur during one's lifetime due to experience. (Skill 1a)

128. **(D)** Narcotics, such as morphine, heroin, or oxycodone, are used primarily for pain relief. Depressants (choice A), such as alcohol, slow down the body by depressing the nervous system. Stimulants (choice B), such as cocaine, lead to an increase in heart rate. They also elevate the blood pressure and speed up body functions. Hallucinogens (choice C), such as LSD, cause a person to perceive the world differently than it really is. Inhalants (choice E) include a number of chemicals that give off vapors, which produce intoxication when they are breathed in. (Skill 1a)

Scenarios

129. **(C)** According to Freud, the symbolic, hidden meaning of the dream is the latent content. While manifest content, Choice A, is a Freudian concept, it refers to a dream's conscious narrative. Choice B, a flashbulb memory, refers to a detailed, emotionally charged memory. A prototype, Choice D, is the best example of a category. When our past experiences shape our interpretation of an event, Choice E, top-down processing occurs. (Skill 1b)

130. **(C)** Alpha waves are present when a person is awake but relaxed. Theta waves, choice A, are associated with both NREM-stage 1 and NREM-stage 2 sleep. Delta waves, choice B, are present during stage-3 sleep, which is deep sleep. Beta waves, choice D, are present when a person is awake and alert but are also present during REM sleep. Sleep spindles, choice E, are bursts of brain activity present during NREM stage 2 sleep. (Skill 1b)

131. **(C)** Narcolepsy is a sleep disorder characterized by periods when a person feels overwhelmingly sleepy and falls asleep at inconvenient times. Since the person drops into REM sleep, he or she loses muscle tone. Sleep apnea, choice A, occurs when a person stops breathing during a night's sleep. Night terrors, choice B, occur during NREM sleep and happen primarily in children. Children who have night terrors experience intense fear during sleep but have no memory of the event the next day. Insomnia, choice D, is a disorder where a person has difficulty going to or staying asleep. Choice E, restless leg syndrome, is a condition where an individual feels an urge to move his or her legs to relieve discomfort. (Skill 1b)

132. **(D)** Since Kenneth is experiencing withdrawal symptoms after discontinuing the use of narcotics, he has developed a physical dependence on the drugs. Choice A is incorrect as such an outcome cannot be determined by the evidence provided in the scenario. Choices B and C are incorrect because narcotics are highly addictive and slow down the nervous system. Because Kenneth is experiencing withdrawal symptoms after he has

stopped taking the drugs, it may be difficult for him to resist taking the drugs again. But there is no reason to predict that he will be "unable" to resist taking the drugs, making choice E incorrect. (Skill 1b)

Names

133. **(D)** Sigmund Freud first suggested that the unconscious mind acts is a repository of unacceptable feelings, thoughts, and wishes that direct our behavior. Carl Jung, choice A, was a prominent Freudian psychologist, but not the first to suggest that the unconscious mind directs human behavior. Carl Rogers, choice B, is a humanistic psychologist known for his suggestion that humans need unconditional positive regard to develop a positive self-concept. Karen Horney, choice C, is a Freudian psychologist but was not the first to propose the idea of an unconscious mind. John Allan Hobson, choice E, is a sleep researcher known for his theory that dreams are a biological byproduct of an active brain during REM sleep. (Skill 1a)

Research Methods

134. **(C)** The dependent variable is the measured outcome of manipulating the independent variable. An operational definition is a specific statement of how researchers measure the outcome. Thus, the operational definition goes beyond judgment, choice E, to how judgment will be measured. In this case, researchers measure judgment by the number of incorrect steps taken by the subjects. A blood alcohol content of 0.08%, choice A, is the variable controlled by the researchers. Thus, it is the independent variable. The same applies to the alcohol consumed, choice B. It is the variable controlled by researchers and is therefore the independent variable. The age of the subjects, choice D, is a subject variable. (Skill 3)

135. **(C)** The belief that a treatment will work can lead to the placebo effect. To control for this, researchers should use a placebo group where participants receive a fake treatment. Doing so will help researchers determine whether it is the alcohol or the preconceived beliefs about alcohol's effects that make a difference in task performance. Choice A is incorrect because this will not control for the placebo effect. The amount of alcohol was controlled by ensuring all subjects drinking alcohol had a blood alcohol content of 0.08%. Random sampling, choice B, helps ensure that the subjects are representative of the population. A correlational study, choice D, looks for relationships among variables. It is not an effective tool to determine cause and effect. Replicating a study, choice E, helps

build confidence in the findings of an earlier study but does not control for the placebo effect. (Skill 3)

Perspectives

136. **(B)** Psychodynamic psychologists focus on unconscious motives. They may interpret the symbolic, or latent, content of dreams to provide insight into what has been repressed to the unconscious. The behavioral perspective, choice A, focuses on observable behavior that has been learned from the environment. Humanistic psychologists, choice C, emphasize the potential for growth and self-fulfillment. Evolutionary psychologists, choice D, explain human behavior through natural selection. Biological psychologists, choice E, center on the workings of the nervous system in explaining human behavior. (Skill 1c)

137. **(E)** Biological psychologists focus on how the functioning of the nervous system produces thoughts and behavior. The activation-synthesis model suggests that dreams are a biological byproduct of an active brain. The explanation of biological psychologists for dreams reflects this perspective. The cognitive perspective, choice A, emphasizes how information is processed. The psychodynamic approach, choice B, stresses the role of the unconscious in influencing behavior. The behavioral perspective, choice C, concentrates on how behaviors are learned from the environment. The evolutionary perspective, choice D, attempts to explain the origin of adaptive human traits through the process of natural selection. (Skill 1c)

CHAPTER 5: SENSATION AND PERCEPTION

Stimulus

138. **(C)** At point [1] in the excerpt, the process of vision is being described. The image from the letters on the page are sensed by the eye as described in choice C. Choice A is not specific to this part of the excerpt. Choices B and D are factually incorrect statements about how language is processed by the brain. Choice E misrepresents the nature of learning. The idea of someone being a "visual learner" is not supported by research. (Skill 1b)

139. **(D)** At point [2] in the excerpt, the viewer is finding meaning from the sensations (reading the words), which is a perceptual process. Choice A is wrong because the sensation process occurred earlier in the excerpt. Choice B, transduction, is a different step in the process. Transduction occurs when sensations are turned into neural impulses. Choice C, potentiation, is out of context. The term *long-term potentiation* refers to how

memories are biologically stored in the brain. Choice E, adaptation, refers to the process of stopping the perception of some sensations because of continuous exposure to those sensations. (Skill 1b)

140. **(E)** Perceptions like the feeling of cold on your skin or the tightness of shoes are perceived in the sensory or somatosensory cortex in the brain. The motor cortex, choice A, is responsible for voluntary movements. Choice B, Broca's area, is involved in speech. The ventromedial hypothalamus, choice C, is part of the system that controls hunger. The frontal lobe, choice D, is a large area of the brain responsible for many different functions, including decision making. However, it is not the primary area where perceptions such as cold or tightness are processed. (Skill 1b)

141. **(A)** All messages received through our senses (except smell) pass through the thalamus first before being sent elsewhere in the brain. Choice B, parietal lobe, is one of the lobes of the brain. Choice C, synaptic gap, is a specific part of the neural transmission process. Choice D, central nervous system, is close to being correct. However, the question asks for a brain structure, and the brain is part of the central nervous system. Choice E, amygdala, is the part of the limbic system that is responsible for strong emotional responses. (Skill 1b)

Definitions

142. **(A)** The term *sensation* refers to the activation of one of our senses (sight, hearing, touch, smell, taste, or the vestibular sense). The example of light activating rods and cones in the retina is the best example in this set. Choices B and E refer to examples (or definitions) of perception, not sensation. Choices C and D are not specific to the concept of sensation. (Skill 1b)

143. **(D)** The term *sensation* refers to the activation of one of our senses. The statement clearly refers to a sensation: hearing. Sound waves are detected in the cochlea by the movements of hair cells, which fire neurons. Choice A is incorrect because the example does not refer to the sounds being interpreted. Choices B, C, and E are not terms relevant to this statement. (Skill 1b)

144. **(B)** The term *perception* refers to the brain interpreting (finding meaning in) sensations. Sensations start in one of the five senses, which sends neural messages to the brain. Perception occurs when the brain makes meaning out of these impulses. The example of feature detectors firing in the optical cortex (located in the occipital lobe) is the best example of perception in this set. Choices A and E refer to examples (or definitions) of sensation, not perception. Choices C and D are not specific to the concept of perception. (Skill 1b)

145. **(C)** Top-down processing is a perceptual process occurring when we use past knowledge or "rules" to help us interpret sensations. Bottom-up processing, choice A, is the opposite. It occurs when we encounter unfamiliar stimuli and have to start at the "bottom," building a perception by looking piece by piece to build an overall perception. Choice B, selective attention, is involved in the process referred to in this question. However, selective attention isn't specifically relevant to the example in the question. Opponent-process theory (choice D) and monocular clues (choice E) are not relevant to this example. (Skill 1b)

146. **(A)** Bottom-up processing is a perceptual process occurring when we encounter unfamiliar stimuli and have to start at the "bottom," building a perception by looking piece by piece to build an overall perception. In bottom-up processing, we use past knowledge or "rules" to help us interpret sensations. Choice B, selective attention, is involved in the process referred to in this question. However, it isn't specifically relevant to this example. Top-down processing, choice C, is the opposite of the bottom-up processing described in the question. With top-down processing, we use past knowledge or "rules" to help us interpret sensations. Opponent-process theory (choice D) and kinesthetic sense (choice E) are not relevant to this example. (Skill 1b)

147. **(E)** The absolute threshold is the minimum amount of a sensation (in this example, sound waves) that we can perceive. Choice A, difference threshold, is a similar concept. However, it refers to how much a sensation needs to change in order for us to detect that change. Choice B, sensory adaptation, refers to the process of our senses becoming less sensitive to stimuli because of constant exposure. Vestibular sense, choice C, is not relevant to this example. Choice D, Weber's law, is also not relevant to this example. (Skill 1b)

148. **(B)** Difference thresholds are the amount stimuli have to change in order for us to perceive a change in the stimulus. For example, a difference threshold is how much louder something needs to be in order for us to be able to tell that it got louder. Choice A is a definition of absolute threshold. Choice C is a definition of top-down processing. Choice D doesn't apply to this example. Choice E refers to sensory adaptation. (Skill 1a)

149. **(D)** Our consciousness, specifically our working memory, focuses on only one or a few stimuli at a time. These stimuli are the ones that get perceived. This process is called selective attention. Choice A, bottom-up processing, refers to the process of building a perception piece by piece. However, it doesn't explain why we perceive only a few stimuli at a time. Kinesthesis, blind spot, and figure-ground (choices B, C, and E) don't specifically help explain why we focus on only a few stimuli at a time. (Skill 1a)

150. **(B)** Humans focus on one or a few stimuli at a time instead of the hundreds of stimuli that bombard us. The stimuli we focus on are the ones that we perceive. This process is called *selective attention*. Choice A, absolute threshold, refers to the minimum amount of a stimulus that we can perceive. However, absolute threshold doesn't explain the scenario in the question. Choice C, mindfulness, is not a relevant sensation and perception term. Precognition, choice D, is a kind of supposed "extrasensory" phenomenon and doesn't really exist. Perception, choice E, is not specifically relevant to this example. (Skill 1a)

151. **(E)** Light enters the eye through the pupil, is focused by the lens, and then activates rods and cones in the retina. Then, nerve impulses travel to the brain via the optic nerve. Choice A includes some parts of the eye. However, it also includes the cochlea, which is part of the ear. The other choices (B, C, and D) all use terms not involved in vision. (Skill 1a)

152. **(D)** The pupil dilates or contracts to let more or less light into the eye. Choice A is a good analogy for the lens of the eye. Choice B is a useful analogy for the retina. Choices C and E are not useful analogies for any structure in the eye. (Skill 1b)

153. **(A)** The lens in the eye changes shape to focus light onto the retina, much like adjusting a telescope can bring an image into focus. Choice B is a useful analogy for the retina. Choice D is a good analogy for the role of the pupil in the eye. Choices C and E are not useful analogies for any structure in the eye. (Skill 1b)

154. **(B)** The retina in the eye is a lot like a movie screen. Light enters the eye through the pupil, is focused by the lens, and is projected onto the retina. (At the retina, specialized neurons like rods and cones fire in response to the focused light.) Choice A is a useful analogy for the lens in the eye. Choice D is a good analogy for the role of the pupil in the eye. Choices C and E are not useful analogies for any structure in the eye. (Skill 1b)

155. **(C)** The place where the optic nerves connect to each retina does not contain receptor cells, creating a blind spot in each eye. Choice A is an incorrect statement about feature detectors. Choice B is true in a sense. Eyes are spaced apart on the human face. However, the visual fields of the two eyes overlap. So, this does not explain the blind spot. Choice D is a factually incorrect statement about the retina. Choice E depends on a cognitive explanation, which is not relevant to the physiological fact of the blind spot. (Skill 1a)

156. **(A)** The place where the optic nerve connects to the retina in each eye does not contain receptor cells, creating a blind spot in each eye. Choices B, C, D, and E all mention an accurate structure in the eye. However, the

optic nerve doesn't connect with any of the structures listed. In addition, none of the phenomena listed are caused by the optic nerve connecting with the structure listed. (Skill 1a)

157. **(D)** Transduction occurs when energy or chemicals are changed into neural impulses. For example, light entering the eye is changed into neural impulses when rods and cones are activated and then send messages to the brain via the optic nerve. In this way, transduction is the last step in sensation and the first step in perception. Choices A, B, and C do not describe transduction because sensations are not being transformed into neural impulses. Choice E describes communication within the brain (neural transmission within the brain). (Skill 1b)

158. **(A)** Transduction occurs when either energy or chemicals are changed into neural impulses. Choices B, C, and D are not relevant to the process of transduction. Choice E, action potential, refers to a step in the process of neural transmission in which the electrical charge moves down the axon. (Skill 1a)

159. **(D)** During transduction, sensations (either energy or chemicals) are changed into neural impulses in our senses. Perception occurs when these neural impulses are interpreted in the brain. Kinesthesis, choice A, refers to our sense of movement and body position. Choice B, Gestalt, refers to a set of principles that describe how we group objects together and perceive them as a whole. Depolarization (choice C) and dissociation (choice E) do not refer to either sensation or perceptual processes. (Skill 1a)

160. **(C)** When sound waves move fluid in the cochlea, tiny hair cells move and then activate neurons that send neural impulses to the brain. This transformation of sound waves into neural impulses is an example of transduction. The tympanic membrane, hammer, and anvil (choices A, B, and D) are all parts of the ear that play a role in transmitting sound waves from the outside world to the inner ear. However, they do not involve transduction. Choice E, thalamus, refers to an area of the brain, not the ear. The thalamus is where all neural impulses from the senses, except the sense of smell, pass through on their way to their final destinations in the brain. (Skill 1a)

161. **(B)** Humans perceive color because combinations of different cones in the eye fire in response to different colors (trichromatic theory) and because cones are linked in opposing color pairs (opponent-process theory). Choices A and D include valid sensation and perception terms. However, neither of these pairs of terms relate to color vision. Choice C refers to opposing perceptual processes but not specifically to the perception of color. Choice E lists important concepts that determine which sensations

we perceive. However, these theories do not specifically relate to color vision. (Skill 1a)

162. **(D)** If you stare at something that is red for long enough and then quickly stare at a white surface, you perceive a green afterimage. You perceive the opposite (complementary) color because the red and green cones are paired in the retina and because the red cones are fatigued due to constant exposure. When you look away at a white surface, the paired cones for green fire at a higher rate than the fatigued red cones, causing you to perceive the color green. This paired-cone theory is the opponent-process theory of vision. Binocular vision (choice A) and retinal disparity (choice B) explain how depth and distance are perceived. Choice C, trichromatic theory, helps explain other examples of color perception but cannot explain color afterimages. Choice E, color constancy, helps explain why an object is perceived as maintaining its color even as lighting conditions change. (Skill 1c)

163. **(C)** Selective attention is one of the major factors determining what stimuli we perceive (because we pay attention to those stimuli). This is similar to the cocktail party effect, instantly noticing when someone says our name even in the midst of a noisy environment. Identity formation (choice A) and egocentrism (choice D) are stages from developmental psychology. Spotlight syndrome, choice B, is the tendency to overestimate how much others pay attention to us. Choice E, self-reference effect, relates to how we learn and remember information better when we relate that information to our own lives. (Skill 1a)

Scenarios

164. **(E)** You use bottom-up processing when you need to build a perception of an unfamiliar object. You examine each piece of the experience and figure out how the pieces all fit together into something you can understand and/or perceive. This is likely the process you would have to use at this very avant-garde art opening. Top-down processing, choice A, is the opposite. When you experience something familiar, you use what you know from the past to understand and/or perceive the experience. Signal detection theory (choice B) and selective attention (choice C) are perceptual processes that you use almost constantly. However, they aren't uniquely suited to this scenario. Choice D, opponent-process theory, refers to a theory about color vision. (Skill 1b)

165. **(A)** This demonstration makes the point that humans perceive the world in ways that may not be accurate according to physics. Humans perceive that the pound of feathers is lighter than the one-pound weight.

That difference in perception is worthy of studying (hence the need for psychology, not just physics). Professor Benjamin's demonstration involves sensation (choice B), which also involves transduction (choice C). However, neither sensation nor transduction explain the point the professor is trying to make. Kinesthesis (choice D) and vestibular (choice E) refer to body movement and position. (Skill 1b)

166. **(B)** The difference threshold is the minimum amount a sensation has to change in order for a difference to be noticed. The volume would have had to exceed the difference threshold for Fred to perceive whether or not this song is louder than the last one. Signal detection theory, choice A, is involved in all perceptual events. However, it wouldn't uniquely help Fred. Binocular cues, choice C, refers to visual depth perception. Trephination, choice D, is out of context. It refers to the history of brain research. Perceptual set, choice E, is involved in all examples of perception. However, it wouldn't help Fred in this scenario. (Skill 1b)

167. **(C)** You do not perceive sensations unless you selectively attend (pay attention) to them. It's possible that you've heard this "lecture" so many times from Mr. Drumknott that you didn't selectively attend to it this time. Choice A, transduction, describes the stage when sensations change into perceptions. Transduction does not help explain the scenario. Choice B, difference threshold, refers to how much louder or softer the speech would have to be for you to notice the change in volume. Projection (choice D) and operant conditioning (choice E) are not sensation and perception terms. So, they don't help explain this situation. (Skill 1b)

168. **(D)** If you want to describe exactly what you are seeing at any given moment, you will need to use a list of the parts of the eye. Choices A, B, C, and E are random collections of terms from the sensation and perception unit. Any of these terms individually might be involved in the process of what you are seeing right now, but they are not specifically all involved in any example of vision. (Skill 1a)

169. **(A)** Hearing involves sound waves moving the eardrum, which moves fluid in the cochlea, which moves hair cells, which cause neural impulses to go to the temporal lobe where they are perceived. Choice B includes the term *frontal lobe*, which is out of place in this list. Choice C includes the terms *pitch* and *tone*, which are helpful when describing sounds but don't help answer how sounds are processed. Choice D includes perceptual terms that might apply to hearing in general but don't help answer this specific question. Choice E includes the terms *frequency* and *amplitude*. They are useful when describing sound waves but don't help explain how sounds are heard. (Skill 1a)

170. **(B)** The sensory systems of kinesthesis (understanding our body's position in space) and vision (getting visual feedback on where we are and where we need to be) are the two most relevant sensory systems responsible for the gymnastics performance. All of the other choices (A, C, D, and E) include at least one irrelevant or incorrect term, such as sense of touch, hearing (inner ear), gustation, olfaction, and transduction. (Skill 1b)

171. **(C)** The absolute threshold is the minimum amount of a sensation that you can perceive. In this case, it's the minimum amount of sound energy you can perceive. The absolute threshold for sound typically goes up as you age and as your hearing deteriorates, which may explain why Rufus hears the song and you don't. Choice A, difference threshold, isn't relevant to the scenario. Choice B, proprioception, refers to knowledge of the position of parts of our body. Choice D, transduction, is a physiological process similar in all humans. Transduction is the process that changes stimuli into neural impulses. Choice E, structuralism, is a movement from the early history of psychology. (Skill 1b)

172. **(D)** The Gestalt psychologists tried to uncover the reasons why people perceive groups of stimuli as a whole instead of just seeing the individual elements of a group. For some reason, your brain reorganized the individual stimuli of those clouds into the whole of the school mascot. Gestalt researchers would be interested in figuring out why you saw the school mascot. Functionalists (choice A) and structuralists (choice B) are historical perspectives from the early history of psychology. Psychodynamic (choice C) and naturalistic observation (choice E) are not terms or schools of thought within the area of sensation and perception research and thinking. (Skill 1b)

173. **(E)** Since this is a drawing class, students learn how to use drawing techniques to create depth, distance, and so on in their drawings. All of these techniques rely on monocular depth cues (cues that you can perceive with one eye) since they are drawn on a two-dimensional surface (the paper). Binocular cues (choice A) and retinal disparity (choice C) aren't correct because this is a drawing class. Binocular cues and retinal disparity help you perceive depth in the real world and rely on you using both eyes. Top-down processing (choice B) and bottom-up processing (choice D) aren't relevant to this scenario because they don't help explain why drawing techniques portray depth in drawings. (Skill 1b)

174. **(A)** Sensory adaptation occurs when a sense is constantly stimulated with the same sensation and a person experiences decreasing responsiveness to that stimuli due to the constant stimulation. If a person is surrounded by the same smell for a long period of time, he or she stops smelling it—like the residents of the town. Sensory adaptation occurs due to

fatigue in the olfactory system. To smell the scent of manure again, the person would need to leave the area, giving the olfactory system time to regenerate. Choice B, habituation, is a similar concept. However, sensory habituation occurs when a person stops paying attention to frequently experienced stimuli rather than a decreased responsiveness in one of his or her senses due to constant exposure. The decreased response is due to a cognitive process. Choice C, perceptual set, helps explain why people interpret and perceive stimuli in the ways they do. Dissociation (choice D) and defense mechanism (choice E) are not relevant to sensation and perception. Instead, they both have to do with levels of consciousness and the idea of the unconscious mind. (Skill 1b)

175. **(B)** Habituation occurred when Samuel stopped noticing a frequently encountered stimulus—the portrait. Habituation is similar to the process of sensory adaptation, choice A. Sensory adaptation, though, is decreased responsiveness of the sense because of constant exposure to a stimulus. There is a physiological blind spot, choice C, in each eye due to the connection to the optic nerve. It would not cause the phenomenon described in the scenario. Choice D, occipital lobe, is responsible for visual perceptions but doesn't explain the scenario. Choice E, perceptual omission, is not a psychological term. (Skill 1b)

176. **(C)** Mr. Slant claims he can see in the infrared and ultraviolet spectrum. Seeing infrared and ultraviolet light waves are beyond the absolute threshold for human eyes, so researchers would likely check his visual absolute threshold carefully in order to check Mr. Slant's claim. Choices A and B are concepts related to perception, but they are not relevant to Mr. Slant's claim of extraordinary sight. Choice D refers to the point at which sensations are changed into perceptions and sent to the brain—that concept is not specifically relevant to this scenario. Choice E is not a sensation/perception concept (Structuralism refers to an early psychological theory). (Skill 1b)

Names

177. **(D)** Ernst Weber and Gustav Fechner performed experiments separately. They theorized about the impact of changes in sensations and how these changes impact a person's perceptions of differences and changes in sensations. The psychologists mentioned in the other choices (choices A, B, C, and E) were not involved in research related to difference thresholds. (Skill 1a)

178. **(A)** David Hubel and Torsten Wiesel won the Nobel Prize for discovering groups of neurons in the visual cortex in animals that respond to specific visual stimuli (feature detectors). The researchers mentioned in choices B, C, and D were all involved in some type of biopsychological research but

not specifically reactions to visual stimuli. Choice E refers to two famous case studies in the history of brain research (Phineas Gage and Clive Wearing). (Skill 1a)

179. **(E)** David Hubel and Torsten Wiesel won the Nobel Prize for discovering groups of neurons in the visual cortex in animals that respond to specific visual stimuli (feature detectors). This research established that a firing neuron can be detected by listening for the sound of that neural firing. The researchers mentioned in choices B and D were involved in brain research but not research specific to this situation. The psychologists mentioned in choices A and C were not primarily involved in brain research. (Skill 1a)

Research Methods

180. **(B)** Since this researcher wants to test the impact of distraction on perception, she is likely to design a way to influence participants' selective attention and then measure how that affects the memory of visual stimuli. Transduction, choice A, is a physiological process that changes stimuli into neural impulses. Absolute threshold, perceptual constancy, and sensory habituation (choices C, D, and E) are all concepts related to perception. However, they could not be used as independent variables because they would be difficult or impossible to manipulate or change for the purposes of the experiment. (Skill 3)

181. **(C)** Operational definitions are used by researchers to measure variables in a study. This researcher would need to define precisely how he or she will measure absolute threshold. That is typically defined as the minimum amount of stimulus a person can detect half the time. Choices A and B are possible elements of the research, but they are not related to the operational definition. Choices D and E are not accurate statements about experimentation or about sensation and perception. (Skill 3)

182. **(D)** Since this study is about color blindness, the researcher would most likely have to use at least two groups of participants: one group of color-blind participants and one group of people who are not color-blind. That is not true random assignment. The other responses (choices A, B, C, and E) include factually incorrect statements about random assignment. (Skill 3)

Perspectives

183. **(A)** The biological perspective researches explanations for human thinking and behavior that are related to biology—genetics, brain chemistry, and/or brain structure. The symptoms this patient is reporting are most likely caused by a biological cause. Potentially, the patient is experiencing

CHAPTER 6

an issue in the visual cortex either in the left hemisphere or on the right side of each retina. The psychological perspectives listed in choices B, C, and D are unlikely to be useful to treat or explain these symptoms. Choice E is concerned with cultural norms and cross-cultural differences/similarities. (Skill 1c)

184. **(D)** The cognitive perspective explains human thinking and behavior by examining how we think about our current experiences and remember past experiences. Perceptual sets relate to our cognitive interpretations of stimuli; they are the "mental rules" we use to change stimuli into perceptions. The perspectives listed in choices A, B, C, and E are not relevant to the concept of perceptual set. (Skill 1a)

185. **(A)** Sociocultural psychologists research how psychological principles impact thinking and behavior differently in different cultures. Most sensation and perception principles operate similarly across cultures. However, some principles, like monocular cues, are culture bound. In other words, these cues influence perception differently in different cultures. Some monocular cues depend on past experiences. For example, growing up in a "carpentered environment" with many right angles influences how individuals interpret two-dimensional cues of lines and angles. Choices B through E are perceptual principles that are primary physiological. So, none of these choices differ among cultures. (Skill 1c)

CHAPTER 6: LEARNING

Stimulus

186. **(C)** In the cell marked with the number 1, Sniffy received a food pellet and then performed the target behavior (standing on her hind legs). This is positive reinforcement—when an organism receives a stimulus and repeats a target behavior. Choices A, D, and E correspond to other cells in the table. Choice B, classical conditioning, describes a different kind of conditioning. It relates a neutral stimulus to a preexisting relationship to a stimulus that already elicits an "unconditioned" response. (Skill 1b)

187. **(A)** In the cell marked with the number 2, one of Sniffy's food pellets was taken away but she still performed the desired behavior (standing on her hind legs). This is negative reinforcement—when an organism gets a stimulus taken away and still repeats a target behavior. Choices C, D, and E correspond to other cells in the table. Choice B, classical conditioning, describes a different kind of conditioning. It relates a neutral stimulus to a preexisting relationship to a stimulus that already elicits an "unconditioned" response. (Skill 1b)

188. **(E)** In the cell marked with the number 3, Sniffy received a food pellet but did not do the desired behavior (standing on her hind legs). This is positive punishment—when an organism receives a stimulus but does not repeat the target behavior. Choices A, C, and D correspond to other cells in the table. Choice B, classical conditioning, describes a different kind of conditioning. It relates a neutral stimulus to a preexisting relationship to a stimulus that already elicits an "unconditioned" response. (Skill 1b)

189. **(D)** In the cell marked with the number 4, one of Sniffy's food pellets was taken away and she did not do the desired behavior (standing on her hind legs). This is negative punishment—when an organism gets a stimulus removed and does not repeat the target behavior. Choices A, C, and E correspond to other cells in the table. Choice B, classical conditioning, describes a different kind of conditioning. It relates a neutral stimulus to a preexisting relationship to a stimulus that already elicits an "unconditioned" response. (Skill 1b)

190. **(D)** For many dogs, seeing a stranger will automatically cause barking, making it an unconditioned stimulus. Hearing a knock, choice A, was previously a neutral stimulus. A neutral stimulus is a stimulus that doesn't automatically cause a specific response. Choice B, barking, is the response. At the beginning of the scenario, it was an unconditioned response. After several pairings of hearing a knock on the door and seeing a stranger, barking became a conditioned response to the knock on the door. Opening the door, choice C, is related to seeing a stranger. However, this option doesn't describe any specific behavior Phinny does when a door opens. Choice E, generalization, is a term related to this example. Phinny is generalizing knocks on the door to anything that sounds like a knock. (Skill 1b)

191. **(A)** Hearing a knock was previously a neutral stimulus. After several pairings of hearing a knock on the door and seeing a stranger (the unconditioned stimulus—choice D), barking (choice B) became a conditioned response to the conditioned stimulus of the knock on the door. Choice C, opening the door, is related to seeing a stranger. However, this choice doesn't describe any specific behavior Phinny does when the door opens. Choice E, generalization, is a term related to this example. Phinny is generalizing knocks on the door to anything that sounds like a knock. (Skill 1b)

192. **(B)** For many dogs, seeing a stranger (choice D) will automatically cause barking. So, seeing the stranger is an unconditioned stimulus causing the unconditioned response of barking. After several pairings of hearing a knock on the door (choice A—the conditioned stimulus) and of seeing a stranger, barking became a conditioned response to the conditioned stimulus of the knock on the door. Choice C, opening the door, is related

to seeing a stranger. However, this scenario doesn't describe any specific behavior Phinny does when the door opens. Choice E, generalization, is a term related to this example. Phinny is generalizing knocks on the door to anything that sounds like a knock. (Skill 1b)

193. (E) Generalization occurs when any stimulus similar to the original conditioned stimulus elicits the conditioned response. In this case, Phinny is conditioned to bark (CR) at any stimulus similar to the knock on the door. Choice A, discrimination, occurs when an organism responds only to the original conditioned stimulus. In this case, if Phinny only barked at a knock on the door, and not other similar sounds, it would be an example of discrimination. Choice B, spontaneous recovery, occurs when an organism responds to a stimulus again after the response was extinct. For example, if Phinny had stopped barking to the sound of a knock on the door, but one day in response to a knock, Phinny barks again. Extinction of a conditioned response, choice C, happens when a conditioned stimulus is repeatedly presented without the unconditioned stimulus. In Phinny's case, her barking (CR) would stop (extinction) if she heard repeated knocks on the door (CS) unaccompanied by a "stranger" (US). Choice D, reinforcement, is an element of operant conditioning, not the classical conditioning scenario referred to in this question. (Skill 1b)

Definitions

194. (B) Classical conditioning involves pairing a neutral stimulus (like the sound of a bell) with a stimulus (like food) that already automatically causes a response (like salivation). Eventually, the previously neutral stimulus (the sound of the bell) will cause the response (salivation) all on its own. Choice A, operant conditioning, involves either providing or taking away a stimulus after an organism responds. Positive reinforcement (choice C) and negative reinforcement (choice D) are types of operant conditioning reinforcements. Choice E, conjoined conditioning, is not a psychological term. (Skill 1a)

195. (A) To condition an organism operantly, a researcher waits until the organism behaves (like a rat pushing a level) and then the researcher provides a stimulus (like a food pellet). At that point the organism may—or may not—repeat the behavior. Classical conditioning, choice B, involves pairing a neutral stimulus with a stimulus that already automatically causes a response. Positive reinforcement (choice C) and negative reinforcement (choice D) are types of operant conditioning reinforcements. Secondary reinforcement, choice E, refers to a learning situation that involves using a reinforcement that has already been previously paired with a primary reinforcer. (Skill 1a)

196. **(E)** The common practice of providing a reward for desired behavior is very similar to the concept of positive reinforcement used during operant conditioning. Choice A, observational learning, is a different kind of learning where researchers learn by watching a model perform behaviors. Rewards are not an element of classical conditioning, choice B. Positive conditioning (choice C) and advantage learning (choice D) are not psychological terms. (Skill 1a)

197. **(C)** Classical conditioning involves pairing stimuli: a neutral stimulus paired with a stimulus that automatically causes a response. Choices A and B describe operant conditioning, not classical conditioning. Choice D doesn't make sense. Researchers don't use reinforcements (operant conditioning) along with unconditioned responses (classical conditioning). Choice E doesn't provide any useful information for this question. The phrase "effective, traditional schedule" isn't useful or meaningful in the context of behaviorism and this question. (Skill 1a)

198. **(D)** Operant conditioning involves providing rewards (positive reinforcements) for behaviors that approximate the desired target behaviors. Choices A and B refer to cognitive interpretations and relationships, which are not a part of either behaviorism or operant conditioning. Choice C describes classical conditioning. Choice E mixes terms from operant and classical conditioning. (Skill 1a)

199. **(B)** Behaviorists research how conditioning influences behavior. They do this by studying how different stimuli, which are external events that elicit behaviors, relate to responses. These responses can be physical reactions or behaviors. Punishment (choice A) and reinforcement (choice E) are kinds of stimuli in the context of operant conditioning. Choice C, instinct, is a specific kind of automatic response that occurs in some nonhuman animals. A response, choice D, is a type of behavior and, therefore, cannot elicit a behavior. (Skill 1a)

200. **(A)** Behaviorists research how conditioning influences human behavior. They do this by studying how different stimuli, which are external events that elicit behaviors, relate to responses. These responses can be physical reactions or behaviors. Choice B is the definition of a reinforcement. Choice C is similar to the definition of a stimulus. However, it is actually a more accurate definition of a sensation. A physical reaction or behavior, choice D, is a response. Choice E is the definition of a punishment. (Skill 1a)

201. **(D)** Behaviorists research how conditioning influences human behavior. They do this by studying how different stimuli, which are external events that elicit behaviors, relate to responses. These responses are physical reactions or behaviors. Punishment (choice A) and reinforcement (choice E)

are kinds of stimuli in the context of operant conditioning. A stimulus, choice B, is something that elicits a behavior, not the behavior itself. An instinct, choice C, is a specific kind of automatic response that occurs in some nonhuman animals. (Skill 1a)

202. **(E)** Behaviorists research how conditioning influences human behavior. They do this by studying how different stimuli, which are external events that elicit behaviors, relate to responses. These responses are physical reactions or behaviors. Choice A refers to cognition (thinking). The context for the term "response" in the question is learning/behaviorism, not the cognitive perspective. Choice B describes a stimulus, which is an external event that elicits a behavior. Choice C is a definition of learning. Choice D is a definition of transduction, which happens in the senses. (Skill 1a)

203. **(B)** An unconditioned stimulus (like food) automatically causes an unconditioned response (like salivation). The term *unconditioned* refers to the fact that the unconditioned stimulus automatically causes the unconditioned response without any prior training or experiences; this is a reflexive relationship. If a conditioned stimulus, choice A, is paired several times with an unconditioned stimulus, the conditioned stimulus will eventually cause the conditioned response, choice C. An unconditioned response, choice D, is the reaction to an unconditioned stimulus. Behavioral contingency, choice E, refers to any stimulus/response relationship in behaviorism. (Skill 1a)

204. **(A)** In classical conditioning, an unconditioned stimulus is paired (presented along) with a conditioned stimulus in order to produce a conditioned response (choice C). Positive reinforcement (choice B) and negative reinforcement (choice E) are types of reinforcement that are used in operant conditioning, not classical conditioning. An unconditioned response (choice D) refers to the response to an unconditioned stimulus. (Skill 1a)

205. **(C)** The four elements listed in choice C are the required elements in any classical conditioning example. An unconditioned stimulus causes an unconditioned response. The unconditioned stimulus is paired with a conditioned stimulus several times until, eventually, the conditioned stimulus causes the conditioned response. Choice A lists the basic elements of one kind of operant-conditioned response. Choices B, D, and E are lists of other terms associated with conditioning, but they aren't specific to classical conditioning. (Skill 1a)

206. **(D)** When a conditioned stimulus (like the sound of a bell) is presented many times without the unconditioned stimulus (like food), eventually the conditioned response (salivation) will become extinct. Discrimination,

choice A, is related to classical conditioning. It occurs when organisms respond only to a specific conditioned stimulus. Shaping, choice B, is not related to classical conditioning. Spontaneous recovery, choice C, is related to classical conditioning. It is the return of a conditioned response after extinction. Overjustification, choice E, is not related to classical conditioning. (Skill 1a)

207. **(B)** Spontaneous recovery can occur only after a classically conditioned response becomes extinct. Extinction of a conditioned response occurs when a conditioned stimulus is presented many times without an unconditioned stimulus. Eventually, the conditioned response becomes extinct. Later, the conditioned response may return spontaneously. Choice A, generalization, is related to classical conditioning. It occurs when an organism responds to any stimulus similar to the conditioned stimulus. Punishment, reinforcement, and deindividuation (choices C, D, and E) do not relate to classical conditioning. (Skill 1a)

208. **(E)** The description in the question describes the process of generalization. The opposite of this process is discrimination, which occurs when an organism responds only to the specific conditioned stimulus. Generalization, choice A, occurs when an organism responds to any stimulus similar to the conditioned stimulus. Behaviorism, choice B, refers to the overall perspective of behaviorism, which includes all types of conditioning. Structuralism (choice C) and overjustification (choice D) are not relevant to learning and conditioning. (Skill 1a)

209. **(C)** John Watson wrote the "Behaviorist Manifesto," which argued that psychology should be the science of behavior. He wrote that psychologists should exclusively study behavior rather than nonobservable phenomena like cognition. The concepts mentioned in choices A, B, D, and E (acquisition, discrimination, extinction, and shaping) are principles behaviorists often research. (Skill 1a)

210. **(B)** The processes of generalization and discrimination can occur during both operant and classical conditioning. In classical conditioning, organisms begin responding to any stimulus similar to the conditioned stimulus (generalization) or only to that specific conditioned stimulus (discrimination). During operant conditioning, an organism may start to generalize the behavior that is associated with reinforcement or may discriminate and do only the exact behavior that is associated with the reinforcement. The terms in choice A, unconditioned stimulus and conditioned response, apply only to classical conditioning. The terms in choice C, shaping and reinforcement, apply only to operant conditioning. The terms in choice D, cognitive map and latent learning, and the terms

in choice E, observational and vicarious learning, aren't specific to either classical or operant conditioning. (Skill 1a)

211. **(A)** By definition, a stimulus that increases the chances that a behavior is repeated is a reinforcement. A stimulus that decreases the chances that a behavior is repeated is a punishment. Choice B refers to interpretation, and behaviorists do not rely on that kind of cognitive process. Choices C, D, and E are incorrect statements. (Skill 1a)

212. **(D)** The schedules of reinforcement differ based on interval and ratio. An interval is the amount of time required between behaviors before a reinforcement is delivered. A ratio is the number of behaviors required before a reinforcement is delivered. The terms listed in choices A, B, C, and E do not have anything to do with different schedules of reinforcement. (Skill 1a)

213. **(A)** Conditioned responses are elicited by conditioned stimuli. The first stage of classical conditioning is the relationship between the unconditioned stimulus and the unconditioned response. The conditioned stimulus is paired with the unconditioned stimulus, which still produces the unconditioned response. When the conditioned stimulus is presented alone and the response occurs, it is a conditioned response. Choice B is incorrect because an unconditioned response is not elicited by a conditioned stimulus. Choices C, D, and E all include inaccurate details about conditioning. (Skill 1a)

Scenarios

214. **(E)** This scenario is an example of classical conditioning because there is a clear, unconditional relationship between the puff of air (unconditioned stimulus) and the eye blink (unconditioned response). The word "puff" (conditioned stimulus) eventually elicits the response of the eye blink (now a conditioned response). The example does not fit the operant conditioning model (choice A) because there is neither a reinforcement nor a punishment in the scenario. Choice B, semantic conditioning, is not a psychological term. Latent learning (choice C) and expectancy effect (choice D) are not relevant to this scenario. (Skill 1b)

215. **(C)** The treatment Dr. Hix is using with this client is an example of operant conditioning because it involves a reinforcement. Dr. Hix and the client created the reinforcement chart to reinforce the client for avoiding smoking. They hope that the reinforcements increase the chances that the client will stay cigarette-free. This scenario is not an example of classical conditioning, choice B, because there is no unconditioned

stimulus–unconditioned response pair in the example. Fixed-ratio schedule, aversive conditioning, and positive punishment (choices A, D, and E) are all terms associated with behaviorism that do not apply to this example. (Skill 1b)

216. **(E)** Any unconditioned stimulus must automatically cause the unconditioned response. The smell of food is the unconditioned stimulus as it would automatically trigger salivation in the dog. Thus, Watch salivating (choice A) is the unconditioned response. If the smell of food was paired with the sound of picking up the food bowl a number of times, Watch may start salivating just at the sound. The sound of the bowl (choice C) has become a conditioned stimulus. Choice B, Watch looking up, is a voluntary response and not classically conditioned. Choice D is not referred to in the example. (Skill 1b)

217. **(D)** When an organism responds only to a specific conditioned stimulus, discrimination has occurred. In this example, discrimination is the dog responding only to Mrs. Ridcully's whistle rather than to a similar stimulus, which is the whistle of the dog's owner. Choice A, instinctive drift, isn't relevant to this example. No instinctive reaction is involved in this example. Selective attention (choice B) and proactive interference (choice C) aren't relevant to operant conditioning. Instead, these terms relate to memory theory. Choice E, extinction, does not apply to this example. The conditioned response is not extinct since it is still elicited by Mrs. Ridcully's whistle. (Skill 1b)

218. **(C)** In operant conditioning, a punishment decreases the chances that the original behavior will be repeated. Mr. Stibbons may intend for the lecture to be punishing. Since his son repeated the original behavior, though, the lecture is probably not a punishment. Choice A includes the phrase "center of attention," and the example doesn't include any details that justify that conclusion. Choice B is factually incorrect. There may be a classical conditioned relationship between frustration and crying. Choice D uses the term "negative reinforcement" incorrectly, so it is also factually incorrect. Choice E may be true, but the example doesn't provide enough details to justify that conclusion as the best choice. (Skill 1b)

219. **(A)** This is an example of negative reinforcement because a stimulus was removed (the students' disruptive behaviors) and Mrs. Whitlow repeated the behavior (having students use laptops). Positive reinforcement, choice B, is incorrect because a stimulus was removed, not added. Aversion training, choice C, is a term used in the context of treating psychological disorders. Positive modeling (choice D) and engagement strategy (choice E) are not psychological terms. (Skill 1b)

220. **(E)** Ms. Brevis can use a fixed-ratio schedule of reinforcement to maintain the desired behavior (the cat jumping into her lap) by not giving a food treat (positive reinforcement) every time the cat jumps into her lap. Now that the behavior is established, Ms. Brevis can give her cat a treat only after the cat does the desired behavior twice. Then she can wait until the cat does the behavior three times to give the reinforcement. Ms. Brevis can continue to increase this ratio until the cat has to jump up ten times (for example) before receiving a treat. In this way, Ms. Brevis maintains the desired conditioned behavior but does not have to give too many cat treats. Choice A is incorrect because operant conditioning will better maintain the desired behavior. In addition, training the cat to jump into her lap using classical conditioning will be difficult to impossible. Choices B and D don't make sense in the context of this scenario. Choice C is incorrect because nothing in this scenario indicates that negative reinforcement will be practical. To use negative reinforcement, Ms. Brevis would have to remove a stimulus that would cause the cat to jump into her lap. Imagining what that stimulus might be is difficult. (Skill 1b)

221. **(B)** The video poker machine described in the scenario delivers a reinforcement (a payout) after a winning hand and after a random amount of time between 10 and 23 minutes. This matches a variable-interval schedule—when a reinforcement is delivered after the desired behavior is performed and a variable amount of time has passed. This scenario is not a fixed-ratio schedule, choice A, because the reinforcement is not delivered after a specific number of times the desired behavior has been performed. The scenario is not a fixed-interval schedule, choice C, because the time between reinforcement varies. This scenario is not a variable-ratio schedule, choice D, because the reinforcement is not delivered after a variable number of times the desired behavior has been performed. Choice E is not a psychological term. (Skill 1b)

222. **(A)** If someone is already intrinsically motivated to perform a behavior (such as a child who loves reading), giving that person a reward (positive reinforcement) can decrease that intrinsic motivation. This is the over-justification effect. Primary reinforcement, choice B, does not help explain this scenario. Ice cream is a primary reinforcement. It doesn't, though, support Dr. Reiman's decision. Secondary reinforcement, choice C, does not help explain this scenario. The coupon is an example of a secondary reinforcement. It doesn't, though, support Dr. Reiman's decision. Latent learning effect (choice D) and proactive interference (choice E) refer to cognitive processes that do not relate to the reward scenario described in the question. (Skill 1b)

223. **(C)** Jason is most influenced by observational learning in this scenario. He watches the behavior of his brother and whether his brother Shawn is rewarded or punished. These observations may influence Jason's behaviors in the future. Positive reinforcement, choice A, is incorrect because Jason is never rewarded or punished for his behavior. Instead, he just watches Shawn as a model. Vicarious reward (choice B) and obedience training (choice D) are not psychological terms. Permissive parenting style, choice E, is not relevant to this example because no information is presented in the scenario about parenting style. (Skill 1b)

224. **(D)** Shaping occurs when a trainer provides a positive reinforcement whenever the organism makes a small step toward the eventual desired behavior. The trainer waits until the organism gets a little closer to the desired behavior, and eventually shapes the organism toward the actual desired behavior. Generalization, choice A, is incorrect because the organism isn't reacting to a similar conditioned stimulus or performing a similar behavior in order to get a reinforcement. Conservation, structuralism, and functionalism (choices B, C, and E) are psychological terms but are not relevant to the context of conditioning. (Skill 1b)

Names

225. **(A)** Ivan Pavlov's research established the classical conditioning model. Other researchers used his initial findings to develop the current principles and vocabulary associated with classical conditioning. The researchers listed in choices B, C, D, and E participated in research related to conditioning but were not involved in the earliest research into classical conditioning. (Skill 1a)

226. **(E)** B. F. Skinner is the most well-known operant conditioning researcher and one of the most well-known psychologists in history. His research using the Skinner box and other apparatuses established operant conditioning as one of the most important and dominant areas of psychology research for much of the 1900s. The researchers listed in choices A, B, C, and D participated in research related to conditioning but not primarily research into operant conditioning. (Skill 1a)

227. **(B)** John Watson wrote the "Behaviorist Manifesto" in 1913. He argued that if researchers wanted psychology to be a science, they needed to restrict their studies to observable, measurable phenomena (like behavior). The researchers listed in choices A, C, D, and E participated in research related to conditioning. However, they were not primarily involved with arguing that behaviorism should be the dominant force in psychology. (Skill 1a)

228. **(B)** This quote is from John Watson's "Behaviorist Manifesto" (actual title: "Psychology as the Behaviorist Views It" in *Psychological Review, 20,* 158–177, 1913). In this essay, Watson argued that if psychology wanted to be a science, researchers needed to restrict their thinking to observable, measurable phenomena (like behavior). The researchers listed in choices A, C, D, and E participated in research related to learning. However, none of them is the most likely author for this quote. The quote makes an overall philosophical argument about the nature of psychology, and Watson is the psychologist most associated with that philosophical viewpoint. (Skill 1a)

229. **(A)** Albert Bandura's research investigated observational learning and modeling. He developed the theory of reciprocal determinism, which included a patient's cognitive interpretations and feelings as a crucial element in the theory. The researchers listed in choices B, C, D, and E were behaviorists and would not have been interested in cognition. Behaviorists thought that psychologists should study observable phenomena like behaviors rather than unobservable events like cognition. (Skill 1a)

Research Methods

230. **(D)** In order to study this research question, this researcher would have to find children who grew up in extremely stressful homes. It would obviously be impossible (and very unethical) to "assign" children to a stressful home. In an experiment, choice A, the researcher must be able to assign participants to either an experimental or a control group. The survey method, choice B, would not be practical. Identifying enough children who grew up in extremely stressful homes would be difficult. Additionally, a survey would not provide useful data for this research question. A correlational study, choice C, requires correlating two variables, which isn't the situation described in this question. Random assignment, choice E, is an element in the experimental method. (Skill 3)

231. **(C)** The operational definition of the dependent variable is how the researcher measures (quantifies) the dependent variable. It is the effect of the independent variable. In this study, the independent variable is the kind of positive reinforcement. So, the dependent variable is how effective that reinforcer is at conditioning the pigeon. The number of times a pigeon pecks the target disk is a good way to measure the effectiveness of conditioning. The descriptions in choices A, B, D, and E don't refer to measuring the dependent variable to determine the effectiveness of conditioning. (Skill 3)

Perspectives

232. **(E)** Cognitive-behavioral therapy is a very commonly used treatment technique. It combines principles of conditioning (usually operant conditioning) with cognitive talk therapy. It strives to help clients change the ways they think about their past and how others treat them. Behavioral psychotherapy (choice A) and humanistic behavioral therapy (choice D) do not combine principles of behaviorism and the cognitive perspective as described in the question. Rational emotive treatment, choice B, is a type of cognitive therapy. However, it does not incorporate conditioning. Reciprocal determinism, choice C, is a theory associated with Albert Bandura. It is not a type of therapy. (Skill 1a)

233. **(B)** Both behaviorism and neuroscience emphasize the need to measure observable variables carefully. Behaviorists measure stimuli and physical responses. Biopsychologists measure neurological responses in the brain and elsewhere in the nervous system. (Biopsychologists also research the influence of genetics and the endocrine system.) Choices A, C, and D all include psychological perspectives. However, none of them focus exclusively on measuring observable phenomena. Note that structuralism in choice D is also a historical perspective, not a current one. The terms in choice E, incrementalism and psychometrics, do not refer to specific psychological perspectives. (Skill 1a)

CHAPTER 7: COGNITION

Stimulus

234. **(E)** When recalling a list of terms, the first and last items in the list will likely be best remembered. This occurs because of increased rehearsal for items early in the list, called the primacy effect. Since the person has recently been exposed to the items at the end of the list, those items may still be stored in short-term memory. This is called the recency effect. Choice A, the spacing effect, refers to the increase in retention if practice is distributed over time. Elaborative rehearsal, choice B, does increase the likelihood that information will be transferred to long-term storage but is not demonstrated in this graph. Ebbinghaus's forgetting curve, choice C, demonstrated that forgetting occurs soon after repetition ends but that forgetting stabilizes over time. Visual imagery, choice D, can impact retention by providing additional retrieval cues. However, this is not illustrated in the graph. (Skill 2)

Definitions

235. **(D)** The three processes necessary for memory formation are encoding—getting information into the information-processing system,

storage—maintaining information over time, and retrieval—getting information out. Sensory, short-term, and long-term (choice A) refer to the three different memory systems. Shallow, intermediate, and deep processing (choice B) refer to how information is encoded into memory. Recall, recognition, and relearning (choice C) refer to how information is retrieved from long-term memory. Space, time, and frequency (choice E) refers to types of information that are automatically processed into the memory system. (Skill 1a)

236. **(C)** Working memory describes the active processing that occurs in short-term memory, such as the integration of information stored in long-term memory with current incoming information. Iconic memory, choice A, refers to visual sensory memory. Explicit memory, choice B, is a specific type of long-term memory that includes information for personal events or general information. Echoic memory, choice D, is auditory sensory memory. Broca's area, choice E, is responsible for speech production and is located in the left frontal lobe. (Skill 1a)

237. **(D)** Explicit memories are those that require conscious recall. They include memories for personal events and general information that have been learned over a lifetime. Choices A, B, C, and E all reflect implicit memories, which are those that occur without conscious awareness. Implicit memories include automatic skills. (Skill 1b)

238. **(E)** Echoic memory is auditory sensory memory. Iconic memory, choice A, is visual sensory memory. Implicit memory, choice B, includes automatic memories for skills. Explicit memories, choice C, are consciously recalled memories, such as for personal events. Working memory, choice D, is a part of short-term memory where current information is combined with long-term memories. (Skill 1a)

239. **(B)** Chunking is the process of grouping items to aid in recall. Choice A refers to a memory mnemonic called the method of loci. Choice C is also a memory mnemonic called the peg word technique. Choice D may take advantage of the spacing effect to increase recall. Although choice E may help in recall by making the information more meaningful, it is not an example of chunking. (Skill 1b)

240. **(A)** The hippocampus is the primary brain region responsible for memory formation. Damage to the hippocampus leads to anterograde amnesia, which is where a person loses the ability to form new memories. The amygdala, choice B, is primarily involved in the emotional responses of fear and anger. The cerebellum, choice C, is responsible not only for coordinating the movements to maintain balance but also for the storage of implicit memory. Choice D, the frontal lobe, contains the centers for

reasoning and movement. The hypothalamus, choice E, regulates homeo-stasis and links the endocrine system to the nervous system. (Skill 1a)

241. **(B)** Priming occurs when exposure to particular stimuli—for example, the words "student," "bus," and so on—unconsciously activates retrieval of specific information, such as the word "school." Source amnesia, choice A, occurs when the origins of stored information are misattributed. Chunking, choice C, is the grouping of information that increases the amount of information that can be held in short-term memory. A flash-bulb memory, choice D, is formed for an emotional or a salient event and has an especially vivid quality. An echoic memory, choice E, is a brief sensory memory for auditory information. (Skill 1b)

242. **(D)** Mood congruent memory occurs when our current mood acts as a retrieval cue. Thus, when Jen feels sad, mood congruent memory trig-gers the recall of other sad events in her life. Choice A refers to the serial position effect. Choice B illustrates anterograde amnesia, which is most likely due to damage to the hippocampus. Choice C is an example of a flashbulb memory. Choice E illustrates the deep processing of informa-tion as Angie tries to make the information she is learning personally meaningful. (Skill 1b)

243. **(E)** Explicit memories require conscious processing. Deliberate effort is needed to locate the stored information about experienced events or acquired facts. Implicit memories become automatically recalled, often through practice. They can be accessed without our conscious awareness. Choice A incorrectly characterizes explicit and implicit memories as both of them are long-term memories. Choice B is incorrect because explicit memories are stored in the cerebral cortex and implicit memories are stored in the cerebellum. Choice C is incorrect because both types of memory can be encoded semantically, visually, or auditorily. Choice D is incorrect because echoic (auditory) and iconic (visual) memory are both types of sensory memory. (Skill 1a)

244. **(C)** Procedural memories are implicit. This means they are performed automatically and involve performing a specific skill. Therefore, knowing how to ride a bike is a procedural memory. Choices A, B, D, and E are all examples of explicit memories for consciously recalled facts or personally experienced events. (Skill 1b)

245. **(C)** Short-term memory is limited to holding approximately 7 units of information (±2) for up to 30 seconds. Echoic memory, choice A, is a sensory memory system. Echoic (auditory) memory holds information for up to 4 seconds. Iconic memory, choice B, is also a sensory memory system. Iconic (visual) memory holds information for up to ½ second.

Semantic memory, choice D, refers to information encoded in memory based on the information's meaningfulness. Long-term memory, choice E, theoretically holds an unlimited amount of information for an indefinite period of time. (Skill 1a)

246. **(E)** Selective attention refers to how we filter extraneous stimuli in order to focus on one aspect of our external world. Framing, choice A, refers to the way information is presented. For example, how a question is asked can impact the choice you give. Confirmation bias, choice B, happens when we look only for information that supports our previous beliefs. Homeostasis, choice C, refers to the way we maintain balance within the body, such as regulating body temperature or hunger. Mental set, choice D, occurs when we consider only solutions that have worked before when dealing with problems. (Skill 1a)

247. **(B)** The prototype is the best example given of a category. Prototypes help us more effectively store and retrieve information by helping us link similar ideas. A concept, choice A, is a grouping of similar items, ideas, or people. Phonemes, choice C, are speech sounds that compose our language. Morphemes, choice D, are the smallest units of language that carry meaning, such as a suffix. A schema, choice E, is a complex set of categories that helps use organize our world. (Skill 1a)

248. **(E)** Convergent thinking requires searching for a single correct choice. Thus, completing a multiple-choice test requires that you eliminate possible choices to find the single correct choice. Trial and error, choice A, is a problem-solving device where you try various solutions until you find one that succeeds. Functional fixedness, choice B, hinders good problem solving because you become unable to see other uses for objects beyond the original intent. Divergent thinking, choice C, is the opposite of convergent thinking. Divergent thinking is the ability to generate multiple solutions to a problem (for example, brainstorming). Incubation, choice D, may promote insight into or the sudden realization of a solution to a problem. When you stop thinking about a problem for a while, the choice may suddenly become clear. (Skill 1a)

249. **(C)** A step-by-step problem-solving strategy that guarantees a solution is called an algorithm. When you follow the step-by-step instructions of a recipe, you are using an algorithm. Trial and error, choice A, is a problem-solving device where you randomly try solutions until you find one that works. Mental set, choice B, can hinder good problem solving because you become limited to considering only solutions that have worked in the past. Belief perseverance, choice D, is also an obstacle to good problem solving because you cling to a belief despite contradictory

evidence. A heuristic, choice E, is a problem-solving shortcut. Such a strategy may save time, but it doesn't guarantee a successful outcome like an algorithm does. (Skill 1b)

250. **(D)** A heuristic is a rule of thumb or a decision-making shortcut. In choice D, you have decided that a 7-foot-tall man must be a basketball player because he fits your prototype. This is an example of the representativeness heuristic. Choice A illustrates the step-by-step process of an algorithm. Choice B is an example of divergent thinking that requires the generation of multiple solutions to a problem. Choice C is an example of trial-and-error problem solving. Choice E demonstrates functional fixedness. This is an obstacle to problem solving because we limit ourselves to seeing only one use for an object. (Skill 1b)

251. **(E)** Confirmation bias occurs when we look only for evidence that supports our preconceived ideas. Thus, Zoe is looking only for evidence to support her view that climate change is a hoax. Choice A is an example of the availability heuristic. Since you left your lights on last week, it's the first thing you think of today. Choice B reflects a mental set. When you continue to use a math solution that has worked in the past, even when it's not working now, you are experiencing mental set. When we can't see another use for an object other than what it was originally designed for, we are experiencing functional fixedness, which is choice C. As you use a shoe to hang a picture when you don't have a hammer, you are demonstrating that you are not functionally fixed. Choice D reflects overconfidence, which is when a person's belief in his or her own ability is greater than the person's actual performance. Brett believes he is a great hitter, but his batting average tells a different story. (Skill 1b)

252. **(B)** How information is presented or how a question is asked can impact the decisions we make. There is no difference between an ice cream that is 20% fat or that is 80% fat free. However, the way the ice cream is framed or described may make a difference for health-conscious consumers who are purchasing the ice cream. The spacing effect, choice A, occurs when recall improves because practice was distributed over time. The spotlight effect, choice C, happens when a person overestimates others' interest in and memory of his or her appearance and behavior. Choice D, the bystander effect, decreases the likelihood of help when more individuals are present. The placebo effect, choice E, occurs when there is an improvement based solely on the belief in a treatment. (Skill 1b)

253. **(A)** Algorithms are logical, step-by-step procedures used to solve problems. When you follow the rules of an algorithm, you are guaranteed to find a solution. In contrast, heuristics are mental shortcuts. Heuristics can

save time but can lead to more problem-solving errors. Choice B, that heuristics take more time to find a solution, is incorrect. Instead, heuristics save time. Choice C, a sudden realization of a solution to a problem, refers to insight, not to the use of either algorithms or heuristics. Choice D is incorrect because it has the definitions of algorithms and heuristics backward. Algorithms use step-by-step procedures. Heuristics are mental shortcuts. Choice E is incorrect because creative thinking can be the result of using either an algorithm or a heuristic. (Skill 1a)

254. **(C)** The availability heuristic involves judging the likelihood of an event on the basis of how easily examples of that event come to mind. Because tornadoes gain more national attention than lightning strikes, tornadoes are more likely to be the first thing a person thinks of in response to being asked what causes more deaths each year. The representativeness heuristic, choice A, is a mental shortcut we use when we make decisions about a current problem based on the prototype stored in memory. Belief perseverance, choice B, occurs when we cling to our previous beliefs even when evidence directly contradicts them. Confirmation bias, choice D, happens when we look for only supporting information and ignore information that contradicts our previous notions. Divergent thinking, choice E, is the process of searching for multiple solutions to solve a problem. (Skill 1b)

255. **(A)** Phonemes are speech sounds that are the basis for language. The speech sounds "n" and "m" differentiate these two almost identical words. Morphemes, choice B, are the smallest units of language that have meaning. Prototypes, choice C, are the best examples of a category. Memes, choice D, are ideas or trends that are culturally specific. Mnemonics, choice E, are memory devices that provide organization and/or visual cues that aid in memory recall. (Skill 1a)

256. **(D)** A morpheme is the smallest unit of language that has meaning. A morpheme can be a word or a part of a word like a suffix or prefix. Babbling, choice A, is the first stage of language development where children practice phonemes (for example, "da da da da"). Phonemes, choice B, are speech sounds. Grammar, choice C, is the set of rules for word order, or syntax, that helps us derive meaning from sounds, called semantics. A prototype, choice E, is the best example of a category (for example, a robin may best represent the category of bird). (Skill 1a)

257. **(C)** At about 10 months of age, a child's babbling starts to sound like the phonemes of his or her native language. Before that, infants can make any sound in any language. Children begin to specialize in the language that they hear. They also lose the ability to discriminate and produce speech sounds in other languages. Prelinguistic, choice A, refers to the time right

after birth when babies communicate through crying. When infants begin cooing, choice B, they are making vowel sounds. The one-word stage, choice D, occurs when a child is typically 1 year of age. The two-word stage, choice E, occurs at 2 years of age. During these later stages, children are acquiring vocabulary and learning the rules of grammar. (Skill 1b)

Scenarios

258. **(A)** Automatic processing does not require conscious attention. When a person practices something enough, it becomes automatic. Since Micah has been practicing the piano piece so often, his finger movements have become automatic. In fact, he no longer has to pay attention to playing the piano and can actually do something else at the same time, like think about school. Framing, choice B, is how information is presented. Cognitive dissonance, choice C, refers to the discomfort someone feels when two thoughts are inconsistent. Stimulus generalization, choice D, happens when an individual responds to a stimulus that is similar to an original conditioned stimulus. Choice E, effortful processing, refers to conscious, deliberate thinking that requires conscious effort.

259. **(A)** Iconic memory is visual sensory memory. Visual information, like the lightning flash, is held briefly in iconic memory. Then the information either decays quickly or is transferred to short-term memory. Choice B, short-term memory, stores 7 ± 2 units of information for up to 30 seconds. Choice C, eidetic or "photographic" memory, occurs when information is retained in great detail after limited exposure. Implicit memory, choice D, is memory for automatic processes, such as tying one's shoes. Flashbulb memories, choice E, are typically detailed for salient and emotional events. (Skill 1b)

260. **(C)** A recognition test, like a multiple-choice test, provides retrieval cues and is a test of familiarity. A recall test, choice A, requires memory reconstruction, such as an essay test. Implicit memory, choice B, does not require conscious thought, such as the ability to ride a bike. Iconic memory, choice D, is visual sensory memory. Mood congruent memory, choice E, occurs when our emotions act as retrieval cues for remembering personal events. (Skill 1b)

261. **(B)** When information is rehearsed repeatedly over time, recall is improved. This is called the spacing effect. The serial position effect, choice A, occurs when we recall items at the beginning and at the end of a list. Semantic encoding, choice C, refers to encoding information based on the information's meaning. The testing effect, choice D, leads to improved recall due to repeated testing of learned information.

Chunking, choice E, is the grouping of information into meaningful units to improve recall. (Skill 1b)

262. **(D)** The hippocampus appears to be the brain region responsible for the formation of new memories. Memory consolidation takes place during sleep when long-term storage of information occurs. Choice A, chunking, helps increase the capacity of short-term memory (by grouping individual memories into larger "chunks"). This is not the process referred to in this question. Serial processing, choice B, occurs when you focus on one aspect of a problem in a deliberate and conscious, step-by-step manner. Priming, choice C, occurs when you are exposed to a particular stimulus that unconsciously leads to the retrieval of specific information later. Convergent thinking, choice E, is a type of problem solving when you are looking for a single solution to a problem. (Skill 1b)

263. **(D)** Content-dependent memory refers to situations when the encoding of information occurs in the same surroundings as where retrieval takes place. The external cue, or context, triggers our recall. Serial position effect, choice A, occurs when we can recall items at the beginning and end of a list but have difficulty recalling terms in the middle. Retroactive interference, choice B, happens when newly learned information blocks our ability to recall information previously learned. Infantile amnesia, choice C, refers to the fact that we have limited recall for personal events that occur before the age of three. Retrograde amnesia, choice E, occurs when individuals are unable to recall events from their past. (Skill 1b)

264. **(D)** Deep processing improves memory recall. In this case, Sara is using elaborative rehearsal by adding personal details and meaning. This type of deep processing is more likely to transfer the information to long-term memory. Choice A relies on maintenance rehearsal. It may keep the information in short-term memory but does not ensure the transfer to long-term memory. Choices B and E rely on shallower processing based on the appearance or sounds of the letters. Making flash cards, choice C, is also a shallow processing method. This method is unlikely to help Sara encode the concepts semantically. (Skill 1b)

265. **(C)** Source amnesia happens when you can't recall where you first acquired information stored in your memory. In this case, when your friend mistakenly says that the joke started with her brother instead of you, this is source amnesia. Mood congruent memory, choice A, occurs when a person's current emotional state acts as a retrieval cue for stored information. Encoding failure, choice B, refers to when information is not stored in memory because you weren't paying attention to it. Retrieval failure, choice D, happens when information is stored but can't

be pulled from long-term memory without a cue. Choice E, retrograde amnesia, is when a person loses memory of his or her past. (Skill 1b)

266. **(D)** Selective attention allows us to narrow our focus on only one aspect of the external world. Cognitive dissonance, choice A, occurs when we have two competing ideas that cause us internal discomfort. To reduce the discomfort, we must change our belief. Social facilitation, choice B, is shown when our performance improves because of the presence of others. The mere exposure effect, choice C, is demonstrated when our liking of an object increases when we are subjected to the object over time. The reciprocity norm, choice E, dictates that when someone helps us, we should help him or her in return. (Skill 1b)

267. **(D)** Inattentional blindness happens when you are focused on one aspect of the environment and do not see another that is in plain view. Thus, while you were focused on texting, you didn't notice that the car in front of you had stopped. Choice A refers to the blind spot. This region of the retina is where the optic nerve leaves the eye. Because there are no rods or cones there, an image that falls on this area disappears. Choice B is referring to change blindness, which is a form of inattentional blindness. Here, an obvious difference in the external world goes unnoticed. In this case, not noticing that your friend is wearing a different shirt later in the school day demonstrates change blindness. Choice C refers to a questionable claim that information presented below an absolute threshold can be unconsciously processed. Choice E refers to a study investigating sensory adaptation in vision. When a stimulus is unchanging, like staring continually at an image of a triangle, the sensory neurons decrease neural firing. This results in no longer "seeing" the complete image. (Skill 1b)

268. **(A)** When we cling to our prior beliefs in the face of contradictory evidence, we are experiencing belief perseverance. Framing, choice B, refers to how information is presented or how a question is asked. Cognitive dissonance, choice C, happens when two thoughts, or our belief and behavior, are inconsistent and lead to discomfort. To reduce our discomfort, we must change what we believe or how we behave. Trial and error, choice D, is when you try a number of solutions to a problem until you find one that works. The misinformation effect, choice E, explains how misleading information can be incorporated into the gaps in memory to create false memories. (Skill 1b)

269. **(D)** Telegraphic speech occurs during the two-word stage of language development when children communicate in grammatically correct sentences. Choice A better reflects the language of a child in the one-word stage. Choices B and E reflect more complex sentences not typical of

telegraphic speech. Choice C is more complex speech and also demonstrates overregularization. After children have learned a grammatical rule, they will often misuse it. In this case, the child has learned to add "-ed" to make something past tense. However, this rule works with regular verbs, not irregular verbs as shown in this case. (Skill 1a)

270. **(C)** Wernicke's area is associated with speech comprehension. Broca's area, choice A, is primarily concerned with speech production. The motor cortex in the frontal lobe, choice B, focuses on generating the impulses that move our bodies. The somatosensory cortex, choice D, is located in the parietal lobe and is responsible for processing sensory information related to touch (for example, pain). The amygdala, choice E, plays an important role in emotional responses, such as anger. (Skill 1b)

271. **(B)** When we fail to notice an obvious change in our environment, change blindness has occurred. Belief perseverance, choice A, happens when a person clings to his or her preconceived notions in the face of contradictory evidence. Episodic memory, choice C, is a type of explicit memory for personal events. Mental set, choice D, occurs when we continue to use a problem-solving strategy because it has worked for us in the past. Source amnesia, choice E, happens when we cannot recall where we learned information that we have stored in memory. (Skill 1b)

272. **(D)** Overconfidence occurs when we believe we know more than we actually do or can perform better than we actually can. For example, not every driver can be in the upper half of the distribution. Mental set, choice A, occurs when we continue to use problem-solving strategies that have worked in the past, even when they may not be effective now. Hindsight bias, choice B, is when we observe an outcome and feel that it was predictable. Source amnesia, choice C, occurs when we have difficulty recalling where we first learned information or when we attribute it to the wrong source. The misinformation effect, choice E, is the source of many of our false memories. When we experience a gap in memory, we often fill it with what makes sense in the context. This misinformation can be incorporated into memory and then become indistinguishable from real memories. (Skill 1b)

Names

273. **(A)** George Miller referred to the number of units we can hold in short-term memory as the "magical number seven." Hermann Ebbinghaus, choice B, is an early memory researcher known for his work on the forgetting curve. Alan Baddeley, choice C, is primarily known for his model of working memory. Richard Atkinson and Richard Shiffrin,

choice D, proposed the three-stage model of memory: sensory, short-term, and long-term. Eric R. Kandel and James H. Schwartz, choice E, revealed the physical basis for memory when they observed changes in the synaptic connections among neurons of a sea slug that was learning a new response. (Skill 1a)

274. **(B)** Hermann Ebbinghaus found that at the time he first learned the nonsense words, he could immediately recall 100% of them. However, he found that memory loss occurred immediately after he stopped rehearsing the words. As time passed, memory loss stabilized as illustrated in the graph below.

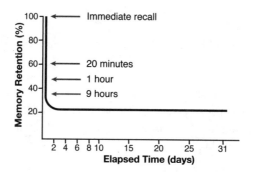

Choice A demonstrates a fixed-interval schedule of reinforcement. On this intermittent schedule, a fixed amount of time must pass before reinforcement is given. An example of this is being paid for your work every two weeks. When reinforced on a fixed amount of time, the response rate falls off after each reinforcement and then picks up as the reinforcer approaches, creating the scalloped appearance of this illustration.

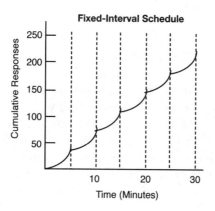

Choice C represents a normal distribution of scores, called a normal or bell curve. Such a distribution is found when the data are clustered around the mean at the center of the curve and when fewer scores lie at the extremes.

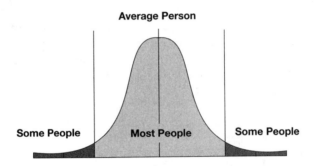

Choice D is a representation of the optimal level of arousal when doing either a difficult or an easy task. Performance of a task is best for difficult tasks when arousal is low. For easy tasks, best performance occurs when arousal levels are high.

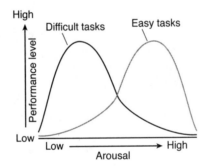

Choice E illustrates acquisition and extinction in classical conditioning. During the acquisition period, the unconditioned stimulus (US) is repeatedly paired with the conditioned stimulus (CS). For example, in Ivan Pavlov's studies, meat powder (US) was paired with the sound of a metronome (CS). The learned or conditioned response (CR) became more likely to occur as the animal learned the association. In Pavlov's experiment, salivation (CR) to the sound of the metronome (CS) increased. However, when the CS was presented over a number of trials without the US, the CR weakened and disappeared. This is called extinction. (Skill 2)

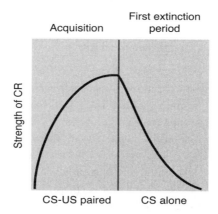

275. **(E)** Elizabeth Loftus's groundbreaking studies demonstrated how malleable memory can be. Participants were given purposefully misleading information concerning a filmed car accident. These participants later altered their memories for the event. Loftus called this phenomenon the misinformation effect. Hermann Ebbinghaus, choice A, is an early memory researcher known for demonstrating how quickly memory decays after rehearsal ends, called the forgetting curve. Mary Cover Jones, choice B, is an early behaviorist who applied classical conditioning principles to help children overcome naturally occurring fears. Alan Baddeley, choice C, is known for expanding our understanding of working memory. George Miller, choice D, is known for his research suggesting that short-term memory is limited to holding 7 units of information ("the magical number seven"). (Skill 1a)

276. **(B)** Benjamin Lee Whorf's linguistic determinism suggests that our language shapes the way we conceptualize the world. Aphasia, choice A, refers to language impairment due to damage in either Broca's or Wernicke's area. The language acquisition device, choice C, was suggested by Noam Chomsky to explain how language is innately acquired. A critical period, choice D, refers to a period during development when specific events must take place. Less-than-ideal conditions during that time may lead to developmental delay. Receptive language, choice E, refers to the language children understand before they can speak. (Skill 1a)

277. **(D)** Sultan used insight, which is also called the "aha experience." Insight occurs when we have suddenly realized the solution to a problem. Mental set, choice A, can be detrimental to good decision making as we have a tendency to rely on solutions that have worked for us in our past. Framing, choice B, is how information is presented that can impact our

decisions. An algorithm, choice C, is a systematic decision-making strategy that guarantees a successful outcome. We use the availability heuristic, choice E, when we judge the probability of an event based on our past experiences. (Skill 1b)

278. **(D)** Noam Chomsky is a nativist who believes that all humans have an inborn ability to acquire grammar rules. B. F. Skinner, choice A, argued that language is learned through interactions with others in the environment. Paul Broca, choice B, suggested that the ability to produce speech is centered in a region located in the left frontal lobe. Carl Wernicke, choice C, argued that our ability to comprehend language is concentrated in a region in the left temporal lobe. Benjamin Lee Whorf, choice E, suggested that language fundamentally shapes our ability to perceive the world. (Skill 1a)

Research Methods

279. **(D)** The speed of the cars reported by the students is the dependent variable. The dependent variable is the measured outcome in the experiment. Choice A, the number of participants, is not manipulated between groups. Therefore, it is not an independent variable. Choices B and E, where students attended school and their educational levels, respectively, refer to potential confounding variables. The independent variable, choice C, is the factor manipulated in the experiment. The wording of the question differs for different groups. (Skill 3)

280. **(D)** Sampling bias occurs when participants in an experiment are not representative of the general population. Since participants in Loftus and Palmer's experiment were all college students from the University of Washington, they are not representative of the general population across a number of characteristics, such as age or education. Confirmation bias, choice A, occurs when an individual seeks only information that supports his or her preconceived ideas. Experimenter bias, choice B, refers to when a researcher's preconceived ideas about the results of an experiment influences his or her actions. Interviewer bias, choice C, occurs when the interviewer influences what the subject says by subtly communicating his or her expectations through, for example, the phrasing of questions. Hindsight bias, choice E, occurs when we perceive that the outcome of an event was predictable and we believe that we "knew it all along." (Skill 3)

281. **(C)** Exposure to either a pleasant or an unpleasant scent is the independent variable as it is the factor that is manipulated. The gender of the participants (choice A) and the educational level of the subjects (choice E) are both subject variables. They can act as potentially confounding

variables but are not manipulated in this study. The dependent variable is the outcome or what is measured in the experiment. In this case, it is participants' attractiveness rating on a scale of 1–9. Therefore, choice D is the dependent variable. Choice B, the ability to recall the pictures, is incorrect because it is not the outcome of the manipulation. (Skill 3)

282. **(A)** From the description of this study, it appears that the subjects were not randomly assigned to different experimental groups. Thus, it is most likely a correlational study. Since there is no manipulation of an independent variable under controlled conditions, researchers would not be able to conclude whether or not there is a cause-and-effect relationship between using textisms and reading ability. Choices B, C, and D are incorrect as this is not an experiment. Choice E is also incorrect as the described study is not a case study, which is an in-depth investigation into a single case. (Skill 3)

283. **(B)** Confirmation bias occurs when we seek out only information that supports our previous beliefs. Once the participants settled on the rule of a "sequence of even numbers," they proposed only sets of numbers that supported that conclusion. Choice A, insight, occurs when we have a sudden realization of the solution to a problem. Choice C, functional fixedness, happens when we cannot see another way an object can be used. Framing, choice D, refers to how information is presented. The misinformation effect, choice E, happens when we fill in the gaps in our memories with what makes sense, leading to the creation of false memories. (Skill 1b)

284. **(A)** Explicit memories for personal events and factual information require conscious recall. These memories are processed by the hippocampus. Implicit memories for skills are automatically recalled and are stored in the cerebellum. In H. M.'s case, he cannot recall doing the puzzle because of the damage done during surgery to his hippocampus. The puzzle is a task. H. M.'s performance can improve with practice and become more automatic; thus, it is implicit. Choices B, C, D, and E are not reflected in the differences in the abilities H. M. demonstrated during testing. (Skill 1b)

285. **(C)** The case study was the research method employed in the long-term study of H. M.'s memory abilities. A case study is an in-depth investigation of a single unique case. A cross-sectional study, choice B, involves the collection of data from individuals of different ages at a set point in time. There is no indication that any correlational analysis, choice A, was performed. Correlational analysis looks at how one variable changes as a second variable changes. A survey, choice D, is a descriptive research method that allows researchers to collect self-report data from a sample of

a population. Randomization, choice E, refers to the process of collecting data using a chance method. (Skill 3)

Perspectives

286. **(B)** Cognitive psychologists are interested in how we process and store information, make decisions, and interpret events. Since Dr. Simonds is interested in techniques students use to improve memory, Dr. Simonds is most likely a cognitive psychologist. Biological psychologists, choice A, center on the workings of the nervous system in explaining human behavior. Evolutionary psychologists, choice C, explain human behavior through natural selection. Sociocultural psychologists, choice D, are sensitive to the social and cultural contexts that influence behavior. Psychodynamic psychologists, choice E, focus on unconscious motives to explain human behavior. (Skill 1c)

287. **(D)** The behavioral perspective, of which B. F. Skinner was a pioneer, concentrates on how we learn our behaviors from the environment. Skinner proposed that a primary way in which we learn is operant conditioning—learning behavior through either reinforcement or punishment. The cognitive perspective, choice A, focuses on internal mental processes, such as problem solving and language. Choice B is incorrect because B. F. Skinner did not describe how language was influenced by any sociocultural factors. Biological psychologists, choice C, focus on how the functioning of the nervous system produces thoughts and behavior. The psychodynamic perspective, choice E, was founded on the beliefs of Sigmund Freud and focus primarily on the role of unconscious forces on behavior. (Skill 1a)

288. **(B)** Behavioral psychologists, like B. F. Skinner, proposed that we learn language through our interactions with the environment. These interactions may include learning associations between words and meanings through operant conditioning or learning by observation. If children imitate the language of adults in their environment, they would not be hearing words such as "tooths" or "foots." Thus, overgeneralization reflects a greater sophistication of language use than behaviorists assumed. Cognitive psychologists, choice A, focus on how we perceive and interpret the world. They focus on the schemas children develop about their world, including the grammatical templates they create and practice. The evolutionary perspective, choice C, attempts to explain the origin of adaptive human traits through the process of natural selection. Biological psychologists, choice D, focus on how the functioning of the nervous system produces our thoughts and behavior. Humanistic psychologists, choice E, emphasize our potential for growth and self-fulfillment. (Skill 1a)

CHAPTER 8: TESTING AND INDIVIDUAL DIFFERENCES

Stimulus

289. **(B)** Intellectual disability is defined as scoring below 70 on a standardized intelligence test. Scores on such tests tend to be normally distributed, with a mean of 100 and a standard deviation of 15. Based on this information, below 70 is 2 standard deviations below the mean. Thus, 2% + 0.1% = 2.1%. Choice A (0.1) is incorrect as it represents only the scores falling below 3 standard deviations below the mean. Choice C (14) is incorrect as it reflects the scores falling between 1 and 2 standard deviations below the mean. Choice D (16.1) is incorrect as it represents the scores falling below 1 standard deviation from the mean (14% + 2% + 0.1% = 16.1%). Choice E (34) is incorrect as it signifies the scores 1 standard deviation below the mean. (Skill 2)

Definitions

290. **(D)** Charles Spearman proposed the idea of general intelligence (*g*) that refers to the mental abilities that underlie all intelligent behavior. Practical intelligence, choice A, is a type of intelligence, suggested by Robert Sternberg, that reflects our street smarts. Multiple intelligences, choice B, was first proposed by Howard Gardner. He suggested that intelligence is composed of 8 separate intelligences, including kinesthetic and intrapersonal intelligence. Crystallized intelligence, choice C, was proposed by Raymond Cattell and refers to knowledge gained through experience. The Flynn effect, choice E, refers to the increase in intelligence test scores over time. (Skill 1a)

291. **(A)** Factor analysis allows researchers to examine patterns in test scores statistically. Intelligence tests tend to measure a number of abilities. Some questions may assess memory abilities, and others might measure processing speed. Factor analysis looks to see if there is a relationship, or correlation, between different items on a test. In other words, if someone scores high on memory-related items, will the person also score high on items measuring processing speed? Charles Spearman believed that if you scored high on one ability, you would also score high on others. He explained that all intelligent behavior has the same underlying factor. He called this *g*, or general intelligence. Factor analysis could not be used for the purposes described in choices B, C, D, or E. (Skill 1a)

292. **(C)** Those with spatial intelligence do extremely well with tasks requiring the ability to think in three dimensions. Such individuals do well at both creating visual images and interpreting them, such as creating art or

solving puzzles. Bodily-kinesthetic intelligence, choice A, is seen in those who have good hand-eye coordination and high physical agility, such as professional athletes. Crystallized intelligence, choice B, refers to knowledge gained over a lifetime of experiences. Practical intelligence, choice D, is illustrated in a person's ability to apply his or her skills to everyday problems that confront the person. Logical-mathematical intelligence, choice E, is the type of intelligence needed for scientific reasoning and for performing mathematical calculations. (Skill 1a)

293. **(E)** Practical intelligence is often referred to as street smarts. Such intelligence is gained through experience. Analytic intelligence, choice A, is the type of intelligence learned in books. It refers to our ability to solve complex hypothetical problems. General intelligence, choice B, is often referred to as *g*. This refers to the underlying ability we possess that allows us to engage in intelligent behavior. Creative intelligence, choice C, is another part of Sternberg's triarchic theory. This type of intelligence allows us to go beyond what is found in a book to generate novel solutions to everyday problems. Emotional intelligence, choice D, is a sensitivity to our own emotions and the ability to regulate those emotions. It also allows us to understand the feelings of others and respond appropriately to their emotional needs. (Skill 1a)

294. **(B)** Analytical intelligence, as suggested by Robert Sternberg, is needed for scientific reasoning, perceiving cause and effect, and problem-solving abilities. These skills are also considered an important part of *g*, or general intelligence. Interpersonal intelligence, choice A, refers to the ability to relate well to others. Emotional intelligence, choice C, is our ability to perceive, understand, and manage our own emotions or those of others. The Flynn effect, choice D, refers to the increase in standardized intelligence test scores over time. Existential intelligence, choice E, is a proposed ninth intelligence from Howard Gardner. Those high in this intelligence are especially able to consider big questions about human existence and life's meaning. (Skill 1a)

295. **(E)** Those high in emotional intelligence are adept at reading others' emotional cues and know what to say when handling conflict. Thus Elizabeth, who can skillfully handle disagreements at work, demonstrates a high level of emotional intelligence. Ken's ability to design buildings, choice A, reflects a high level of Gardner's spatial intelligence. Rik's skills on the basketball court, choice B, demonstrates a high level of Gardner's bodily-kinesthetic intelligence. Jane's ability to discern musical skill, choice C, reflects Gardner's idea of musical intelligence. Jim's research abilities, choice D, suggest a high level of Gardner's logical-mathematical intelligence. (Skill 1b)

296. **(E)** An achievement test measures what people have learned. For example, the AP Psychology exam, which attempts to gauge what you know about psychology, is an achievement test. Choices A and B measure specific underlying skills associated with a particular definition of intelligence. These skills would be largely unlearned. A specific mathematical formula, not an achievement test, is used to determine a standard deviation from a distribution of scores. Thus, choice C is incorrect. Many measures can be used to check the reliability of an assessment, choice D, such as the test-retest. (Skill 1a)

297. **(B)** Mental age refers to the age when a child demonstrates intellectual performance like the average person at that same physical age. Aptitude, choice A, refers to an individual's ability to learn. Criterion, choice C, is what a test is designed to measure. Intrapersonal intelligence, choice D, is one of Howard Gardner's multiple intelligences. General intelligence, choice E, refers to the underlying abilities behind intelligent behavior. (Skill 1a)

298. **(D)** The formula for determining the intelligence quotient (IQ) is $\frac{\text{mental age (MA)}}{\text{chronological age (CA)}} \times 100$. In this case, $\frac{10}{8} \times 100 = 125$. Choice A, 80, incorrectly divides the chronological age by the mental age before multiplying by 100. Choice B, 100, is the IQ of someone whose mental age equals his or her chronological age. Choice C, 110, and choice E, 150, cannot result from the scenario provided. (Skill 1a)

299. **(E)** When a test is standardized, it is pretested with a representative sample. This method allows individuals to compare their scores against the norm. Factor analysis, choice A, is a statistical measure that allows researchers to group similar abilities. A test has content validity, choice B, when questions measure the intended knowledge or characteristic. Heritability, choice C, refers to the percentage that a specific trait occurs in a population due to heredity. Reliability, choice D, concerns the consistency of test scores across different administrations. (Skill 1a)

300. **(E)** In a set of scores that are normally distributed, 50% of the population scores above the mean. In this example, the mean is 100. With a standard deviation of 15, a score of 70 falls 2 standard deviations below the mean. Approximately 48% of the scores fall into this range (34% + 14% = 48%). Thus, 50% + 48% = 98%. The percentages listed in choices A, B, C, and D do not correspond to percentages as described by the normal curve in relation to the proportion of scores that are 2 standard deviations below the mean or higher. (Skill 2)

301. **(C)** James Flynn first documented the rise in intelligence test scores in the 1920s. This increase in performance has been noted in many countries and has caused scientists to investigate its possible causes. Some suggest that better nutrition, health care, and educational opportunities may have contributed to this change. Choices A, B, D, and E are incorrect definitions of the Flynn effect. (Skill 1a)

302. **(D)** A test has reliability if, over repeated administrations, the scores are consistent. If a test is valid, choice A, it is testing what it has been designed to measure. A standardized test, choice B, has been pretested with a representative sample to provide comparison scores. Heritability, choice C, is an estimate of the role genetics plays in the differences in a specific trait in a population. A test that is positively skewed, choice E, has the majority of scores less than the mean score. (Skill 1a)

303. **(C)** Fluid intelligence refers to our ability to reason quickly and abstractly while integrating key information into our decision-making process. It is the type of intelligence that appears to decrease as we age. Crystallized intelligence, choice A, is the knowledge that we gain over a lifetime of experiences. Practical intelligence, choice B, was proposed by Robert Sternberg and is often referred to as street smarts. Intrapersonal intelligence, choice D, was described by Howard Gardner. It is found in those who are closely connected to their own feelings and needs. A person with savant syndrome, choice E, has cognitive limitations but also demonstrates an extraordinary ability, such as an incredible memory or a superior artistic ability. (Skill 1a)

304. **(B)** Heritability is an estimate that reflects what causes a variation in traits within a population. It is a correlational term from 0 to 1. The closer the number is to 1, the more likely that genetics accounts for the differences in a trait within a population. In this case, the environment that the seeds are raised in are identical within each tray (either deprived or ideal). Thus, height differences in the plants within one of the trays (for example, within the deprived tray) are most likely due to the genetic diversity of the seeds. Heritability within the deprived tray would be high, probably close to 1. A statistically significant result, choice A, indicates that any differences between two tested groups are not likely due to chance. Factor analysis, choice C, is used by researchers who wish to group specific traits that are correlated together. Predictive validity, choice D, is found in tests that predict the future behavior they are designed to predict. Grit, choice E, is reflected in those who have passion and perseverance to complete a goal over a long period of time. (Skill 1b)

Scenarios

305. **(E)** According to Robert Sternberg, creative intelligence includes the ability to use existing knowledge to deal with novel problems. In this case, Sue was able to take what she already knew, which is the structure of a paper clip, and apply it to a new situation, fixing her glasses. Practical intelligence, choice A, is referred to as street smarts or being able to adapt and thrive in an individual's environment. Analytical intelligence, choice B, is closest to Spearman's concept of *g*. It includes skills related to academic success, such as hypothetical reasoning. Bodily-kinesthetic, choice C, is part of Gardner's multiple intelligences and refers to the ability to handle one's body with skill and agility. Spatial intelligence, choice D, is also one of Gardner's intelligences. It refers to the ability to think about and design three-dimensional objects. (Skill 1b)

306. **(A)** Emotional intelligence consists of the ability to perceive and understand others' emotions while being able to manage your own and use emotions effectively. Thus, the managers in the given scenario were being trained to develop their emotional intelligence. Creative intelligence, choice B, refers to one of Sternberg's triarchic intelligences. It refers, in part, to the ability to solve problems in novel ways. Analytical intelligence, choice C, is also one of Sternberg's intelligences. It refers to our ability to engage in academic problem solving. Choice D, linguistic intelligence, is one of Gardner's eight intelligences. It encompasses a facility for using language to communicate effectively. General intelligence (*g*), choice E, refers to the mental abilities that underlie all intelligent behaviors. (Skill 1b)

307. **(B)** When a test is standardized, the procedures are uniform for all those who take it. Such an approach helps ensure that differences in scores are due to differing abilities and not other variables. Thus, Mrs. Nielsen should be certain that students have the same amount of time to answer the same question. Choice A concerns a question of content validity, not standardization. Choices C and D reflect a concern with testing the reliability, or the consistency, of the test. The double-blind technique, choice E, is when the experimenter does not know if the subject has been assigned to either an experimental or a control condition. This technique is used to control for experimenter bias. (Skill 3)

308. **(E)** In order to determine predictive validity, the test score must be correlated with some criterion or to a specific behavior related to future performance. Thus, Mrs. Coburn would be able to determine predictive validity if the scores on the PAT are positively correlated with students' grade performance in her AP Psychology class. Choice A reflects

a test-retest reliability measure, not a measure of validity. If the mean, median, and mode of the PAT were all the same number, choice B, the distribution of test scores would be normally distributed. Choice C reflects measures to ensure standardization for different students taking the test. Fluid intelligence is reflected in abstract reasoning. Crystallized intelligence refers to knowledge learned over time. Distinguishing between these concepts, choice D, does not help determine a test's predictive validity. (Skill 3)

309. **(E)** One way to determine the reliability, or consistency, of a test is to split the test in half (odds and evens) and look at the correlation between the groups' scores. The higher the correlation is, the higher the reliability of the test is. Standardization, choice A, occurs when the measure is pretested with a representative sample to provide comparison scores for later test takers. If scores are normally distributed, choice B, they appear like a bell curve with 68% of the scores within 1 standard deviation away from the mean, 95% of the scores within 2 standard deviations from the mean, and 99.7% of the scores falling within 3 standard deviations from the mean. General intelligence, also called g, choice C, refers to the abilities that underlie intelligent behaviors. Tests have predictive validity, choice D, when they predict the behavior they are designed to measure. (Skill 1b)

310. **(D)** Raymond Cattell suggested that there are two types of intelligence, one of which is crystallized. Crystallized intelligence is based on the knowledge and skills that are acquired during a lifetime based on experiences. Fluid intelligence, choice A, is the other type of intelligence suggested by Cattell. This refers to the ability to reason quickly and abstractly. Heritability, choice B, refers to the extent to which variations in a specific trait within a group, like intelligence, can be attributed to genetics. A person with high naturalistic intelligence, choice C, according to Howard Gardner, demonstrates a sensitivity to and appreciation of nature. Analytical intelligence, choice E, was suggested by Robert Sternberg and refers to the ability to reason and problem solve. (Skill 1b)

311. **(C)** The Wechsler Adult Intelligence Scale (WAIS) assesses not only a person's general intelligence but also measures a person's verbal and performance abilities across 15 subtests, including tests of vocabulary. It is widely used today and provides detailed information helpful in assessing a wide variety of cognitive abilities. The Stanford-Binet, choice A, was developed by Lewis Terman and generates an intelligence quotient to measure overall general intelligence. The Myers-Briggs Type Indicator (MBTI), choice B, is a widely used scale to separate personality characteristics into four different areas. This assessment has been widely criticized

as lacking scientific validity and reliability. The Binet-Simon intelligence scale, choice D, was developed by Alfred Binet and his colleague
Theodore Simon. It is used to assess a child's mental age and is used to
place children into appropriate school classes. The Minnesota Multiphasic
Personality Inventory (MMPI), choice E, is used primarily in the diagnosis of mental disorders. (Skill 1b)

312. **(B)** Gardner suggests that we have eight different intelligences, or abilities, including musical intelligence. Brain damage can impact one type of
intelligence while leaving the other intelligences undamaged. Savants tend
to score below 70 on traditional IQ tests, which is considered intellectually disabled. However, they can demonstrate brilliance, like Leslie, in
one area. Spearman's concept of *g*, choice A, suggests that intelligence is
one thing that underlies all intelligent behavior. Emotional intelligence,
choice C, taps into our ability to read and manage our own, and others', emotions. Cattell's fluid intelligence, choice D, refers to our ability
to solve abstract problems speedily. Binet believed that our mental age,
choice E, corresponds to a particular level of cognitive performance for
others of the same chronological age. (Skill 1c)

313. **(E)** Those with a fixed mindset believe that a particular trait, like intelligence or talent, is something they are born with and that cannot be
changed. When such individuals face academic challenges, they are
likely to give up. This fixed mindset is reflected in the statement, "I just
can't learn this." The statements in choices A, B, C, and D all reflect
a growth mindset. A growth mindset is the understanding that basic
abilities, including intelligence, can change with dedication and hard
work. (Skill 1b)

Names

314. **(A)** Alfred Binet was hired by the French government to develop a measure to determine if a child needed remedial help when he or she entered
school. Binet developed an assessment that measured a child's mental
age. Binet assumed that for a given chronological age, a child would
have attained a set of specific abilities. These abilities were measured as
the child's mental age. Lewis Terman, choice B, developed the Stanford-
Binet intelligence test. Francis Galton, choice C, is known for first using
the phrase "nature versus nurture" and for focusing on how intelligence
is inherited. Charles Spearman, choice D, first identified *g*, or general
intelligence. L. L. Thurstone, choice E, suggested that intelligence is comprised of seven clusters of primary mental abilities, such as word fluency
or spatial ability. (Skill 1a)

315. **(C)** Lewis Terman developed the Stanford-Binet test by adapting the test Alfred Binet originally made and creating his own. The Stanford-Binet test is still a widely used intelligence test. Alfred Binet, choice A, did not develop the Stanford-Binet test, although his work was used in developing the test. Francis Galton, choice B, is known for his belief that intelligence is inherited. Galton also founded the eugenics movement. Charles Spearman, choice D, developed the idea that general intelligence, or *g*, underlies all intelligent behavior and can be quantified. David Wechsler, choice E, developed another widely used intelligence test with subtests measuring both verbal and performance abilities. (Skill 1a)

316. **(A)** Francis Galton first used the term "nature versus nurture" and was a strong proponent that intelligence was inherited. He was the founder of the eugenics movement that worked to restrict reproduction among those considered to be "unfit." Carol Dweck, choice B, proposed that intelligence can be impacted by our own belief in our abilities to change our brains. Howard Gardner, choice C, believed that we all have eight multiple intelligences represented in us but to different degrees. He believed that we can learn and improve in certain intelligences through life experiences. Raymond Cattell, choice D, suggested that there are two types of intelligence, fluid and crystallized. Crystallized intelligence grows throughout the lifetime as we continue to learn from experience. Alfred Binet, choice E, was hired by the French government to develop a test able to place children into remedial classes if needed. Binet believed that low-performing children could improve in their intellectual performance if their educational opportunities improved. (Skill 1a)

317. **(A)** Howard Gardner proposed that intelligence is comprised of eight different abilities: naturalist, interpersonal, intrapersonal, bodily-kinesthetic, spatial, musical, logical-mathematical, and linguistic intelligences. Gardner suggested that we have all eight abilities but that some are more developed than others. Yet, he claimed, we have the ability to develop and improve them. Gardner, however, did not support the idea of learning styles. This idea suggests that students can learn only through one modality, such as kinesthetic (hands-on) or verbal (lecture). Robert Sternberg, choice B, proposed the triarchic theory of intelligence. Albert Bandura, choice C, was a social-learning theorist known for his research in observational learning. Raymond Cattell, choice D, divided intelligence into fluid and crystallized forms. L. L. Thurstone, choice E, opposed Spearman's idea of *g* (general intelligence) and suggested that we instead have seven clusters of primary mental abilities. (Skill 1a)

Research Methods

318. **(D)** If a test that has been designed to predict future performance successfully does, the test has predictive validity. This is ascertained by establishing whether there is a positive correlation between the test (the college entrance exam) and some related behavior (freshman grade point average). Reliability, choice A, refers to whether or not a test yields consistent scores. A test with content validity, choice B, contains questions that pertain to and measure a specific behavior. Bias, choice C, refers to the impact of a preconceived belief on performance. If a test has been standardized, choice E, it has been pretested with a representative sample. (Skill 1b)

319. **(B)** To measure the reliability of a test, a researcher will often administer the test, wait for a period of time, and then give the test to the same people again to compare scores. If the test is reliable, there will be a correlation between the scores. The higher the correlation is, the higher the reliability of the measure is. Choice A is incorrect as it describes a negative correlation. The test-retest format is not used to determine the validity of a measure. Thus, choices C and E are incorrect. Statistical significance, choice D, allows a researcher to determine if differences in group outcomes are likely due to chance. (Skill 3)

320. **(E)** When researchers follow the same group for many years to learn about how factors in early life influence later development, they are conducting a longitudinal study. A double-blind procedure, choice A, is carried out to prevent experimenter bias. In a double-blind procedure, both the subjects and experimenter are blind to which group the subject has been assigned to, experimental or control. A cross-sectional study, choice B, tests people of diverse ages at the same time. A naturalistic observation, choice C, allows a researcher to observe carefully and record the behavior of a person or an animal in his or her natural environment. An experiment, choice D, involves the random assignment of participants to different conditions in order to observe the impact of manipulating a variable on behavior. (Skill 1b)

321. **(D)** Because researchers randomly assigned subjects to differing conditions, the researchers used an experiment. In a correlational study, choice A, researchers look at preexisting information and look to see if a relationship exists. There is no manipulation of an independent variable across the different groups in a correlational study. A researcher using a survey, choice B, collects self-report data concerning an individual's behavior or attitudes. A naturalistic observation, choice C, includes carefully recording observed behaviors in the natural environment of the organism. A case study, choice E, involves an in-depth analysis

of a single person or of a small group that shares a common, unique characteristic. (Skill 3)

322. **(D)** Control groups receive no manipulation and serve as a comparison to the groups where a manipulation has taken place. In this study, the third group acted as the control. Its members were told the test has nothing to do with intellectual ability but, instead, was just a challenging task. Members of this control group received similar instructions as did members of groups 1 and 2. Members of group 3 were expected to perform like members of group 2. Choice A is incorrect because group 3 was the control group. Choices B, C, and E are incorrect because only group 3 is the control group. Because of the information given to members of groups 1 and 2, these groups were manipulated. (Skill 3)

323. **(E)** When people are aware of a negative stereotype pertaining to a group with which they identify, they are likely to experience a decrease in performance when they believe others will judge them through that lens. The fundamental attribution error, choice A, occurs when we judge others based on perceived personality characteristics and discount the role of environmental forces. Fixation, choice B, occurs when we are unable to view a problem from a new perspective. Belief perseverance, choice C, happens when we have been presented with overwhelming evidence but continue to cling to a previous belief. Framing, choice D, refers to how a question or a statement is presented to us. How the question or statement is framed can influence the decisions we make. (Skill 1b)

Perspectives

324. **(C)** Behavior genetics is the study of the influence of the environment and of genetics on behaviors. Researchers in this field often use twin studies as part of their methodology. Psychoanalysts, choice A, focus on the role of the unconscious in producing behaviors. Humanists, choice B, are interested in the factors that influence our potential. Sociocultural psychologists, choice D, investigate the influence of societal factors on our cognition and behaviors. Behaviorists, choice E, focus on how our behaviors are learned through our interactions with the environment. (Skill 1c)

CHAPTER 9: DEVELOPMENTAL PSYCHOLOGY

Stimulus

325. **(E)** The chart reflects a difference in outcomes regarding the stability of intelligence test scores over time. Longitudinal studies, which retest the same sample over time, suggest that intelligence test scores remain fairly

stable across the life span. Cross-sectional studies, which test different age groups at the same time, tell a very different story about intelligence. Based on the chart, there is a steady drop in intelligence test scores across the different ages. Choices A, B, C, and D all summarize the information incorrectly. (Skill 2)

Definitions

326. **(C)** Proponents of the nature position suggest that our behaviors are determined by our genetic inheritance. Thus, Konrad Lorenz is a proponent of nature in the debate because he believed that ducklings were predisposed to imprint, or attach, to the first moving thing they saw after hatching. The other responses (choices A, B, D, and E) reflect the alternative influences of nurture, including learning, parenting styles, and experience. (Skill 1a)

327. **(C)** A zygote is the single cell that forms as a result of uniting the sperm and egg cell at conception. A gene, choice A, is a section of a DNA molecule that carries instructions for making proteins that support cell functions. An ovum, choice B, is a mature egg cell in a woman. The ovum can unite with a sperm cell to form a zygote. A teratogen, choice D, is a substance, such as a drug, that is able to cross the placenta. A blastocyst, choice E, is a ball of cells that forms after several days of cell division following conception. (Skill 1a)

328. **(C)** From the beginning of the ninth week after conception to birth, a developing human organism is called a fetus. A zygote, choice A, refers to the fertilized egg directly after conception. A neonate, choice B, is a newborn baby. A gamete, choice D, is a reproductive cell—a sperm cell or an egg cell. An embryo, choice E, describes the developing human organism from 2 to 8 weeks after fertilization. (Skill 1a)

329. **(D)** A teratogen is a substance that can cross the placenta during prenatal development and that has the ability to disrupt fetal development or lead to physical malformations. Choice A, a monocular cue, is a visual cue for depth perception, such as relative height, that requires the use of one eye. Glial cells, choice B, are found in the nervous system and provide support and nourishment for neurons. Dizygotic, choice C, typically refers to fraternal twins that develop from two separate fertilized cells. Heritable, choice E, refers to a characteristic that can be passed down from parents to their offspring. (Skill 1b)

330. **(D)** Maturation refers to the orderly developmental processes. Thus, the universal sequence of motor skill development in infancy is considered

a maturational process. Assimilation, choice A, refers to the cognitive process of incorporating new information into existing schemata. Scaffolding, choice B, occurs when an adult provides modeling of a new skill to a child and then allows the child to practice that ability in order to master it. Imprinting, choice C, occurs in specific animals, such as ducklings, when they attach to the first moving object they see after hatching. Accommodation, choice E, is a cognitive process where a child must change an existing schema to account for newly learned information. (Skill 1b)

331. **(C)** The hippocampus is primarily responsible for the formation of new memories. This brain region is immature in young children and therefore inhibits the formation of long-term memories. The reticular formation, choice A, is located in the brainstem and activates the brain in regulating arousal and attention. The medulla, choice B, is responsible for regulating autonomic functions, such as breathing and heart rate. The somatosensory cortex, choice D, interprets signals related to the skin senses, including pressure on the skin. The pituitary gland, choice E, is the master gland of the endocrine system and regulates growth processes. (Skill 1b)

332. **(D)** Jean Piaget suggested that object permanence is a cognitive milestone achieved during the sensorimotor stage. Beginning at 8 months, children understand that physical objects continue to exist when outside of their visual field. Thus, Brackstyn understands that his toy continues to exist even though he can't see it under his blanket. Therefore, Brackstyn understands that the bunny toy has object permanence. Choice A illustrates a child who is not yet able to conserve. In other words, Amanda doesn't know that despite changes in shape, the amount of pancake remains the same. Whitney demonstrates egocentrism in choice B. She has difficulty perceiving the world from her mother's perspective. Curtis, in choice C, demonstrates conservation as he understands that the amount of juice may appear different in separate glasses, yet the amount remains the same. Beau, in choice E, represents a child who believes in animism, that all inanimate objects have human-like characteristics. (Skill 1b)

333. **(E)** Piaget's four stages of cognitive development, in order, are the sensorimotor, preoperational, concrete operational, and formal operational. Choices A, B, C, and D all list the stages in incorrect order. (Skill 1a)

334. **(D)** Formal operational children are able to think abstractly and creatively about how the world could be, not necessarily how it is. Thus, Devin's response better illustrates formal operational thinking than Brad's. Brad's thinking is a more accurate representation of concrete operational thinking because his response is more accurate to how the world

actually operates. Choices A, B, and E are earlier stages of Piaget's theory. Choice C is the second stage of Kohlberg's theory of moral development. (Skill 1b)

335. **(B)** Imprinting is vital for the survival of certain animals. Ducklings must imprint so that they can follow their parents to obtain food and protection. Imprinting occurs during a critical period for learning this crucial behavior. The sensorimotor stage, choice A, is the first of Piaget's stages of cognitive development. The identity stage of psychosocial development, choice C, happens during adolescence according to Erik Erikson's psychosocial stages. According to Lev Vygotsky, a zone of proximal development, choice D, occurs when a behavior is modeled by a parent so that the child may learn it with support. The preconventional stage, choice E, is the first stage of Lawrence Kohlberg's theory of moral development. (Skill 1b)

336. **(C)** Authoritarian parents tend to be strict disciplinarians and expect their orders to be followed without question. Authoritative parents, choice A, are responsive to their children's needs. Authoritative parents are demanding and controlling but have a more democratic style of parenting than authoritarian parents. Responsive parenting, choice B, is a larger category described in Baumrind's parenting styles theory. Baumrind included both the authoritative and permissive parents in the overall "responsive parenting" category. Permissive parents, choice D, are undemanding and rarely use punishment. Neglecting parents, choice E, are inattentive to the needs of their children and are emotionally withdrawn. (Skill 1b)

337. **(E)** Postconventional reasoning is characterized by an internalized sense of morality. Those in this stage believe in a social contract, where governments exist because of the will of its citizens. These citizens have the right and responsibility to disobey unjust laws. According to postconventional reasoning, human life and the desire for justice may take precedence over the law. Formal operational (choice A) and preoperational (choice C) are both stages in Piaget's theory of cognitive development. Preconventional morality, choice B, focuses on self-interest: avoiding punishment or gaining a reward. Conventional reasoning, choice D, focuses on upholding the law or on gaining approval from others. (Skill 1c)

338. **(D)** Arnett found that individuals between the ages of 18 and 25 postpone adult responsibilities. During this in-between and unstable period of emerging adulthood, young people are focused on establishing their identities and feel that the world is open to all possibilities. Those in Piaget's concrete operational stage, choice A, do not focus on self-exploration and lack abstract thinking. Erikson's psychosocial stage of initiative versus guilt, choice B, is the focus of preschool children. Freud's psychosexual

stage of latency, choice C, is the time between the age of 6 and puberty. During this stage, according to Freud, sexual feelings are repressed. Kohlberg's preconventional morality stage, choice E, is primarily for children younger than age 9. (Skill 1c)

339. **(E)** Erikson suggested that the psychosocial crisis of young adulthood is intimacy versus isolation. In this stage, individuals seek out others to form long-term personal relationships but must struggle with the fear of rejection. If individuals are not willing to make the commitments and sacrifices that relationships require, they will become isolated and lonely. (Skill 1c)

340. **(C)** Pruning refers to the process of removing neurons and the connections among them that are not being used in the adolescent brain. This process makes the brain work more efficiently. The all-or-none response, choice A, refers to how a neuron fires with the same intensity each time it reaches threshold. A refractory period, choice B, is a brief pause after a neuron fires so that it can recharge to fire again. Habituation, choice D, is the decrease in responsiveness to a stimulus that is repeatedly presented. Sensory adaptation, choice E, occurs when a constant external stimulation is present and leads to a decrease in neural firing that creates a diminished sensitivity to the stimulus. (Skill 1a)

341. **(E)** Prospective memory is the ability to remember to carry out planned actions, such as remembering to take daily medications. A flashbulb memory, choice A, is an emotionally salient memory that is encoded into memory with a "photographic" quality. An implicit memory, choice B, is demonstrated without conscious recall, such as a skill like tying one's shoe. An iconic memory, choice C, is a brief sensory memory of a visual stimulus stored in the sensory receptors. A mood congruent memory, choice D, is a memory triggered by an emotion that acts as a retrieval cue. (Skill 1b)

342. **(C)** Repetitiveness is an early symptom of Alzheimer's disease. It may be evident by the individual asking the same question or repeating the same story many times in a short period. Failing to recognize a close family member, forgetting personal events from the past, difficulty communicating, and having difficulty learning new tasks (choices A, B, D, and E) are associated with a progression of the disease. (Skill 1a)

343. **(A)** Telomeres are the DNA at the end of the chromosomes. The telomeres protect the chromosomes during cell division. Without these endings, cells would lose genes. As cells continue to divide as they must, the telomeres shorten. When the telomeres get too short, the cell can no longer divide and the cell dies. Research has demonstrated that regular exercise can protect the telomeres and slow aging. Agonists, choice B, are chemicals that activate receptors in the brain. The myelin sheath,

choice C, insulates the axon and speeds neural impulses. Synapses, choice D, are the spaces between nerve cells. Glial cells, choice E, provide support and nourishment for neurons. (Skill 1a)

344. **(B)** Sex refers to the biological differences, including genitalia and genetics, between males and females. Sexual orientation, choice A, relates to which sex one is sexually attracted to. Androgyny, choice C, is the blending of male and female personality characteristics in one individual. Gender, choice D, refers to the cultural expectations held for men and women in a specific society. Identity, choice E, is an individual's personal conception of himself or herself. (Skill 1a)

345. **(D)** Gender identity is a personal sense of knowing if you are a man, a woman, or a combination of both. Choice A refers to gender roles. Choice B is a description of androgyny. Social learning theory is illustrated in choice C. Choice E is the definition for sex, which is based on a biological category defined by genetics. Sex is often confused with gender and gender identity. (Skill 1a)

Scenarios

346. **(E)** Temperament refers to characteristic emotional reactivity in infancy. Gerald's behaviors are consistent with being a "difficult" baby. Habituation, choice A, refers to the decrease in responsiveness with the repetition of a stimulus. Children show object permanence, choice B, when they demonstrate an understanding that an object continues to exist when outside of their visual field. Animism, choice C, is a child's belief that inanimate objects have human characteristics, such as believing a doll feels pain when dropped. Androgyny, choice D, refers to the blending of masculine and feminine characteristics in an individual's personality. (Skill 1b)

347. **(A)** When we are exposed to new information, we try to make it fit our current schema. This is called assimilation. When Risa was exposed to a new flavor of candy, she had difficulty accepting as a flavor something she associated with a scent. Thus, she was having difficulty assimilating musk as a flavor. Children exhibiting egocentrism, choice B, have difficulty perceiving an experience from another's point of view. Conservation, choice C, is the understanding that the basic properties of objects remain the same if the objects change in appearance. When preoperational children believe that all objects have been manufactured by humans, they demonstrate artificialism, choice D. Choice E, habituation, occurs when a response decreases with repeated presentations of a stimulus. (Skill 1b)

348. **(B)** When a child develops a theory of mind, he or she is able to make inferences about others' mental states. The child in this example assumes that the dog knows what the child knows, that there are candles in the box. Conservation, choice A, is the understanding that despite changes in shape, the basic properties of an object remain the same. Artificialism, choice C, is the belief that everything in the world has been manufactured by humankind. Object permanence, choice D, is understanding that an object exists when not perceived. Developing basic trust, choice E, is the result of a favorable outcome in Erik Erikson's psychosocial stages. A child whose basic needs are met learns that the world is a predictable and safe place. (Skill 1b)

349. **(E)** Stranger anxiety begins around 8 months of age and corresponds to the development of object permanence. A child experiencing stranger anxiety shows distress in the presence of an unknown person. Imprinting, choice A, occurs in animals, such as ducklings, as they attach to the first object they see moving after hatching. Habituation, choice B, is demonstrated when an individual's response to an external stimulus decreases when the stimulus is continually presented. Conservation, choice C, is an ability demonstrated by those in the concrete operational stage who understand that a specific quantity remains the same even if the object's appearance changes. Animism, choice D, is the belief of preoperational children that inanimate objects have human-like characteristics. (Skill 1b)

350. **(A)** According to Jean Piaget, preoperational children lack the ability to conserve. The test described in the scenario is a common test for the conservation of a solid quantity. If a child can conserve, he or she knows that despite changes in appearance, the basic properties of the substance remain the same. Children in the sensorimotor stage, choice B, are between birth and 2 years of age. The test as described would not be used with children this age because they lack language ability. Formal operational thought, choice C, typically begins after puberty when a child begins thinking abstractly. Postformal thought, choice D, has been suggested by psychologists who have furthered Piaget's initial work. They suggest that older adults' thinking is more flexible, complex, and able to deal with uncertainties. Concrete operational children, choice E, comprehend conservation because they think logically about events in the physical world. (Skill 1b)

351. **(B)** The experimental procedure described in the scenario is called "the rouge test." It is used to test the development of self-concept. A child who understands that he or she is separate from others and has individual thoughts and needs has self-concept. As this child looks in the mirror, the child recognizes himself or herself as an individual and notices that

something is on his or her face. Thus, the child touches his or her nose. Object permanence, choice A, is first attained during the sensorimotor stage of Piaget's cognitive development. A child with this ability understands that objects continue to exist outside of his or her ability to see them. Basic trust, choice C, is the first stage of Erikson's psychosocial stages. As a result of responsive parenting, a child develops the belief that the world is predictable and safe. A child with a secure attachment, choice D, develops a trusting relationship with his or her primary caregiver. Concrete operational thought, choice E, is the third of Piaget's stages. In it, a child first develops logical reasoning concerning how the physical world operates. (Skill 1b)

352. **(B)** According to Kohlberg, preconventional morality focuses on self-interest—avoiding punishment or gaining a reward. If Katie's main concern is avoiding a ticket, she is preconventional. Preoperational thinking, choice A, is the second stage of Piaget's theory of cognitive development. Conventional reasoning, choice C, focuses on upholding the law or gaining approval from others. If Katie did not speed because speeding is "against the law," she would be in this stage. Concrete operational, choice D, is Piaget's third stage in his theory of cognitive development. Those who are in the postconventional stage of moral development, choice E, are guided by an internalized sense of right and wrong. If Katie believed that speeding might be justified if a person's life was in danger, even if it broke the law, she would be a postconventional thinker. (Skill 1b)

353. **(D)** The last stage of Erik Erikson's psychosocial stages is integrity versus despair. This is a time for older adults to reflect on their lives. Those with integrity, like Lillie described in the scenario, feel a sense of satisfaction with their lives. Establishing basic trust, choice A, in a predictable world is the crisis of infancy. Establishing a firm sense of identity, choice B, is the concern of adolescents. Generativity, choice C, is the concern of middle adulthood, where adults use their talents to guide the next generation. Competence, choice E, is the task of older elementary-school-aged children who find joy in learning that they can succeed at hard tasks. (Skill 1b)

354. **(B)** Children acquire gender by watching adult models and imitating what those models do. When the children are praised for this behavior, like Jackie is, they become more likely to repeat it. This is social learning. Gender schema theory, choice A, explains that we form schemata to organize the world around us. We learn from our environment about how boys and girls are supposed to behave. Then we organize the world around these frameworks. Psychodynamic theorists, choice C, believe that we adopt our gender identity as a way to resolve the unconscious conflict

associated with the phallic stage. Biological psychologists, choice D, focus on how our nervous system and other body systems influence behavior. Evolutionary psychologists, choice E, focus on how our behaviors have allowed us to survive in our environment. (Skill 1c)

355. **(E)** Egocentrism, according to Jean Piaget, is the inability of a child to take the perspective of another person. When a child reports that the doll perceives the same scene as himself or herself, the child reflects this type of egocentric thought. Conservation, choice A, is the understanding that even if an object changes in appearance, its basic properties remain unchanged. Preconventional reasoning, choice B, is the first stage of Lawrence Kohlberg's stages of moral development. A child reflecting this type of reasoning determines if something is right or wrong based on an expectation of punishment or reward. Insecure avoidant attachment, choice C, refers to a pattern of behavior exhibited in Ainsworth's strange situation. This child avoids connection with his or her caregiver and does not seem to care about a caregiver's presence, absence, or return to the playroom. Generativity, choice D, is the psychosocial crisis of middle age according to Erik Erikson. At this stage, adults consider their legacy and the impact they can have on future generations. (Skill 1b)

356. **(B)** According to Jean Piaget, formal operational thinking is characterized by abstract reasoning. Adolescents who become formal operational begin to consider what is possible in the world, leading them to consider their own beliefs within the context of what they have been taught in childhood. This questioning can lead to conflicts with parents. The postconventional stage, choice A, is the final stage of Kohlberg's theory of moral development. Identity versus role confusion, choice C, is the psychosocial conflict of adolescence according to Erik Erikson. Choice D, insecure attachment, is incorrect as it concerns social, not cognitive, development. Choice E reflects a Freudian view of development. (Skill 1b)

357. **(D)** Some authors suggested that empty-nest syndrome occurs when children leave the family home and, as a result, parents experience negative emotions. However, recent research questions this as a universal experience. The recent research suggests that having an empty nest is not necessarily a negative experience for middle-aged adults. A midlife crisis, choice A, which is a period of self-reflection that is supposed to occur during midlife, has also been questioned. Identity versus role confusion, choice B, is the psychosocial crisis proposed by Erik Erikson for adolescents. Stranger anxiety, choice C, occurs during infancy when object permanence is first observed. Insecure attachment, choice E, is an early childhood attachment style described by Mary Ainsworth. (Skill 1b)

358. **(E)** The social clock refers to a particular age or period in one's lifetime when certain social events should take place, such as marriage. Lev Vygotsky suggested that the zone of proximal development, choice A, is the time period when a child needs help from an adult to master a new task. Heritability, choice B, concerns the impact of genetics on observed differences in a trait within a population. A critical period, choice C, is the time when specific development must occur. The theory of mind, choice D, refers to the ability to infer what another person is thinking or feeling. (Skill 1b)

Names

359. **(C)** Harlow found that the infant monkeys spent most of their time with the soft, warm, rocking mother and went to the wire mother only to eat. He concluded that the warmth associated with close body contact was the key factor that led to attachment. Prior to Harlow's research, it was commonly believed that the nourishment provided by the mother, choice D, was the most important element leading to infant attachment. Choices A, B, and E were not factors Harlow included in these attachment studies. (Skill 1b)

360. **(D)** According to Lev Vygotsky, children advance in their cognitive development through social interactions. Parents play a key role by modeling new skills. This is necessary in helping a child advance from novice to veteran during this zone of proximal development. A period of assimilation, choice A, occurs when we try to incorporate new information into our existing schemata. The theory of mind, choice B, refers to the ability to infer what others are perceiving. Formal operational thinking, choice C, is the fourth stage of Piaget's theory of cognitive development. According to Erik Erikson, the psychosocial conflict of autonomy versus shame and doubt, choice E, occurs when a toddler learns to do tasks for himself or herself. (Skill 1b)

361. **(D)** Ainsworth found that mothers who were caring and responsive to their child's needs were more likely to have a secure attachment. Postconventional reasoning, choice A, refers to a type of moral reasoning based on internalized principles. However, it was not the primary feature in the parenting style of those tested in Mary Ainsworth's strange situation procedure. Demands for obedience (choice B) and little use of punishment (choice C) are characteristic of authoritarian and permissive parenting styles, respectively. Neither one was the key factor in developing a secure attachment. An extroverted personality, choice E, or having an outgoing, sociable personality, was not the key element in Ainsworth's procedure. (Skill 1a)

362. **(B)** Jean Piaget suggested that infants younger than 6 months of age do not exhibit object permanence, that is, knowing that items continue to exist when they are not in direct view. Researchers have demonstrated object permanence in children at earlier ages, such as in the described scenario. Erik Erikson, choice A, focused on the psychosocial crises that occur during eight stages (trust, autonomy, initiative, competence, identity, intimacy, generativity, and integrity). Lawrence Kohlberg, choice C, focused on moral development, not cognitive development. He suggested that our moral reasoning can be categorized into three stages (preconventional, conventional, and postconventional). Lev Vygotsky, choice D, studied cognitive development and suggested that social interaction was the key to fostering cognitive growth. Mary Ainsworth, choice E, designed the strange situation procedures to investigate the quality of attachment between child and caregiver. (Skill 1b)

363. **(E)** Carol Gilligan criticized Kohlberg for drawing conclusions about moral development for both men and women when his sample was entirely male. She felt that the highest level of moral reasoning, postconventional, reflected a male bias with the emphasis on justice in making moral decisions. Gilligan felt that women are socialized to be compassionate and caring, traits that are reflected in the second stage of moral development, conventional reasoning. The potential problems described in choices A, B, C, and D were not emphasized by Gilligan in her critiques of Kolhberg's research. (Skill 1a)

Research Methods

364. **(C)** In a correlational study, researchers look for associations among naturally occurring variables. When researchers find a correlation, they must consider that a third variable might exist that is the source of the relationship. For example, a genetic predisposition shared by parents and children for social competence might be the third variable that produces the correlation between parenting style and social competence. Thus, choice A is incorrect as correlations do show the relationship between two variables. Choices B, D, and E are all concerns related to using experimentation. (Skill 3)

365. **(B)** Longitudinal studies retest the same variable in the same group of people over time. It is an important tool in investigating developmental changes across the life span. A case study, choice A, studies a single case in depth. An experiment, choice C, investigates the impact of an experimental variable across randomly assigned groups to investigate causal relationships. A cross-sectional study, choice D, tests different people of

varying ages at a single point in time. A naturalistic observation, choice E, involves studying subjects in their natural environments. (Skill 1b)

366. **(A)** Habituation occurs when responsiveness to a stimulus decreases with repeated presentations. This is a simple form of learning that is used to study cognition in infants. When a stimulus, like a red circle, is first presented, infants will spend a long time looking. However, this response will grow weaker over time. When a new stimulus is presented, the green square, time spent looking will increase. Choice B is a test for object permanence. Choice C is used primarily by physicians to detect developmental delay. Choice D describes the strange situation test used to study infant attachment. Choice E is a test for self-concept. (Skill 1b)

367. **(C)** Replication involves repeating a study using the same methods but different subjects and researchers. Replicating the results of a study is vital in order to build confidence in the validity in and reliability of the results. The description of the 2018 research in the question does not include the research elements mentioned in choices A, B, D, and E. (Skill 3)

368. **(B)** Critics argue that monkeys are social creatures and to isolate them for a lengthy period of time, knowing that doing so would cause excessive distress, violates the current American Psychological Association (APA) guidelines. Informed consent (choice A), lack of scientific value (choice C), debriefing (choice D), and confidentiality (choice E) are included in the APA ethical guidelines. However, these guidelines concern human subjects, not nonhuman subjects. Harlow did have a clear scientific purpose in investigating processes underlying development (choice C). However, the extreme negative impact of social deprivation on his subjects calls into question his design. (Skill 3)

Perspectives

369. **(C)** Psychodynamic psychology has its roots in the Freudian tradition. Erik Erikson trained as a psychoanalyst and believed in the basic teachings of Sigmund Freud. Erickson differed from Freud in that Erickson focused on the development of the ego throughout the life span and downplayed sexual crises as the bases of personality development. Erikson's work did not reflect the psychological perspectives listed in choices A, B, D, or E. (Skill 1a)

370. **(E)** Evolutionary psychologists believe that certain innate behaviors allow us to adapt to our environment, thus promoting our ability to survive. Behavioral psychologists, choice A, believe that we learn our behaviors from our interactions with the environment. Cognitive psychologists,

choice B, are primarily interested in how we process and store information. Humanistic psychologists, choice C, emphasize our potential for growth and self-fulfillment. Sociocultural psychologists, choice D, emphasize the role that society plays in shaping our development. (Skill 1a)

371. **(E)** Albert Bandura is associated with the social-cognitive perspective. His beliefs about how we learn draws from the behavioral perspective. However, he also has cognitive roots. Bandura believes that when a child observes a model and sees the model reinforced, the child is likely to imitate the behavior, called vicarious learning. In addition, if a child is positively reinforced for a behavior he or she has imitated, the child is likely to repeat that behavior. Bandura goes beyond behavioral theory because he believes that cognition also plays an important role in learning. When a child watches a model, the child must pay attention and store the information for when he or she later is motivated to reproduce the behavior. Psychodynamic psychologists, choice A, focus on the unconscious forces that shape behavior. Humanistic psychologists, choice B, emphasize the human potential for growth. Biological psychologists, choice C, focus on the workings of the nervous and other biological systems in determining behavior. Evolutionary psychologists, choice D, investigate the role of natural selection in shaping adaptive human behaviors. (Skill 1a)

372. **(C)** Biological psychologists focus on the workings of the nervous and other body systems in determining cognition and behavior. Thus, moral reasoning is impacted by the workings of specific brain regions, such as the brain's reward system. Choice A reflects the position of Lawrence Kohlberg. He suggested that as moral questions come up in our lives, our mental processes are stimulated. Through such cognitive challenges we develop a sense of right and wrong. Social learning psychologists would focus on the role of observational learning, choice B, on a child's moral development. The psychodynamic perspective, choice D, illustrates the role of unconscious conflict during psychosexual development that is central to an individual's moral reasoning. The sociocultural perspective is demonstrated in choice E. (Skill 1a)

CHAPTER 10: MOTIVATION AND EMOTION

Stimulus

373. **(B)** Based on Carter's and Ava's statements, Carter seems to be motivated by grades, which are an external reward for effort. So, Carter is influenced by extrinsic motivation. Choice A, achievement motivation, best fits Danny's statements, which indicate that he is motivated to master this

specific task and become skilled at it. Mastery motivation (choice C) and instrumental motivation (choice E) are not psychological terms. Intrinsic motivation, choice D, best fits Ava's statements. She seems motivated to do a good job on this task only because she wants the internal satisfaction of doing good work. (Skill 1b)

374. **(D)** Ava's statements indicate that she is motivated to do a good job on this task only because she wants the internal satisfaction of doing good work. So, Ava is influenced by intrinsic motivation. Choice A, achievement motivation, best fits Danny's statements, which indicate that he is motivated to master this specific task and become skilled at it. Carter seems to be motivated by grades, which are an external reward for effort. So, Carter is influenced by extrinsic motivation, choice B. Mastery motivation (choice C) and instrumental motivation (choice E) are not psychological terms. (Skill 1b)

375. **(A)** Danny's statements indicate that he is motivated by achievement motivation because he seems motivated to master this specific task and become skilled at it. Carter seems to be motivated by grades, which are an external reward for effort. So, Carter is influenced by extrinsic motivation, choice B. Ava's statements indicate that she is motivated to do a good job on this task only because she wants the internal satisfaction of doing good work. So, Ava is influenced by intrinsic motivation, choice D. (Mastery motivation (choice C) and instrumental motivation (choice E) are not psychological terms. (Skill 1b)

376. **(C)** The Yerkes-Dodson law describes the relationship between stress/arousal and performance on a task. For many tasks, if stress/arousal is very low or very high, performance suffers. This seems to be what Guy is experiencing. Danny's statements indicate that he is motivated by achievement motivation, choice A. Danny seems motivated to master this specific task and become skilled at it. Ava's statements indicate that she is motivated to do a good job on this task only because she wants the internal satisfaction of doing good work. So, Ava is experiencing intrinsic motivation, choice D. Carter seems to be motivated by grades, which are an external reward for effort. So, Carter is experiencing extrinsic motivation, choice B. The law of effect, choice E, is a term from learning (conditioning) research. The law of effect states that an organism's reaction to a stimulus determines whether that stimulus is a reinforcement or a punishment. (Skill 1b)

Definitions

377. **(E)** An instinct is a complex behavior that all organisms within a species are born with (instead of acquiring later through experience). Instinctual

behavior follows a fixed pattern; organisms of that species perform the complex behavior in the same way in response to the same conditions. For example, newborn humans turn toward a touch on the cheek and suck to get milk. Choice A is incomplete because it does not include the details that the behavior must be complex and follow a fixed pattern. Choice B is incorrect because many basic drives are related to survival but are not instincts. Choice C is incorrect because many behaviors evolved over time but are not instincts. Choice D is incorrect because it refers to conditioning, but instincts are unlearned. (Skill 1a)

378. **(B)** An instinct is a complex behavior that all organisms within a species are born with (instead of acquiring later through experience). A drive, choice A, is a physiological need that motivates some of our behaviors. We act on drives in order to regain physiological balance. Autonomic, choice C, refers to the autonomic nervous system. Homeostasis, choice D, is physiological balance. Basal, choice E, refers to the basal metabolic rate, which is the rate at which our body uses energy at rest. (Skill 1a)

379. **(D)** The Yerkes-Dodson law describes how very low or very high levels of arousal (such as stress) can have a detrimental impact on performing some tasks. Achievement motivation (choice A) and extrinsic motivation (choice B) are different kinds of motivation. However, neither one is relevant to the question about the impact of stress or arousal. Homeostasis, choice C, refers to biological balance. Homeostasis is an aspect of what motivates behaviors but is not related to the impact of stress or arousal. Choice E, performance anxiety, is not a psychological term. (Skill 1a)

380. **(C)** The Yerkes-Dodson law describes how very low or high levels of arousal (such as stress) can have a detrimental impact on performing some tasks. Choice A is an interesting question but is not related to the Yerkes-Dodson law. Choices B and E are related to the motivation principles of intrinsic, extrinsic, and achievement motivation. However, the Yerkes-Dodson law doesn't relate to those concepts. Choice D is relevant to emotion research, but the Yerkes-Dodson law applies to motivation, not emotion. (Skill 1b)

381. **(B)** Extrinsic motivations, like money or food treats, can be very effective at quick, short-term behavior changes, especially when working with strangers. Choice A, achievement motivation, is a different kind of motivation but is not uniquely "faster" than extrinsic motivators. Choice C, two-factor motivation, is not actually a motivation term. Instead, two-factor theory is an emotion theory. Intrinsic motivation, choice D, depends on knowing people well and would not be an effective choice for working with strangers. Choice E, autonomic motivation, is not actually a kind of motivation. Instead, the autonomic nervous system is part of the peripheral nervous system. (Skill 1a)

382. **(D)** Intrinsic motivation is generally longer lasting than extrinsic motivation (choice B). When someone is motivated only because of internal satisfaction, he or she is more likely to keep performing that behavior for a long time, even when no one else is paying attention and giving the person any external rewards. Choice A, achievement motivation, is incorrect because the question doesn't imply that anyone is working to achieve mastery of a skill or set of knowledge. Choice C, two-factor motivation, is not actually a motivation term. Instead, two-factor theory is an emotion theory. Choice E, autonomic motivation, is not actually a kind of motivation. Instead, the autonomic nervous system is part of the peripheral nervous system. (Skill 1a)

383. **(A)** Drive reduction theory describes how a drive is created when we experience a physiological deficit (like hunger). The drive reduces the need, resulting in a behavior (like eating) that helps a person regain balance. Instinct theory, choice B, is a motivation theory. However, it is much more specific than the description of the theory in this question. Maslow's hierarchy of needs, choice C, refers to physiological needs. However, it includes many more elements than described in the question, like safety needs, a sense of belonging, and so on. Homeostasis, choice D, is a balanced internal state. It is not a motivation. The limbic system, choice E, is an area of the brain. (Skill 1a)

384. **(E)** Drive reduction theory describes how a drive is created when we experience a physiological deficit (like hunger). The drive reduces the need, resulting in a behavior (like eating) that helps a person regain homeostasis, which is a balanced state. Choice A is like the theory of achievement motivation but is not a complete definition. Choice B refers to instinct theory. Choice C is similar to Maslow's hierarchy of needs. Choice D is like Freud's psychodynamic theory. (Skill 1a)

385. **(C)** Homeostasis is an internally balanced state without physiological deficits (like hunger) that create drives. Choice A, autonomic, references the autonomic nervous system, which is part of the peripheral nervous system. Choice B, hypothalamus, refers to a part of the brain. Choice D, refractory period, is part of the sexual response cycle. Choice E, self-actualization, is part of Maslow's hierarchy of needs. (Skill 1a)

386. **(D)** Homeostasis is an internally balanced state without physiological deficits (like hunger) that create drives. Choice A refers to some accurate information about neural transmission in the brain but is not relevant to drive reduction theory. Choices B, C, and E each refer to some ideas related to motivation but are not relevant to drive reduction theory. (Skill 1a)

387. **(B)** Maslow believed that people are motivated to satisfy needs in a specific order: physiological needs, safety needs, love and belongingness, self-esteem, and finally self-actualization. (A top level of self-transcendence is sometimes included.) Choices A, C, D, and E reference some motivation concepts but include incorrect information about Maslow's hierarchy of needs. (Skill 1a)

388. **(B)** According to Maslow's theory, the correct order of the levels is physiological needs, safety needs, love and belongingness, self-esteem, and self-actualization. Choices A and C include many valid motivation terms, but they are not part of Maslow's theory. Choice D lists the stages of Piaget's cognitive development theory. Choice E doesn't refer to any psychological stage theory or list of needs. (Skill 1a)

389. **(A)** The hypothalamus regulates several physiological processes, including hunger. The lateral hypothalamus is associated with the feeling of hunger. A separate part, the ventromedial hypothalamus, is associated with the feeling of fullness. The amygdala, choice B, is involved with basic, extreme emotions. Choice C, the thalamus, receives all the sensory impulses from the rest of the body (except the sense of smell) and routes them to the correct places in the rest of the brain. Choice D, the pons, deals with several basic life support functions but not hunger/satiation. The sensorimotor cortex, choice E, involves voluntary muscle movements. (Skill 1a)

390. **(E)** The hypothalamus regulates several physiological processes, including hunger. The lateral hypothalamus is associated with the feeling of hunger. A separate part, the ventromedial hypothalamus, is associated with the feeling of fullness. Choices A, B, C, and D are incorrect because they describe aspects of motivation that are not controlled or primarily influenced by the hypothalamus. (Skill 1a)

391. **(C)** The hypothalamus regulates several physiological processes, including hunger. The lateral hypothalamus is associated with the feeling of hunger. A separate part, the ventromedial hypothalamus, is associated with the feeling of fullness. Choices A, B, and E mention motivation terminology, but these motivations are not associated with the lateral hypothalamus. The hypothalamus is involved in sexual responses, but damage to the lateral hypothalamus would not impact the refractory period. Therefore, choice D is incorrect. (Skill 1a)

392. **(D)** The hypothalamus regulates several physiological processes, including hunger. The lateral hypothalamus is associated with the feeling of hunger. A separate part, the ventromedial hypothalamus, is associated with the feeling of fullness. Choices A, B, and E use valid psychological terms

related to motivation. However, the terms are not used accurately and are not specifically tied to the hypothalamus. Choice C is an incorrect statement about the functions of the hypothalamus. (Skill 1a)

393. **(A)** Set-point theory maintains that our brains have a set point of weight that our brains interpret as the balanced point (homeostasis). If we are below this weight, set-point theory states that our brains will increase hunger motivation. If we are above the set point, the theory states that our brains will decrease hunger impulses. Set-point theory does not apply to intrinsic/extrinsic motivations (choice B), achievement motivation (choice C), drive reduction theory (choice D), or two-factor theory (choice E). In fact, two-factor theory is about emotions, not motivations. (Skill 1a)

394. **(B)** Anorexia and bulimia are both eating disorders, but they are associated with very different sets of behaviors. Anorexia causes an individual to avoid eating or to eat, infrequently, very small amounts or very low calorie foods. Bulimia is associated with a cycle of binging and purging. Individuals may eat a regular or large amount of food but then purge what they ate through vomiting, laxatives, or extreme exercise. Craving (choice A) and pathway (choice D) are not specific psychological terms and are not relevant to the differences between anorexia and bulimia. Choice C, the hypothalamus, is associated with all eating behaviors. However, this brain structure does not define the difference between anorexia and bulimia. Choice E, etiology, is a term that refers to the causes of disorders. (Skill 1a)

395. **(E)** Both the James-Lange and Cannon-Bard theories try to explain how humans experience emotions. The James-Lange theory states that our physiology changes first and that we experience emotions because of those changes. The Cannon-Bard theory states that we experience emotions first and then our physiology changes because of the emotions that we experience. Choices A, B, and D are questions about motivation, which are not relevant to the emotion theories of James-Lange and Cannon-Bard. Choice C is somewhat like the two-factor theory of emotion. However, that theory attempts to explain emotional experiences, not interpreting others' reactions. (Skill 1a)

396. **(C)** Two-factor theory states that our experience of emotion results from a combination of both physiological changes and how we label (think about) an experience. The statement in the question supports two-factor theory and contradicts James-Lange theory (choice A). The James-Lange theory states that our physiology changes first and then we experience emotion. The most important evidence against the James-Lange theory

is that there are many emotions that involve the same physiological response. Choices B, D, and E are motivation theories, which are not relevant to this question. (Skill 1a)

Scenarios

397. **(B)** Instincts are fixed patterns of behavior that organisms are born with and that happen in response to specific stimuli. Some researchers dispute whether humans have "instincts," but Levi's rooting and sucking behaviors seem to meet this definition. Choice A, Yerkes-Dodson law, refers to the optimal level of arousal for performing certain tasks, which is not relevant to this scenario. Operant conditioning (choice C) and conditioned response (choice D) are learning/conditioning principles. Choice E, reciprocal determinism, is Albert Bandura's overall theory of what causes behaviors. (Skill 1b)

398. **(D)** Drive reduction theory describes how a drive is created when we experience a physiological deficit (like hunger). The drive reduces the need and results in a behavior (like eating) that helps a person regain balance. Instinct theory, Yerkes-Dodson law, and self-actualization theory (choices A, B, and C) are motivation theories. However, they are not as applicable to this scenario as is drive reduction theory. Choice E, satiation theory, is not a psychological term. (Skill 1b)

399. **(B)** The Yerkes-Dodson law describes the relationship between stress/arousal and performance on a task. For many tasks, if stress/arousal is very low or very high, performance suffers. However, experience and practice can lead performers, like Jim, to know exactly how much stress (or arousal) will facilitate an excellent performance. Choice A, drive reduction theory, helps describe many human motivations. However, it doesn't explain why this stress enhances Jim's performance. The autonomic nervous system, choice C, is involved in this scenario. Stress causes the autonomic nervous system to raise blood pressure. However, this choice doesn't explain how performance is either helped or hurt. Performance anxiety, choice D, is a term commonly used by people who experience the kind of stress that Jim experiences before the competition. However, it doesn't relate to Jim's success in the finals. Naturalistic observation theory, choice E, is a research methodology, not a motivation term. (Skill 1b)

400. **(A)** It is clear from the scenario that Daniel is intrinsically motivated to volunteer. His grandmother is mistaken when she thinks that an extrinsic reward, like money, will help motivate him more. Choice B lists motivation principles, but they don't specifically apply to this scenario. Choice C is not relevant because no conditioning is taking place in this scenario.

Choice D lists two stages of Piaget's theory of cognitive development. The terms in choice E are like the cognitive concepts of retroactive and proactive interference, which are also not relevant to this scenario. (Skill 1b)

401. **(E)** Homeostasis is an internally balanced state without physiological deficits (like hunger) that create drives. Self-actualization, choice A, is a motivation concept. However, it is not related to the concept of internal balance described in this scenario. Reciprocal determinism, choice B, refers to Bandura's theory about how past experiences and the social environment influence behaviors. Social facilitation, choice C, is a concept from social psychology. It states that sometimes the presence of other people can enhance our performance. Transduction, choice D, is a concept from sensation and perception research. Transduction occurs when energy or chemicals from the outside world are changed into neural impulses. (Skill 1b)

402. **(C)** Set-point theory maintains that our brains have a set point of weight that our brains interpret as the balanced point. If we are below this weight, set-point theory states that our brains will increase hunger motivation. If we are above the set point, the theory states that our brains will decrease hunger impulses. This psychological concept might help the roommate in the scenario find research about how to change habits safely that promote long-term weight loss, which the cabbage soup diet is unlikely to do. Instinct, choice A, is a motivation concept that is not likely to be helpful. Instincts cannot be changed. Id, choice B, is a concept from Freud that some would argue is related to hunger. However, talking about the id isn't likely to be helpful. Refractory period (choice D) and amygdala (choice E) are not related to hunger. (Skill 1b)

403. **(D)** The hypothalamus controls several basic physiological functions: feeding, the fight/flight response, and mating. All of CMOT's behaviors relate to these four basic functions. So, his hypothalamus may be malfunctioning. If CMOT's brainstem, choice A, was malfunctioning, he would be experiencing much more dire symptoms. Since the brainstem controls basic life support functions, CMOT might not be able to breathe on his own. The amygdala, choice B, is associated with strong emotions (including fighting) but not with the other symptoms listed. Fungiform papillae, choice C, are bumps on the tongue with taste buds on the upper surface. Transduction, choice E, is a concept from sensation and perception research. Transduction occurs when energy or chemicals from the outside world are changed into neural impulses. (Skill 1b)

404. **(B)** Achievement motivation theory describes a person's desire to master tasks and problem solve. It is likely that this intrinsic desire to master skills may be correlated with long-term success in school. In addition,

achievement motivation would be much more difficult to measure (operationally define) than the variables in choices A and D (grade point average and attitude toward school). Choice C, extrinsic motivation, is often important in school. However, extrinsic motivations are less effective long term than intrinsic motivations. Choice E, psychosocial maturational stage, refers to Erikson's psychosocial developmental stage theory. (Skill 3)

405. **(A)** Two-factor theory explains that our experience of emotions depends on a combination of how we label an experience and our physiological response. If we are in an emotionally stressful situation and for some reason our physiological reaction is heightened (perhaps because of medication, as in this scenario), we will "feel" the emotion more deeply. This is sometimes called the spillover effect. The James-Lange theory, Cannon-Bard theory, and Yerkes-Dodson theory (choices B, D, and E) are motivation theories but don't help explain the experience described in the scenario. Drive reduction theory (choice C) is a motivation theory, not an emotion theory. (Skill 1c)

406. **(E)** Maslow's hierarchy of needs theory predicts that people are motivated to satisfy needs in a specific order: physiological needs, safety needs, love and belongingness, self-esteem, and finally self-actualization. (A top level of self-transcendence is sometimes included.) Mr. Gassama's heroic act put his physiological and safety needs at risk. So, Maslow's hierarchy of needs theory might struggle to explain Mr. Gassama's motivation more than the other motivation theories. Intrinsic motivation (choice A), achievement motivation (choice B), and extrinsic motivation (choice C) might all explain Mr. Gassama's heroism because of his internal drives or the possibility of external rewards. Choice D, altruism, is a synonym for a selfless act, not a motivation theory. (Skill 1c)

Names

407. **(C)** Later in his career, Abraham Maslow became interested in something he called self-transcendence, which refers to the motivation to seek meanings in our lives that are "beyond the self." Carl Lange (choice A) and William James (choice D) are associated with the James-Lange theory of emotion. Alfred Kinsey, choice B, was involved in sexual response research. Walter Cannon, choice E, developed the Cannon-Bard theory of emotion along with Philip Bard. (Skill 1a)

408. **(A)** Carl Lange and William James are credited with the James-Lange theory, which states that physiological changes precede our cognitive awareness of emotion. The researchers listed in choice B, Virginia Johnson and William Masters, investigated the human sexual response cycle.

Philip Bard and Walter Cannon, choice C, established a theory that directly contradicts the James-Lange theory. The researchers in choice D, Henry Murray and Abraham Maslow, each investigated motivation but not the research described in this question. B. F. Skinner and John Watson, choice E, were behavioral researchers, not motivation researchers. (Skill 1a)

409. **(B)** Alfred Kinsey developed a carefully worded survey about sexual habits and sent it to a nationwide, representative sample. Results of the survey helped describe both common and uncommon sexual habits of Americans for the first time. The other researchers mentioned in choices A, C, D, and E (Carl Lange, Abraham Maslow, William James, and Walter Cannon) were all motivation researchers but were not involved in sexual behavior research. (Skill 1a)

410. **(D)** The principal disagreement between the James-Lange and Cannon-Bard theories of emotion are whether physiological responses occur before our conscious awareness of an emotion (James-Lange) or after (Cannon-Bard). Schachter and Singer's research indicates that an emotional experience is a combination of a physiological response and our cognitive interpretation of that physiological response. Choices A, B, and E are statements that are not relevant to Schachter and Singer's research. Choice C is a description of the James-Lange theory of emotion. (Skill 1c)

411. **(C)** Robert Zajonc demonstrated that some emotional responses occur without any conscious awareness of the experience. These "priming" experiments indicate that we can experience an emotion (such as liking something) because of experiences that occurred too quickly for us to be consciously aware of them. Philip Bard's (choice A) emotion theory (with Walter Cannon) argued that cognitive interpretation was central to emotional experiences and occurred before physiological reactions. Albert Bandura, Daniel Kahneman, and Robert Garcia (choices B, D, and E) were not emotion researchers. (Skill 1a)

Research Methods

412. **(E)** Homeostasis is an internally balanced state without physiological deficits (like hunger) that create drives. Since homeostasis appears to be the dependent variable in this experiment, the operational definition would need to be a way to measure this balanced internal state. Physiological instruments, such as blood pressure and respiration sensors, might be able to measure homeostasis. The rest of the choices (choices A, B, C, and D) are not ways to measure homeostasis. (Skill 3)

413. **(B)** Intrinsic motivations are, by definition, personal and internal. The primary way researchers investigate intrinsic motivations is to ask people about their intrinsic motivations. A careful survey with a sample of elementary school teachers could provide data to help answer these questions. This research method is called a self-report or a survey. An experiment (choice A), a correlation (choice C), and a naturalistic observation (choice D) cannot be used for this research question because intrinsic motivations cannot be observed. Choice E, empirical (data based), is not a specific research method. All psychological research is empirical (data based). (Skill 3)

414. **(A)** Since achievement motivation is not a variable that a researcher can manipulate, the researcher would first need to measure achievement motivation in the sample. Then the researcher would have to assign participants with high achievement motivation to one group and those with low achievement motivation to another group. As a result, this would be a quasi-experiment rather than a true experiment. Choice B is incorrect because the double-blind technique is not related to random assignment. Choices C and D include statements that are factually incorrect about experimental design and statistics. Choice E is a definition of random sampling, not random assignment. (Skill 3)

415. **(D)** Maslow's hierarchy of needs begins with physiological needs, and the next level is safety needs. Therefore, the most likely reason for the denial from the Ethics Review Board is that the research puts these basic needs at risk. There is no indication that this research inevitably involves coercion (choice A), outdated theory (choice B), lack of informed consent (choice C), or nonhuman animals (choice E). (Skill 3)

416. **(C)** The refractory period is part of the sexual response cycle. Studying this element using naturalistic observation would obviously be an unacceptable intrusion into people's privacy. (Using naturalistic observation would also be very awkward for both researchers and participants!) The research methods listed in choices A, B, and D (focus group, interview, and survey) involve asking participants about their sexual response cycle, which is a more realistic alternative to naturalistic observation. Choice E, qualitative analysis, can be used with any research method. (Skill 3)

Perspectives

417. **(E)** The overjustification effect occurs when someone receives a positive reinforcement (behaviorism) for a behavior that he or she is already intrinsically motivated to perform. This reward may result in a decrease in the person's intrinsic motivation for the behavior. Choices A, B, C, and D

all include psychological perspectives and terms from motivation theories, but none of the terms are relevant to the overjustification effect. (Skill 1a)

418. **(D)** Drive reduction theory involves biological drives produced by physiological needs/deficits. Researchers with a biological perspective (biopsychologists) would be most interested in these biological drives and how these drives might explain motivation better than cognitions. The sociocultural (choice A), behaviorism (choice B), evolutionary (choice C), and behavioral-genetics (choice E) perspectives would not be specifically more interested in why drive reduction theory explains behaviors better than does a cognitive-based motivation theory. (Skill 1a)

419. **(B)** Concluding that hunger is almost exclusively a biological process and that cognition ("conscious control") has little impact argues for the primacy of biology over cognitive psychology. Choice A is incorrect because it argues that cognition is a major factor in hunger, which contradicts the statement in the question. Choice C references humanism, which is not relevant to this statement. Choices D and E assume details about the research in the journal article, and these assumptions are not justified. In addition, choice E includes an incorrect statement about fMRI data. (Skill 3)

420. **(C)** Two-factor theory explains that our experience of emotions depends on a combination of how we label an experience (cognitive perspective) and our physiological response (biological perspective). Display rules (choice A), Yerkes-Dodson law (choice B), top-down processing (choice D), and drive reduction theory (choice E) are not theories of emotion. Display rules are related to emotions and how emotions are physically expressed. However, display rules are not inevitably the product of a combination of the cognitive and biological perspectives. (Skill 1a)

CHAPTER 11: PERSONALITY

Stimulus

421. **(B)** Reliability refers to the consistency of a psychological instrument—whether the same respondent gets similar results each time the test is taken. One way to determine the reliability of a personality test is to ask a group of people to take the test repeatedly to see if they get similar results each time. Choices A and C are validity checks, not reliability checks. Choices D and E are factually incorrect. (Skill 3)

422. **(D)** A test is valid to the extent that it actually measures what it was designed to measure. One way to check the validity of a personality test

is to check the results against another personality test that is known to be valid. Choices A and C refer to statistical procedures, which would not help determine validity. Choice B is a reliability check, not a validity check. Choice E is somewhat true—valid psychological instruments should be based on psychological theories. However, checking the underlying theory would not guarantee the validity of a personality test. (Skill 3)

423. **(E)** Trait theorists believe that human personalities can be explained by describing a set of traits, or patterns of thinking and behaving, that are stable across different contexts. This personality test must be a trait theory test because respondents are asked to choose which words in the boxes best describe them and because the test designers must believe that the words people choose align with underlying personality traits. Psychodynamic theory (choice A), projection theory (choice B), reciprocal determinism (choice C), and locus of control (choice D) do not have any obvious connection to this personality test. (Skill 1b)

424. **(C)** This personality test is likely to be reliable; a person is likely to choose the same box each time he or she takes this test. Reliability is a necessary condition for validity. Just because a test is reliable, though, does not mean the test is valid. This personality test is not likely to measure anything about personality because human personalities are complex. Choice A is incorrect because this is not a projective test. Choice B is incorrect because this test is not likely to measure personality after asking people simply to choose 1 out of 9 boxes. Choice D is often true; we should think critically about psychological information shared via social media. However, this choice is an overstatement. Choice E is nearly correct, but valid personality tests do not have to include scenarios. (Skill 3)

Definitions

425. **(A)** Sigmund Freud's theory of personality—psychoanalytic theory— described the influences of unconscious stresses and anxieties on thinking and behavior. Trait (choice B) and reciprocal determinism (choice E) are personality theories. However, they do not use the unconscious in their explanations. Cognitive (choice C) is a psychological perspective, not a personality theory. The psychosexual theory of development (choice D) is related to the psychoanalytic perspective but is not a personality theory. (Skill 1a)

426. **(D)** Psychoanalysts search for unconscious influences on thinking and behavior. The terms mentioned in choice D all relate to the supposed unconscious mind. Choice A lists traits from personality trait theory

tests. The terms shown in choice B are statistical terms used by psychometricians. The acronyms in choice C refer to different personality and aptitude tests. The terms in choice E are related to personality but are not relevant to psychoanalysis. (Skill 1a)

427. **(A)** Freud believed that the unconscious mind is governed by a combination of three different elements: the id, the ego, and the superego. Freud thought that the id expresses animalistic, base impulses like greed and sexual impulses. Oedipal (choice B) is used in other parts of psychodynamic theory but is not the correct choice to this specific question. The ego (choice C) is one of Freud's three elements. However, he thought that the ego negotiates and tries to find compromises between the id and the superego. Psychosexual (choice D) is used in other parts of psychodynamic theory but is not the correct choice to this specific question. The superego (choice E) is another one of Freud's three elements. However, he thought that the superego expresses our moralistic reasoning and conscience. (Skill 1a)

428. **(E)** Freud believed that the unconscious mind was governed by a combination of three different elements: the id, the ego, and the superego. Freud thought that the superego expresses our moralistic reasoning and conscience. The id (choice A) is one of Freud's three elements. However, he thought that it expresses animalistic, base impulses like greed and sexual impulses. Postconventional (choice B) is part of Kohlberg's theory of moral reasoning. The ego (choice C) is another one of Freud's three elements. However, it negotiates and tries to find compromises between the id and the superego. Formal operational (choice D) is a stage in Piaget's cognitive developmental theory. (Skill 1a)

429. **(C)** Freud believed that the unconscious mind was governed by a combination of three different elements: the id, the ego, and the superego. Freud thought that the ego negotiates and tries to find compromises between the id (animalistic impulses) and the superego ("higher self"). The id (choice A) is one of Freud's three elements. However, he thought that the id expresses animalistic, base impulses like greed and sexual impulses. Working memory (choice B) is a part of cognitive/memory psychology theory but is not relevant to a question about psychodynamic theory. The medulla (choice D) is a brain structure, which is not relevant to this question. The superego (choice E) is another one of Freud's three elements. However, he thought that the superego expresses our moralistic reasoning and conscience. (Skill 1a)

430. **(B)** Psychotherapy refers to any kind of psychological treatment of a psychological disorder other than medical interventions. Psychoanalysis is a tradition of psychotherapy based on Freud's theory of the unconscious mind (psychodynamic perspective). Choices A, C, and E are

factually incorrect. Choice D is almost correct, but the reverse is true. Psychotherapy is the overall category, and psychoanalysis is a specific kind of psychotherapy. (Skill 1a)

431. **(D)** The theory behind projective personality tests is based on the idea that people will reveal unconscious beliefs by interpreting open-ended stimuli (like inkblots or visual images). Establishing reliability and validity for projective tests (choice A) are more difficult. Choices B and C are factually incorrect. Both types of tests are "self-report" measures, which means they are based on respondents' self-reports. Therefore, choice E is incorrect. (Skill 1a)

432. **(E)** The Thematic Apperception Test (TAT) asks respondents to "fill in the story" behind a series of visual images (drawings, paintings, and so on). The theory behind this test, like all projective personality tests, is based on the idea that people will reveal their unconscious beliefs by interpreting open-ended pictures. The MBTI—Myers-Briggs Type Indicator (choice A), MMPI—Minnesota Multiphasic Personality Inventory (choice C), and Big Five trait theory test (choice D) are all trait-based personality tests. Note that many researchers feel the MBTI does not meet validity requirements for a trait theory test. IQ—intelligence quotient (choice B) is an intellectual aptitude test. (Skill 1a)

433. **(A)** If a personality test returns different results each time a person takes the test, the test is, by definition, not reliable. A personality test must be reliable (returning consistent results) in order to be valid since personality is supposed to be a relatively stable, unchanging pattern of thinking and behaving. Since reliability is a necessary condition for validity, choices B and C are incorrect. Choices D and E are incorrect because if a researcher knows that a test is not reliable, no further evidence is needed in order to determine the test's validity. (Skill 1a)

434. **(C)** Personality tests must be reliable (return consistent results) in order to be valid since personality is supposed to be a relatively stable, unchanging pattern of thinking and behaving. In this way, reliability is a necessary (but not sufficient) condition for validity. Therefore, choice A is incorrect. Both reliability and validity must be established by empirical results. So, choices B and D are therefore incorrect. Choice E is incorrect because it is the opposite of the correct choice. A test must be reliable for it to be considered valid, not vice versa. (Skill 1a)

435. **(D)** The phrase in the question indicates that for a test to be valid, it must first be reliable ("a necessary condition"). Even though a test is reliable, other evidence is still needed to establish its validity ("a sufficient condition"). Choices A and C communicate inaccurate information about how

validity is analyzed. Choices B and E inaccurately describe the "necessary but not sufficient" element of the statement in the question. (Skill 1a)

436. **(C)** The MMPI (Minnesota Multiphasic Personality Inventory) is an empirically derived (based on evidence from the past) personality test that is well established by researchers to be reliable and valid. The MBTI—Myers-Briggs Type Indicator (choice A) is based on Jungian personality archetypes, and researchers debate the reliability and validity of this instrument. Choice B, Kohlberg theory test, refers to Lawrence Kohlberg, who studied moral development, not personality. Rorschach theory test (choice D) and Thematic Apperception Test (choice E) refer to projective personality tests, which are difficult to confirm in reliability and validity tests. (Skill 1a)

437. **(B)** This choice lists the Big Five personality traits, which are the most supported set of personality traits (based on empirical data and techniques such as factor analysis). Choice A lists the dichotomies of the Myers-Briggs Type Indicator (MBTI) test, which is not well supported by research. Choice C lists the elements of Freud's conception of the unconscious mind. Choice D lists terms related to personality theory but are not elements of a trait theory test. Choice E lists elements of Bandura's reciprocal determinism theory. (Skill 1a)

438. **(E)** Trait theorists believe that our personalities, which are ways of thinking/feeling that are consistent across contexts, can be explained by sets of traits or characteristics. These characteristics are useful categories for describing different aspects of personality. Not all (or many) trait theorists use Jung's theory (choice A). Choice B is a better description of Freud's theory of the unconscious. Aspects of choice C are true; many trait theorists research trait theory across different cultures. However, the statement in this choice does not describe the underlying assumption behind trait theory. Choice D describes IQ testing and theory. (Skill 1a)

439. **(A)** Bandura's theory of reciprocal determinism explained our personalities through the interactions among three elements: what we've learned from past experiences, our internal feelings and cognitive interpretations of events, and the environmental influences within which we are acting. Choices B and D are not personality theories. Choice C is a psychological perspective. Choice E is not related to the three elements mentioned in the stem of the question. (Skill 1a)

440. **(C)** The statistical process of factor analysis can determine whether a set of items on a personality test all actually measure the same personality trait. The statistical methods mentioned in choice A (measures of central tendency) and choice B (inferential statistics) might be involved when a

researcher investigates the validity of a personality test. However, these methods are not uniquely suited to this process. (Measures of central tendency and inferential statistics are involved in almost every quantitative psychological study.) Qualitative analysis (choice D) refers to research that analyzes words rather than numbers. This technique does not apply to this question. The double-blind technique (choice E) is a detail from research methodology, not a statistical technique. (Skill 3)

Scenarios

441. **(E)** The Thematic Apperception Test (TAT) asks respondents to "fill in the story" behind a series of visual images (drawings, paintings, and so on). The theory behind this test, like all projective personality tests, is based on the idea that people will reveal their unconscious beliefs by interpreting open-ended pictures. Obviously basing a hiring decision on a test that depends on revealing the unconscious mind isn't the best policy. The MBTI—Myers-Briggs Type Indicator (choice A), MMPI—Minnesota Multiphasic Personality Inventory (choice C), and Big Five (choice D) are all trait-based personality tests. These tests may or may not be useful during a hiring decision, but they are not the projective test described in the question. Note that many researchers feel the MBTI does not meet validity requirements for a trait theory test. An IQ—Intelligence Quotient—test (choice B) is an intellectual aptitude test, not the projective test described in the question. (Skill 1b)

442. **(D)** Since each of the participants received a different result on day 2 than each of them did on day 1, this personality test is not reliable. Choice A is incorrect because a personality test cannot be valid if it is not reliable. Nothing indicates that the research involves a projective test (choice B) or needs to use factor analysis (choice E). Choice C is incorrect because personality is defined as a relatively stable set of traits over time, especially over two days. (Skill 1b)

443. **(B)** Psychoanalysts use the technique of free association (speaking whatever comes to mind, especially in response to a list of single word cues) to help clients reveal unconscious desires and conflicts. Reciprocal determinism (choice A) is Bandura's personality theory. Introspection (choice C) and functionalism (choice E) are historical references to earlier psychology theories and techniques. If someone has an internal locus (choice D), he or she has the sense of being in control of what happens to him or her. (Skill 1b)

444. **(A)** Displacement occurs when we unknowingly misapply our strong feelings (such as anger) on another target instead of the actual person

or situation causing the strong feelings. Regression (choice B), denial (choice C), dissociation (choice D), and reaction formation (choice E) are all defense mechanisms that do not help explain W. M. Arthur's angry behaviors. (Skill 1b)

445. **(B)** Regression occurs when we unconsciously seek stress-relieving behaviors that we used when we were children, such as holding comfort objects and thumb sucking. Projection (choice A), denial (choice C), dissociation (choice D), and reaction formation (choice E) are all defense mechanisms that do not help explain Ms. Humpeding's stress-relief behaviors. (Skill 1b)

446. **(C)** Priming research indicates that stimuli that are presented too quickly for our conscious minds to perceive may still have some influence on our later attitudes. This means that there may be an unconscious mind, or at least a level of our consciousness that we are not aware of. Free association (choice A) and dream analysis (choice D) relate to Freudian psychoanalytic theory but are not empirical evidence for the unconscious mind. Trait theory (choice B) and reliability (choice E) do not relate to the unconscious mind. (Skill 1b)

447. **(E)** Carl Jung's ideas about the collective unconscious might be interesting to Frida because Jung thought that every person responds to certain symbols. Jung believed we are all connected to the "collective unconscious mind" where these symbols reside. The big five (choice A) refers to the personality traits that have been empirically validated. These would not be useful for Frida's paintings. Reciprocal determinism (choice B) references Bandura's overall theory of personality, which is not likely to help Frida's art. Structuralism (choice C) and social facilitation (choice D) do not relate to personality and are not related to symbols or other concepts that help answer Frida's question. (Skill 1b)

448. **(D)** A valid test measures what it is designed to measure. In this scenario, the test is designed to measure employee productivity. The corporation president wants to investigate whether the test results are accurate by testing current employees. Reliability (choice A) refers to the consistency of test results. Accuracy (choice B) is a general term. However, the correct choice—validity (choice D)—is a better, more specific choice for this scenario. Correlation (choice C) is a statistical technique. Generalization (choice E) is a term from psychological research referring to whether findings from a specific sample can be generalized to the population. (Skill 1b)

449. **(A)** Reliability refers to the consistency of test results. Since personality is supposed to be relatively stable over time, personality tests should return

similar results each time. Trait theory (choice B) assumes that person-alities can be described by categorizing personalities into a set of traits. Validity (choice C) is an indication of whether or not a test measures what it intends to measure. Inferential statistics (choice D) and descrip-tive statistics (choice E) are different kinds of statistical analysis. They might be useful in research into personality tests but are not specifically relevant to Agnes's experience. (Skill 1b)

450. **(D)** Bandura's theory of reciprocal determinism explains our personali-ties through the interactions among three elements: what we've learned from past experiences, our internal feelings and cognitive interpretations of events, and the environmental influences within which we are acting. Collective unconscious (choice A) and psychosexual stages (choice E) would not be useful in the conversation with your father because they rely on the theory of the unconscious mind, which is not relevant to your father's objections. Trait theory (choice B) may be the theory that your father objects to due to its tendency to reduce personality to "numbers." Behaviorism (choice C) is a psychological perspective that would not effectively respond to your father's argument in this scenario. (Skill 1c)

451. **(C)** The process described in the scenario is an empirical process: using evidence from the past (in this case, data from the field test) to develop the test. Nothing in the scenario implies that the test is projective (choice A). A projective test involves asking people to interpret ambiguous stimuli (such as inkblots or open-ended images) that may reveal the unconscious mind. Nothing in the scenario indicates that Professor Magpyr uses the humanistic perspective (choice B). The researchers may have used correla-tional techniques (choice D), but nothing in the scenario implies that this is inevitable. There is no guarantee that the Magpyr Personality Test uses the big five personality traits (choice E). In fact, these are very commonly used personality traits for empirically derived tests, but using other traits is possible. (Skill 1b)

452. **(B)** Freud believed that the unconscious mind was governed by the combination of three different elements: the id, the superego, and the ego. He claimed that the id expresses animalistic, base impulses like greed and sexual impulses. Freud stated that the superego expresses moralistic reasoning and conscience. Finally, he believed that the ego negotiates and tries to find compromises between the id and the superego. These three elements are like the speaker's concepts of selfishness, moral conscience, and compromise. Choices A, C, D, and E all list terms that are not similar or relevant to the speaker's literary argument. (Skill 1c)

Names

453. **(E)** Freud established the psychodynamic perspective based on the idea that thinking and behavior are significantly influenced by repressed anxieties/stresses in the unconscious mind. None of the psychological theories listed in choices A, B, C, and D are associated with Freud. In fact, collectivism and individualism theory (choice D) is neither a personality theory nor a perspective. (Skill 1a)

454. **(A)** Albert Bandura's theory of reciprocal determinism explains our personalities through the interactions among three elements: what we've learned from past experiences, our internal feelings and cognitive interpretations of events, and the environmental influences within which we are acting. Abraham Maslow (choice B) is associated with humanistic personality theories. Gordon Allport (choice C) is associated with trait theories of personality. Carl Jung (choice D) and Karen Horney (choice E) were both neo-Freudians. (Skill 1a)

455. **(C)** One of the techniques that trait theorist Gordon Allport used to research personality was organizing hundreds of words from the dictionary that are associated with personality. Albert Bandura (choice A) is associated with reciprocal determinism theory. Choices B, D, and E are all researchers associated with psychodynamic theory. (Skill 1a)

456. **(D)** Humanistic psychologists like Carl Rogers were interested in human growth and potential. Rogers may have been interested in a personality test that examines an individual's internal image of who he or she wants to be versus who he or she actually is because that difference might help a person become his or her ideal self. Choices A and E describe trait theory personality tests, not tests that would interest humanistic psychologists like Rogers. Choice B describes a test that would interest psychodynamic therapists. Choice C is a version of the definition of personality, not a description of a personality test. (Skill 1a)

Research Methods

457. **(B)** The most likely technique this researcher would use is correlation—using a scatter plot to look at the relationship between scores on the new personality test with the big five personality test. This analysis could determine whether scores on one test predict scores on the other test. The scenario described is not an experiment (choice A). It does not contain an experimental group, a control group, or an independent variable. Inferential statistics (choice C) and descriptive statistics (choice D) are categories of statistics. These might be useful during the analysis, but

correlation is a more specific and correct choice. Factor analysis (choice E) is often used during personality test development but would not be useful in the scenario described in this question. (Skill 3)

458. **(A)** The dependent variable in this hypothesis is the results on personality tests, and the independent variable is sleep deprivation. The operational definition of the dependent variable is a way to measure the dependent variable. In this case, the only correct choice is a trait theory personality test. Choices B, C, and D refer to the independent variable. Choice E refers to sampling procedures. (Skill 3)

459. **(E)** This is the only choice that uses the big five personality traits as the independent variable. Remember that the independent variable causes changes in the dependent variable, which is the number of friends at age 50. The hypotheses in choices A, C, and D use the big five personality traits as a dependent variable. Choice B describes a correlational study without either a specific independent or specific dependent variable. (Skill 3)

Perspectives

460. **(E)** Bandura's theory of reciprocal determinism explains our personalities through the interactions among three elements: what we've learned from past experiences (behaviorism), our internal feelings and cognitive interpretations of events (cognitive), and the biological influences upon our behavior. Choices A and C list psychological perspectives. However, these lists are not as close to Bandura's theory as is the list in choice E. Choice B lists historical psychological perspectives along with the more current term, empiricism. Choice D lists three psychological perspectives that are related to the area of biological psychology, none of which are closely related to Bandura's theory. (Skill 1a)

461. **(D)** The psychodynamic perspective is a tradition of psychotherapy based on Freud's theory of the unconscious mind, which involves the superego and defense mechanisms. Choice A references trait theory. Choices B and C are related to research about personality tests (how researchers establish the validity of personality tests). Choice E references Bandura's theory of reciprocal determinism and locus of control theory. (Skill 1a)

462. **(B)** Cognitive psychologists investigate how we remember events and mentally interpret what happens around us. They also study how these cognitions impact our behaviors. These researchers would be interested in investigating how our memories of stories relate to personality traits. Choices A and C are psychological perspectives, but these perspectives would not be specifically interested in how we recall stories. Choices D

and E are psychological perspectives. However, neither psychodynamic theory nor humanism are specifically related to the research mentioned in the question. (Skill 1a)

CHAPTER 12: ABNORMAL PSYCHOLOGY

Stimulus

463. **(D)** Identical twin studies, like the finding described in this choice, indicate that genetics play a significant role in schizophrenia. This finding contradicts one of the claims on Dr. Xenu's poster: "Environmental origins of all psychological disorders." Choices A and E argue for primarily environmental origins of psychological disorders, which does not contradict the claims on the poster. Choice B is not relevant to this situation. Choice C is incorrect information about the DSM. (Skill 3)

464. **(B)** Psychologists and psychiatrists use several criteria in order to determine whether behaviors may be symptomatic of a psychological disorder. Three common criteria used in this process are whether the behavior is common (atypical), whether it is an obstacle in the person's life (maladaptive), and whether it is considered disturbing in that culture. Choices A, C, D, and E do not include specific criteria used in this process of diagnosing psychological disorders. (Skill 3)

465. **(C)** Over time, the psychological disorders listed in the DSM have changed. Many diagnoses (including homosexuality) have been removed as research and cultural attitudes have evolved. Choices A and B are inaccurate statements about the DSM and how diagnoses are added or removed. Choice D is incorrect because, although psychological medications are essential in alleviating the symptoms of many psychological disorders, psychoactive drugs don't "cure" psychological disorders. Choice E is completely inaccurate about the purpose of the DSM. One of the major purposes of the DSM is to list diagnostic labels for the medical community. (Skill 1b)

Definitions

466. **(C)** In the context of psychological disorders, a maladaptive behavior is an obstacle in a person's life that gets in the way of daily living. Psychologists and psychiatrists use several criteria in order to determine whether behaviors may be symptomatic of a psychological disorder. Three common criteria used in this process are whether the behavior is common (atypical), whether it is an obstacle in the person's life (maladaptive), and whether it is considered disturbing in that culture. Therefore,

choice A (the third criterion) and choice D (atypical, the first criterion) are incorrect. The term *maladaptive* doesn't have anything to do with a person's ability to adapt. So, choice B is not correct. The term *maladaptive* also doesn't have anything to do with the term *malady*, making choice E incorrect. (Skill 1a)

467. **(E)** The DSM listed homosexuality as a psychological disorder from 1952 through 1973. Psychologists during this era mistakenly believed that homosexuality was a set of disordered behaviors that should be treated to improve the lives of their clients. Research eventually led psychologists to conclude that homosexuality should be removed from the DSM. Choices A, B, C, and D are inaccurate descriptions of how psychological thinking evolved about homosexuality. (Skill 1a)

468. **(A)** The medical model describes the causes, impacts, and treatments of psychological disorders using terminology from medicine and medical doctors. Other choices list terms related to psychological disorders but are not specifically associated with the medical model. Choice B lists some criteria used to determine whether behaviors may be related to psychological disorders. Choice C contains psychological perspectives. Choice D lists terms connected to the biopsychosocial model. Choice E contains different categories of psychological disorders. (Skill 1a)

469. **(B)** Epigenetics and diathesis-stress model both refer to interactions between the environment and genetic predispositions, which are key components of the biopsychosocial model. Other choices list terms related to psychological disorders but are not specifically associated with the biopsychosocial model. Choice A lists different categories of psychological disorders. Choice C contains terms from cognitive psychological research. Choice D refers to two psychological perspectives. The terms in choice E are most relevant to motivation theories. (Skill 1a)

470. **(D)** The medical model describes the causes, impacts, and treatment of psychological disorders using terminology (like *cure, diagnosis,* and *symptoms*) from medicine and medical doctors. The biopsychosocial model, choice A, explains some aspects of psychological disorders. However, therapists using the biopsychosocial model are less likely to use the terms listed in the question. The classical model (choice B) and the treatment model (choice E) do not explain psychological disorders. The psychodynamic model, choice C, refers to a psychological perspective. It is not a model explaining psychological disorders. (Skill 1a)

471. **(A)** Epigenetics and the diathesis-stress model both refer to interactions between the environment and genetic predispositions, which are key components of the biopsychosocial model. The biopsychosocial model

of psychological disorders focuses on the interactions among biological, psychological, and social influences when dealing with issues related to psychological disorders. The behavior genetics model (choice B) and the humanistic model (choice C) refer to psychological perspectives. Note that the behavior genetics perspective is similar in some ways to the biopsychosocial model, but behavior genetics doesn't focus specifically on disorders. The medical model, choice D, is a model of psychological disorders. However, it is not specifically interested in either epigenetics or the diathesis-stress model. The cognitive-behavior model, choice E, is a common combination of treatment orientations but is not relevant to the situation described in the question. (Skill 1a)

472. **(D)** The DSM-5 is used by mental health care practitioners to identify which labels should be used for which psychological disorders. The DSM-5 lists symptomatic behaviors for each disorder and provides the most current diagnostic label for each. These labels are used for insurance and other official purposes. The descriptions in choices A, B, C, and E imply that the focus of the DSM-5 is more comprehensive than describing psychological disorders. (Skill 1a)

473. **(C)** Insanity is used only in the context of the court system; it is a legal term used by lawyers and others during the trial process. In the context of psychological research and mental health care, the term *psychological disorders* is used. Choices A and E imply that psychological disorders and insanities are subcategories of each other, which is incorrect. Choices B and D are incorrect because they imply that the DSM is only a historical document and that the difference between the terms is related to the environment or to genetics. (Skill 1a)

474. **(B)** Researchers often investigate whether different practitioners (anyone who uses the DSM) choose the same diagnosis for the same set of symptoms. In fact, this is one way to study the reliability of the DSM. Choices A and C describe statistical analyses that aren't relevant to the context of the DSM. Choices D and E describe issues that aren't relevant to the DSM. (Skill 1a)

475. **(E)** Researchers often field test diagnoses in the DSM by giving the same descriptions of behaviors to different psychologists/psychiatrists in order to determine whether they assign the same diagnostic labels. Choice A describes potentially interesting research, but it is not related to reliability issues. Choices B and C describe research studies that do not follow ethical standards for research. Choice D is a somewhat random collection of research method terminology. (Skill 3)

476. **(D)** Psychological disorders, in general, are not usually associated with cases of violent crime; most crimes are not associated with mental health issues. In fact, most people who are diagnosed with psychological disorders are never associated with violent crime. Choices A, B, and E are factually incorrect statements. Choice C includes some correct information (for example, *insanity* is a legal term). However, the rest of this choice describes incorrect information about psychological disorders and violence. (Skill 1a)

477. **(C)** About 9–10% of Americans are diagnosed with some kind of depressive disorder each year. Social anxiety disorders (choice A), post-traumatic stress disorder (choice B), antisocial personality disorder (choice D), and bipolar disorder (choice E) are all diagnosed at a far lower rate. (Skill 1a)

478. **(A)** Research indicates that the first symptoms of most psychological disorders usually occur before age 25. Obviously, many instances occur of symptoms appearing at different ages. Choices B, C, D, and E are factually incorrect statements about how and when symptoms of psychological disorders usually begin. (Skill 1a)

479. **(B)** Generalized anxiety disorder is a diagnostic label in the DSM. It is a type of anxiety disorder. The term *free floating* describes the feeling of anxiety experienced by some people who are diagnosed with generalized anxiety disorder. Their anxiety isn't attached to anything specific; they just feel anxious. These terms are not likely to be used with depressive disorders (choice A), dissociative disorders (choice C), schizophrenia (choice D), and phobias (choice E). (Skill 1a)

480. **(A)** The most commonly diagnosed psychological disorder is major depressive disorder. This is what some people think of when they say a person has been diagnosed with depression. Bipolar disorder is less commonly diagnosed. However, it is categorized as a depressive disorder because it includes two phases—a manic phase and a depressed phase. Choices B, D, and E all include diagnostic labels, but these labels are not categorized as depressive disorders. Note that antisocial personality disorder in choice E is more properly known as antisocial personality disorder. Choice C is incorrect because reactive disorder is not an actual diagnostic label. (Skill 1a)

481. **(B)** All the somatic disorders (like conversion disorder and illness anxiety disorder) share the same characteristic: the symptoms of the disorders are experienced and perceived physically (as pain, a loss of physical capabilities, or similar). Choice A lists some parts of neural anatomy, which is not relevant to somatic disorders. Choice C references mood and anxiety disorders, which are not relevant to somatic disorders. Choice D is

describing dissociative disorders. Choice E describes two symptoms that are not typically associated with any of the somatic disorders. (Skill 1a)

482. **(C)** Deficits in serotonin in the brain are commonly associated with mood/depression disorders. Acetylcholine (choice A), glutamate (choice B), and gamma-aminobutyric acid/GABA (choice D) are neurotransmitters not typically associated with mood/depression disorders. Selective Serotonin Reuptake Inhibitors (SSRIs), choice E, can be helpful in treating depression since SSRIs help the brain use available serotonin more efficiently. (Skill 1a)

483. **(D)** People who experience symptoms of depressive disorders often report that extremely stressful events occurred before they started experiencing these depressive symptoms. Depressive disorders are not caused exclusively by either genetics (choices A and E) or environmental stresses (choice C). Environmental stresses do not alter genetic predispositions (choice B). (Skill 1a)

484. **(E)** Negative symptoms of schizophrenia involve symptoms that are absences—a lack of emotions, a lack of typical movements/reactions, and so on. Choices A, B, C, and D all describe what may be positive symptoms of schizophrenia. Positive symptoms are those that are present (added), such as hallucinations, disturbances in speech, inappropriate emotional reactions, or delusions. (Skill 1a)

485. **(A)** The DSM groups psychological disorders with similar impacts on behavior into overall categories. The different depressive disorders listed in the DSM impact an individual's mood and emotions in different ways. The DSM is not organized chronologically (choice B), based on a yearly conference (choice D), or due to the neurotransmitters associated with the disorder (choice E). Many disorders listed within a category may have similar recommended treatments, choice C, but that is not the main organizational scheme of the DSM. (Skill 1a)

Scenarios

486. **(C)** Reliability is a characteristic of any psychological instrument that describes the ability of that instrument to produce consistent results over time. If this new version of the DSM is highly reliable, psychiatrists should choose the same diagnostic label for the same descriptions of symptoms. Validity, choice A, is related to reliability. A psychological instrument must be reliable in order to be considered valid. However, reliability is the most accurate term for this scenario. Accuracy (choice B), authenticity (choice D), and consistency (choice E) are words that seem similar to the term reliability. However, reliability is the most

accurate term for this idea in the context of psychological research and practice. (Skill 1b)

487. **(B)** Dissociative disorders often involve people dissociating from their previous lives and identities. This may involve abandoning a previous identity and moving to a different city, seemingly developing new identities or personalities, or experiencing other disruptions in a person's identity. Mr. Oleron's behaviors are not depressive (choice A), anxiety (choice C), schizophrenic (choice D), or somatic (choice E). (Skill 1b)

488. **(C)** Depression symptoms that include at least one period of mania, which is a period of intense activity accompanied by behaviors like reckless spending and risk taking, are indicative of bipolar depression. Mr. Vimes's initial symptoms were typical of major depression, choice A. Somatic depression, choice B, is not a diagnostic label. Antisocial personality disorder, choice D, does not fit Mr. Vimes's behaviors. Post-traumatic stress disorder, choice E, is an anxiety disorder related to trauma (either long-term trauma or an acute traumatic event). However, trauma is not present in the scenario. (Skill 1b)

489. **(D)** People who are diagnosed with major depressive disorder commonly express self-defeating cognitions: thought patterns that reinforce their depressed thinking and behavior. Three common characteristics of self-defeating cognitions are that they are stable (the feeling that these thought patterns will last forever), global (the thought patterns affect everything in the person's life), and internal (the individual is responsible for the cognitions). Choice A lists three categories of psychological disorders. Choice B lists three of the big five personality traits. Choice C lists the three stages of the stress cycle. Choice E are three elements of Sternberg's triarchic theory of love. (Skill 1b)

490. **(E)** People who suffer from panic disorder experience intense, terrifying episodes of anxiety that feel like an emergency medical situation. They are often convinced that they will die and/or that they are having a heart attack or some other emergency physical problem. Some people who are diagnosed with specific phobias (choice A) or with generalized anxiety disorder (choice B) may also experience panic attacks. However, no details in Mr. Lipwig's description hint at those diagnoses. Post-traumatic stress disorder (choice C) and somatic symptom disorder (choice D) are not relevant to the panic attack described in the scenario. (Skill 1b)

491. **(A)** Behaviors typical of Obsessive-Compulsive Disorder (OCD) involve recurring unwanted thoughts and recurring unwanted behaviors that the individual feels compelled to perform. Ms. Dinwiddie's repetitive checking of her desk and her out-of-proportion reactions to her colleagues may

cause the company counselor to talk with her about OCD. Panic disorder (choice B), generalized anxiety disorder (choice C), social anxiety disorder (choice D), and bipolar disorder (choice E) do not involve repetitive checking or obsessive orderliness. (Skill 1b)

492. **(B)** Dissociative Identity Disorder (DID) is a controversial diagnosis involving clients who express additional personalities, often after experiencing severe trauma and sometimes during the process of therapy. Somatoform disorder, choice A, describes disorders that involve physical symptoms. Schizophrenia (choice C) and schizotypal personality disorder (choice D) refer to different diagnoses relating to a split from reality (schizophrenia), not multiple personalities. Dissociative amnesia with fugue, choice E, is also a dissociative disorder. However, it involves an individual abandoning his or her previous identity and often physically moving to a different place, often in a confused and disoriented state. (Skill 1b)

493. **(D)** Dissociative Identity Disorder (DID) is a controversial diagnosis involving clients who express additional personalities, often after experiencing severe trauma and sometimes during the process of therapy. Schizophrenia, choice A, involves hallucinations or delusions, not the development of multiple personalities. Social anxiety disorder, choice B, is an anxiety disorder associated with social situations. Obsessive-compulsive disorder (choice C) and antisocial personality disorder (choice E) are accurate psychological disorders but are not relevant to the scenario in the question. (Skill 1b)

494. **(C)** Individuals who are eventually diagnosed with antisocial personality disorder often have a long history of disturbing behaviors, including violence, theft, and other socially unacceptable compulsive behaviors. Post-traumatic stress disorder, choice A, is not a psychological disorder that fits the description in the question well. Dissociative identity disorder, choice B, describes individuals who develop multiple personalities. Bipolar disorder (choice D) and schizophrenia (choice E) do not fit the symptoms listed in the scenario. (Skill 1b)

495. **(E)** People who suffer from bulimia nervosa sometimes avoid eating. However, they sometimes binge on a large amount of food, which is then followed by a purge—using vomiting, laxatives, or excessive exercise. They feel compelled to get rid of the calories they ate. People with anorexia nervosa, choice A, try to avoid eating when possible. Those with binge-eating disorder, choice B, binge on food at times but do not purge. Obsessive-compulsive disorder, choice C, is an anxiety disorder and is not specific to eating behavior. Fugue disorder, choice D, is a dissociative disorder and is not specific to eating behavior. (Skill 1b)

496. **(B)** Eating disorders like anorexia nervosa may vary widely among cultures because eating disorders are influenced by cultural pressures about what body types are socially desirable. Schizophrenia (choice A), major depressive disorder (choice C), bipolar disorder (choice D), and Alzheimer's disease (choice E) are highly influenced by genetic predispositions, so they are less likely to vary among countries. (Skill 1b)

497. **(A)** A conversion disorder often involves an individual experiencing a stressful, traumatic event followed by an unexplained severe physical symptom (such as blindness, paralysis, or other major physical deficit). Illness anxiety disorder, choice B, is a type of somatic disorder. However, it involves people interpreting symptoms of common illnesses as symptomatic of extremely serious diseases. Schizotypal personality disorder, choice C, dissociative disorder (choice D) and catatonic schizophrenia (choice E) are not applicable to the scenario in the question. (Skill 1b)

498. **(B)** Research has established that there seems to be an excess of dopamine receptors in the brains of people diagnosed with schizophrenia. This research indicates that the brains of those with schizophrenia may overrespond to dopamine, and this may be connected to hallucinations and delusions. Generalized anxiety disorder (choice A), conversion disorder (choice C), dissociative amnesia (choice D), and anorexia nervosa (choice E) are not known to be connected to either dopamine underactivity or overactivity. (Skill 1b)

Names

499. **(D)** Freud established the psychodynamic psychological perspective, which explains thinking and behavior in the context of unconscious conflicts and stresses. Freud would have explained psychological disorders using this perspective. Choices A and B describe the influences of biopsychological, cultural, and cognitive perspectives. Choices C and E are incorrect statements. (Skill 1a)

500. **(C)** David Rosenhan executed the thud study, which involved psychology professors and graduate students pretending to have psychological disorders and getting themselves admitted to psychiatric hospitals. The study indicated that psychological labels strongly influenced how these people were treated, even after they stopped feigning any symptoms. Carl Jung (choice A) and Sigmund Freud (choice B) were not specifically interested in the influence of labels. Philippe Pinel (choice D) was an early advocate for the humane treatment of the mentally ill. Aaron Beck (choice E) developed cognitive therapies used in the treatment of depression. (Skill 1a)

501. **(D)** Philippe Pinel worked in the early 1800s to convince others that people who suffered from psychological disorders deserved empathy and humane treatment and shouldn't be locked away in asylums and forgotten. Albert Ellis (choice A) and Sigmund Freud (choice B) influenced the treatment of psychological disorders but not the specific issue of humane treatment. David Rosenhan, choice C, researched how psychological labels influence treatment. John Watson, choice E, was a behaviorist, not a clinical psychologist. (Skill 1a)

Research Methods

502. **(E)** Rosenhan's thud study investigated whether the fact that individuals were labeled as having psychological disorders would influence how they were treated by medical professionals even when the individuals were free of symptoms. The study involved psychology professors and graduate students pretending to have psychological disorders and getting themselves admitted to psychiatric hospitals. Then the participants stopped exhibiting those symptoms. The study indicated that the psychological labels strongly influenced how these people were treated, even after they stopped feigning any symptoms. Choices A, B, C, and D all incorrectly identify independent variables or do not correctly describe the study. (Skill 3)

503. **(A)** Reliability is the degree to which a psychological instrument (such as the DSM) produces consistent results (such as the same label being used for the same symptoms across a group of psychiatrists). Choice B is an attempt to measure validity, not reliability. Choices C and D are somewhat random collections of psychological terms. Choice E is a generic description of the experimental method. (Skill 3)

504. **(B)** Random assignment is used by researchers to make sure their groups (often the experimental group and the control group) are balanced by randomly assigning participants to each group. Choice A misuses the terms "independent variable" and "dependent variable." Choice C refers to random sampling. Choices D and E do not use research methodology correctly. (Skill 3)

505. **(D)** Observing video footage without interfering with these individuals or trying to add or measure changes in variables in any way is an example of a naturalistic observational study. It is not a case study, choice A, because multiple individuals are involved. It is not an experiment, choice B, because an independent variable is not used. Inferential statistics, choice C, is a statistical method and not a research method. Correlation, choice E, involves determining the relationship between two variables, which is not described in this scenario. (Skill 3)

506. **(C)** In a double-blind study, neither the participants nor the researcher doing the data analysis knows which participants are in the experimental group and which participants are in the control group. Choices A, D, and E partly accurately describe different forms of a single-blind study. Choice B does not use psychological terms accurately. (Skill 3)

Perspectives

507. **(D)** Since schizophrenia is highly influenced by genetic predisposition and brain chemistry, biological research is most likely to produce useful results about schizophrenia. Humanism (choice A), cognitive research (choice B), behaviorism (choice C), and sociocultural research (choice E) are not as likely to produce useful research because they are not likely to produce insights about either genetics or brain chemistry. (Skill 1a)

508. **(E)** Offering a reward for behavior (behaviorism) gives positive reinforcement to individuals who are willing to put themselves in the anxiety-producing situations that cause their phobias. Researchers interested in the sociocultural perspective (choice A), humanism (choice B), the cognitive perspective (choice C), and the biological perspective (choice D) are not likely to try to treat phobias using positive reinforcements. (Skill 1c)

509. **(B)** One of the most common treatments for major depression involves cognitive interventions. These interventions help individuals change the ways they think about and remember events in their lives. Individuals with schizophrenia (choice A), antisocial personality disorder (choice C), dissociative identity disorder (choice D), and bipolar disorder (choice E) are less likely to respond to cognitive interventions. (Skill 1c)

510. **(E)** Case studies of people suffering from bulimia from around the world would be of interest to sociocultural psychologists. These international case studies might reveal the influences of different cultures on the cause and process of this psychological eating disorder. Researchers in behaviorism (choice A), the cognitive perspective (choice B), humanism (choice C), and the biological perspective (choice D) would not be specifically interested in case studies that contrast international influences on bulimia. (Skill 1c)

CHAPTER 13: TREATMENT OF PSYCHOLOGICAL DISORDERS

Stimulus

511. **(C)** Rational Emotive Behavior Therapy (REBT) is a cognitive therapy technique developed by Albert Ellis. Ellis believed that illness stems from

irrational thinking. Thus, he believed that self-defeating and illogical thoughts have to be directly confronted. When a person confronts the negative ways he or she has been thinking, those negative thoughts can be replaced by more adaptive, healthier ways of viewing the world. Active listening, choice A, is a humanistic technique advanced by Carl Rogers. It involves a restating and clarifying of what a client says. This approach creates an environment based on acceptance, empathy, and genuineness, which are necessary for growth. Free association, choice B, is a psychoanalytic technique developed by Freud. A session typically begins with an open-ended question, followed by the patient speaking whatever comes to mind. Counterconditioning, choice D, is a behavioral technique that involves continual exposure to an anxiety-producing stimulus so that the fear is eventually replaced with a new response. Eye Movement Desensitization and Reprocessing (EMDR), choice E, is a controversial therapy technique where a person imagines a traumatic experience while watching the therapist's finger move. (Skill 1b)

Definitions

512. **(E)** A therapist with an eclectic approach uses a number of approaches and techniques to treat an individual's specific concerns. Thus, Megan is eclectic because her approach includes providing unconditional positive regard (humanistic), focusing on changing illogical thinking (cognitive), and role playing with the goal of learning more adaptive ways of behaving (behavioral). Emily, choice A, focuses on a psychodynamic approach to therapy. Shannon, choice B, provides an example of a humanistic therapeutic approach. Jake, choice C, uses systematic desensitization, which is derived from the principles of behaviorism. Jill, choice D, refers to changing thinking ("cognitive restructuring"), which is a focus of the cognitive perspective. (Skill 1b)

513. **(D)** Repression is a central concept to the psychoanalytic approach. Psychoanalysts believe that trauma is pushed from the consciousness to protect the individual from anxiety. Such memories may be out of awareness but still exist and direct our behavior. Repressed trauma can be a source of mental disorders. To treat illness, the psychoanalyst must uncover what has been repressed. Resistance, choice A, occurs during psychoanalysis when the patient changes a subject during free association as a way of protecting himself or herself. Free association, choice B, is the primary tool of psychoanalysis. As a person freely speaks in response to an open-ended question, the psychoanalyst looks for clues into what has been repressed. Active listening, choice C, is a humanistic technique that involves rephrasing a client's feelings. Transference, choice E, is a

psychoanalytic concept. A therapist expects that during a session, the patient may transfer his or her feelings toward a family member, for example, onto the therapist. (Skill 1a)

514. **(D)** Psychoanalysis, which is an insight therapy with the goal of uncovering unconscious trauma, was developed by Sigmund Freud. Aversive conditioning (choice A) and flooding (choice E) are both based on behavioral principles. Active listening, choice B, is a technique used by humanistic psychologists. Cognitive restructuring, choice C, which refers to the process of challenging and changing illogical thoughts, is a technique used by cognitive psychologists. (Skill 1a)

515. **(E)** During free association, a person freely speaks in response to an open-ended question. The psychoanalyst looks for clues into what has been repressed and that may have led to the current issue. Choice A is an example of active listening, which is a tool of humanistic therapy. Choice B reflects systematic desensitization and is based on behavioral principles. Antidepressants, choice C, are most likely prescribed by a psychiatrist. Choice D reflects the approach of a cognitive psychologist. (Skill 1a)

516. **(B)** Transference is an expected aspect of psychoanalysis. It occurs when a patient redirects emotions or feelings onto the therapist, whether these feelings are positive or negative. When transference occurs, the psychoanalyst has an opportunity to help the patient gain insight into his or her repressed feelings. A token economy, choice A, is a behavioral therapeutic approach based on operant conditioning. Client-centered therapy, choice C, describes the approach of humanistic psychologists. Resistance, choice D, is a psychoanalytic concept that describes when a patient quickly changes the subject during free association as a way to protect sensitive information. Exposure therapy, choice E, is based on behavioral principles of extinction. A patient is repeatedly exposed to an object as a way to reduce his or her fear of the object. (Skill 1a)

517. **(A)** Client-centered therapy is based on the humanistic principle of providing others with unconditional positive regard. Carl Rogers suggested that it is necessary to receive this acceptance in order to develop positive self-concept. Psychoanalysis, choice B, is based on the Freudian concept that repressed trauma leads to illness. Aversive conditioning (choice C) and flooding (choice E) are both based on the behavioral principles of classical conditioning. Rational Emotive Behavior Therapy (REBT), choice D, is a cognitive therapy, developed by Albert Ellis, that leads to changes in illogical thinking due to direct challenges made by the therapist. (Skill 1a)

518. **(B)** Developed by Joseph Wolpe, systematic desensitization is a counter-conditioning therapy used successfully to treat phobias. While relaxed, patients are exposed to their fear-producing stimuli in increasing increments. The goal is to replace the fear with a new response, relaxation. Choice A reflects another behavioral treatment called aversive conditioning where an unpleasant state (bad taste) is associated with an undesirable behavior (chewing fingernails). Identifying and restructuring one's thinking, choice C, reflects a cognitive approach to psychotherapy. Dream interpretation, choice D, is consistent with the use of psychoanalysis. Choice E illustrates Electroconvulsive Therapy (ECT), a biological approach to treatment. (Skill 1b)

519. **(A)** Aversive conditioning is a behavioral therapy, a type of counterconditioning, that involves pairing something unpleasant with an unwanted behavior. The use of aversive conditioning as described in the scenario was acknowledged to be dangerous by the American Psychological Association in 1994. Many individuals subjected to this technique experienced increased depression and anxiety. Today it is considered a violation of professional conduct to engage in such practices. Systematic desensitization, choice B, is also a form of counterconditioning where a relaxed state is paired with stimuli that progressively produce more anxiety. Transference, choice C, occurs when a patient begins to treat the psychoanalyst like someone else important in his or her life. Flooding, choice D, is a behavioral technique where the individual becomes immersed in the stimulus that produces a phobic response. Rational Emotive Behavioral Therapy (REBT), choice E, is a cognitive therapy where an individual's illogical thought processes are directly challenged. (Skill 1b)

520. **(B)** Although in group therapy an individual may have less one-on-one interaction with a therapist, group therapy can still be an effective approach primarily because it provides interaction with others. These interactions help an individual feel more connected to others who share similar problems with himself or herself. Because the group members have things in common, they can watch as others work on specific issues and recognize certain patterns in themselves. Choices A, C, D, and E are positive outcomes for therapy in general. (Skill 1a)

521. **(E)** Antagonists are chemicals that prevent other chemicals from binding with a receptor site. In this case, antipsychotics are close in structure to dopamine and can occupy dopamine's receptor sites, thus blocking the action of dopamine. Hallucinogens, choice A, such as LSD, produce hallucinations. Depressants, choice B, such as alcohol, slow down the central nervous system and produce feelings of relaxation. Agonists, choice C, increase a chemical's action. Stimulants, choice D, such as cocaine, speed

up the central nervous system and produce increased energy and a rush of euphoria. (Skill 1a)

522. **(B)** Depression is associated with decreased amounts of serotonin and norepinephrine. SSRIs block the reuptake process of serotonin, thus making more serotonin available. SSRIs do not appear to be helpful in reducing the primary symptoms of schizophrenia (choice A), Dissociative Identity Disorder—DID (choice C), specific phobias (choice D), or borderline personality disorder, (choice E). (Skill 1a)

523. **(C)** Lithium, which is a simple salt, is a mood stabilizer. Although researchers are unsure of how it works to lessen extremes in mood, it can be very effective. Antipsychotics, choice A, are primarily used to treat psychotic illnesses, such as schizophrenia. Antidepressants, choice B, are used to treat the lows of depression as well as anxiety disorders. Antianxiety drugs, choice D, such as Xanax, depress the activity in the central nervous system and can be used to treat obsessive-compulsive disorder. Electroconvulsive Therapy (ECT), choice E, is primarily used to treat severe depression in those who do not respond well to drug therapies. (Skill 1a)

524. **(B)** Although Electroconvulsive Therapy (ECT) can be very effective in treating severe depression, one side effect is memory loss. Repetitive Transcranial Magnetic Stimulation (rTMS), choice A, is used to treat depression. However, rTMS does not seem to have memory loss as a side effect. Lithium (choice C), deep brain stimulation (choice D), and Selective Serotonin Reuptake Inhibitors—SSRIs (choice E) do have side effects. However, memory loss is not primarily associated with each treatment. (Skill 1a)

Scenarios

525. **(C)** When patients change the subject, make a joke, or forget relevant details, psychoanalysts believe that they are trying to protect themselves from anxiety-producing information. Psychoanalysts call this *resistance* and expect it to occur during psychoanalysis. Transference, choice A, is another part of psychoanalysis. In transference, patients transfer their feelings about a person close to them onto the therapist. Counterconditioning, choice B, is a behavioral technique based on classical conditioning. Cognitive restructuring, choice D, occurs when a therapist challenges illogical beliefs and helps patients create new, healthier ways of thinking. Meta-analysis, choice E, is a statistical technique used to combine the findings of numerous studies about a common phenomenon. (Skill 1b)

526. **(E)** Active listening involves the therapist restating and clarifying the statements made by the client. It is a way for the therapist to demonstrate acceptance, genuineness, and empathy for the client and to provide an atmosphere where the client can grow. Free association, choice A, involves speaking without censoring thoughts. The psychoanalyst's goal is to help the client discover repressed memories. Counterconditioning (choice B) and aversive conditioning (choice D) are both behavioral techniques based on classical conditioning. Cognitive restructuring, choice C, results from challenges made by the therapist to illogical thinking. (Skill 1b)

527. **(B)** Carl Rogers suggested that unconditional positive regard, shown through accepting and valuing others regardless of their actions or beliefs, was central to the development of positive self-concept. Resistance (choice A) and transference (choice C) are both a part of psychoanalysis. Resistance occurs when a patient changes the subject during free association as a way of protecting the ego. Transference happens when a patient begins to treat the therapist as a proxy for someone else by transferring the emotions he or she has for that person onto the psychoanalyst. Cognitive restructuring, choice D, is the change from illogical to logical thinking. Aversive conditioning, choice E, is based on counterconditioning. It involves pairing an unwanted behavior with a negative stimulus. (Skill 1b)

528. **(E)** Counterconditioning is based on behavioral principles. Phobias are likely learned through classical conditioning. Based on this, if a conditioned stimulus (for example, seeing a spider) is repeatedly presented without the unconditioned stimulus (being surprised by a spider floating in a swimming pool), the conditioned response (fear) will decrease and eventually become extinct. Counterconditioning techniques, such as systematic desensitization, require repeatedly exposing the individual to the stimulus that causes fear so that, eventually, the fear will be replaced with a new response. Psychoanalysis, choice A, involves techniques to uncover repressed trauma, such as free association. Client-centered therapy, choice B, is the primary technique of humanistic psychologists. A token economy, choice C, is an operant conditioning technique based on receiving rewards for appropriate behavior. Cognitive restructuring, choice D, involves identifying and changing illogical thinking patterns. (Skill 1b)

529. **(D)** Cognitive restructuring was developed by cognitive psychologist Aaron Beck. It involves developing an awareness of illogical thoughts and then challenging and changing such self-defeating ways of thinking. Resistance, choice A, occurs during free association with a psychoanalyst when the patient changes the subject whenever asked about potentially sensitive information. Active listening, choice B, is a humanistic

technique advanced by Carl Rogers. It involves a restating of what the client has said to provide a sense of empathy and genuineness. Counterconditioning, choice C, is a behavioral technique that involves continual exposure to an anxiety-producing stimulus so that, eventually, the fear is replaced with a new response. Aversive conditioning, choice E, is a type of counterconditioning that involves pairing something unpleasant with an unwanted behavior. (Skill 1b)

530. **(D)** Antipsychotics would be most effective in helping decrease Greg's delusions and hallucinations. Such drugs are similar in their chemical composition to dopamine and can occupy dopamine's receptor sites, reducing the amount of available dopamine. Increased levels of dopamine appear to play a role in psychotic symptoms. Antidepressants, choice A, such as Prozac, work to increase levels of serotonin at the synapse. Antianxiety drugs, choice B, such as Xanax, depress the central nervous system. Electroconvulsive Therapy (ECT), choice C, is currently used to treat severe depression. Stimulants, choice E, such as cocaine, increase nervous system activity and would not decrease Greg's symptoms. (Skill 1b)

531. **(E)** Electroconvulsive Therapy (ECT) is primarily used for depressed patients who don't respond well to psychotherapies or standard drug treatments. Although how it works is still largely a mystery, it can be very effective in alleviating severe symptoms of depression. Choice A is a description of Repetitive Transcranial Magnetic Stimulation (rTMS), which has also been found to be effective in treating depression. Choice B describes deep brain stimulation, which shows some promise in treating the symptoms of Parkinson's disease. Choice C describes a lobotomy, which is no longer used in the treatment of mental illness. Choice D illustrates the controversial use of light to treat depression tied to seasonal changes. (Skill 1a)

532. **(B)** The description of Mary's symptoms appears to be related to severe depression. Antidepressants, such as Selective Serotonin Reuptake Inhibitors (SSRIs), may be effective in reducing her symptoms. Arnold's symptoms, choice A, appear to be psychotic, possibly schizophrenia, which are best treated with antipsychotics. Don's symptoms, choice C, seem to illustrate antisocial personality disorder, which does not appear to respond to antidepressant medications. Jessica's specific phobia, choice D, is best treated with behavioral therapies such as systematic desensitization. Vivian, choice E, appears to have illness anxiety disorder, whose symptoms don't respond to drug therapies. (Skill 1b)

533. **(E)** Cognitive-Behavioral Therapies (CBT) assumes that what an individual thinks impacts his or her behavior. If Vickie is thinking self-defeating

thoughts, it can lead to depression. To help Vickie, her therapist will help Vickie identify and change her illogical thinking. In addition, her therapist will use techniques that will give Vickie more activities that produce positive emotions, such as scheduling one pleasant activity per day. Psychoanalysis, choice A, focuses on the analyst interpreting dreams or free associations for unconscious conflict that has led to illness. A token economy (choice B) and systematic desensitization (choice C) are behavioral techniques used to change the target behavior only, not the underlying thoughts that produce it. Active listening, choice D, involves an echoing of a client's statements during therapy. It is a humanistic technique used to promote an environment where the client can reach his or her full potential. (Skill 1b)

534. **(B)** Stress inoculation training is based in cognitive therapy. It focuses on helping individuals become more resistant to stressors in their lives. It teaches people about how their bodies respond to stress as well as the illogical thinking they might engage in that causes stress. Much like an inoculation to stop disease, clients design in advance steps to take when they are feeling stressed. For Kai, planning positive statements to think before class might help him control the stress that is inhibiting his performance. Exposure therapy, choice A, is a behavioral technique based on classical conditioning. In exposure therapy, a fear-producing stimulus is paired with a new response, such as relaxation. A token economy, choice C, is a behavioral technique based on operant conditioning. In a token economy, an individual earns small rewards, or tokens, in order to earn other reinforcers. Active listening, choice D, is a technique where the therapist restates what the client has said and asks the client for clarification with the goal of helping the individual feel total acceptance. Free association, choice E, is a psychoanalytic technique to discover unconscious trauma. Free association begins with the therapist asking an open-ended question that allows the person to speak freely without censoring his or her thoughts. (Skill 1b)

Names

535. **(C)** Carl Rogers was a major influence in humanistic psychology. He developed client-centered therapy and urged psychologists to create therapeutic environments that demonstrated their genuineness, acceptance, and empathy. Therapists using active listening would echo, restate, and clarify clients' statements, thereby establishing the human connection that served as the bases for growth. Sigmund Freud, choice A, focused on the role of the unconscious. He used free association as a vehicle to uncover repressed trauma. Aaron Beck (choice B) and Albert Ellis (choice E) were

both cognitive psychologists who helped patients identify faulty thinking as a way to help them establish more adaptive ways of viewing their lives. B. F. Skinner, choice D, was a behavioral psychologist who studied the role of reinforcement and punishment in shaping behavior. (Skill 1b)

536. **(E)** Mary Cover Jones's therapy techniques were known as counterconditioning. They were grounded in behavioral principles. Mary Cover Jones believed she could remove a phobia if she paired the trigger stimulus, in this case a rabbit, with a new response, relaxation. Thus, the fear was countered by relaxation because such opposing states cannot be experienced simultaneously. Free association, choice A, is a technique of psychoanalysis and was developed by Sigmund Freud. Electroconvulsive therapy, choice B, is a biological intervention used to treat severe depression. Active listening, choice C, was proposed by the humanistic psychologist Carl Rogers. Rational emotive behavior therapy, choice D, is a cognitive therapy developed by Albert Ellis. (Skill 1b)

537. **(D)** Aaron Beck developed a form of cognitive therapy aimed at treating depression. He believed that people are depressed because they form self-defeating ways of thinking about themselves. Beck's technique, called cognitive restructuring, uses gentle questioning that helps individuals discover their own illogical thinking patterns as well as develop new ways of interpreting events in their lives. Sigmund Freud, choice A, developed psychoanalysis to help individuals gain insight into the unconscious forces impacting their behavior. Carl Rogers (choice B) and Abraham Maslow (choice C) were humanistic psychologists. Carl Rogers developed client-centered therapy techniques, including active listening, while Maslow focused on discussing which unmet needs might be blocking a client's progress. Joseph Wolpe, choice E, built upon the work of Mary Cover Jones in developing counterconditioning techniques, such as systematic desensitization. (Skill 1a)

538. **(B)** B. F. Skinner was a major figure in behaviorism. He furthered our understanding of the law of effect, that reinforced behavior is maintained and that behavior that is punished is eliminated. Therapies, such as a token economy, are based upon these operant conditioning principles. Aaron Beck (choice A) and Albert Ellis (choice C) were cognitive psychologists who focused on how our thinking influences our behavior. Carl Rogers, choice D, was a humanistic psychologist who stressed the importance of unconditional positive regard in developing a positive self-concept. Joseph Wolpe, choice E, was also a behaviorist. He developed the method of systematic desensitization to treat phobias. This method is based on classical conditioning principles. (Skill 1a)

Research Methods

539. **(C)** Case studies allow researchers to study an unusual instance in detail. Freud published numerous case studies that served as the foundation for his psychoanalysis, including "Dora," "Little Hans," and the "Rat Man." Surveys, choice A, provide researchers with self-report data on individuals' attitudes. Experiments, choice B, involve the random assignment of subjects to two groups where one group receives the independent variable while all other conditions remain constant. Correlational studies, choice D, involve using a statistical measure, called a correlation coefficient, to determine how closely two variables are related. Naturalistic observations, choice E, are conducted within the natural environment of the organisms so the researcher can closely study their behavior. (Skill 3)

540. **(D)** The placebo effect occurs when an individual believes in a treatment and a change in symptoms occurs. To control for the power of belief, researchers include a placebo group, one that receives a fake treatment. The inclusion of Group B does not impact the ethics of the study, making ethical concerns (choice A) incorrect. For example, to adhere to the ethical guidelines, Dr. Pozniak would need to obtain informed consent before beginning the experiment. Subject bias, choice B, could be controlled for by using either a single- or double-blind technique. Perceptual adaptation, choice C, is not related to the placebo effect. Sampling bias, choice E, which can lead to having an unrepresentative sample, can be controlled for by obtaining a random sample from the population. (Skill 3)

541. **(D)** The dependent variable in an experiment is the outcome that is measured. That variable is called "dependent" because it depends on the manipulation of the independent variable. In this case, the number of anxiety-related symptoms as reported by the subjects was the measured outcome. The independent variable, choice A, is the administration of the antianxiety medication. Choices B, C, and E were identical in both groups, meaning that none were variables. (Skill 3)

Perspectives

542. **(C)** Psychodynamic psychologists focus on the unconscious forces that shape our behavior. Cognitive psychologists, choice A, look at how our thinking influences our actions. The behavioral perspective, choice B, concentrates on how our actions are learned from the environment. Evolutionary psychologists, choice D, investigate the role of natural selection in shaping adaptive human behaviors. The sociocultural perspective, choice E, looks to the role of a person's cultural background in affecting his or her behavior. (Skill 1c)

543. **(D)** The behavioral perspective provides the basis for this approach. Token economies are based on the principles of operant conditioning, which were studied extensively by B. F. Skinner. If a behavior is reinforced, that behavior will likely be repeated. The tokens act as reinforcers to be exchanged for other reinforcers. The cognitive perspective, choice A, focuses on how our thinking impacts our behavior. The biological perspective, choice B, emphasizes the role of the nervous and other systems on our behavior. The humanistic perspective, choice C, looks to human fulfillment as its primary focus. The psychodynamic perspective, choice E, stresses the role of the unconscious in influencing behavior. (Skill 1c)

544. **(C)** Since rTMS focuses on changing how the brain operates, it is coming from the biological perspective. The cognitive perspective, choice A, emphasizes the thought processes that influence our behavior. Evolutionary psychology, choice B, stresses the role of natural selection in shaping adaptive human behaviors. Behavioral psychologists, choice D, highlight the role of environmental forces on our behavior. Psychodynamic psychologists, choice E, focus on the unconscious forces that shape our behavior. (Skill 1c)

545. **(A)** Behavioral psychologists focus on changing maladaptive behavior using learning principles. Exposure therapies are based on classical conditioning. Using virtual reality provides a safe environment for the individual to be exposed to the fear-producing stimulus. Biological psychologists, choice B, focus on how the workings of the brain and the body systems influence behavior. Psychodynamic psychologists, choice C, stress how unconscious thought processes impact our behavior. Humanistic psychologists, choice D, believe in the power of the individual to fulfill his or her potential. Evolutionary psychologists, choice E, seek choices to human behavior using the Darwinian principle of natural selection. (Skill 1c)

546. **(C)** The sociocultural perspective stresses how an individual's culture influences the way he or she thinks and learns. Cultural differences can impact the effectiveness of a therapist. As shown in the scenario, a therapist with an individualistic cultural background may focus on meeting with the client individually and speaking with the client about his or her life goals. That therapist might neglect including the family in treatment, which may be very important to the client with a collectivist perspective. The psychodynamic perspective, choice A, focuses on helping the patient develop insights into the unconscious forces that shape his or her behavior. The biological perspective, choice B, focuses on how the workings of the nervous and other body systems shape behavior. The humanistic perspective, choice D, believes that people are basically good and work toward fulfilling their potential. The evolutionary perspective, choice E, looks to the forces of natural selection in determining the behaviors that allow humans to survive in their environment. (Skill 1c)

CHAPTER 14: SOCIAL PSYCHOLOGY

Stimulus

547. **(B)** Zimbardo's prison study has been criticized for potentially violating ethical requirements for research with human participants. Some participants in the prison study asked to leave and were not allowed to (although Zimbardo and others dispute this criticism). The prison study took place on the Stanford campus (choice A). Choice C is incorrect because the Zimbardo study also investigated authority. Choices D and E include incorrect statements about the Zimbardo prison study. (Skill 3)

548. **(D)** Asch studied conformity—whether people changed their behaviors to be in line with the unanimous group decision. The study in the newspaper explicitly focuses on authority, which is related to obedience—following orders from a perceived authority figure. Choices A, B, and E include incorrect information about Asch's study. Choice C is incorrect because nothing in the newspaper ad implies that this is a case study. (Skill 3)

549. **(C)** Milgram's study famously depended on keeping participants from knowing that deception/confederates were involved. The "learners" in the study did not know that the "teachers" were confederates. However, the newspaper ad specifically states that deception and confederates will be used. Choices A, D, and E include incorrect information about the Milgram study. Choice B is incorrect because nothing in the newspaper clipping implies that the researcher is a behaviorist. (Skill 3)

550. **(A)** The newspaper clipping says that the research is about "responses to different kinds of authority." This means that perception of authority is the independent variable. Nothing in the newspaper clipping implies that conformity (choice B) or age (choice E) are elements of the study. Choice C, perception of behavior, is very general, and behavior is more likely to be an aspect of the dependent variable. The response to authority, choice D, is the dependent variable. (Skill 3)

Definitions

551. **(B)** The goal of attribution theory is to investigate how we explain behaviors. People usually explain the behaviors of others by attributing them to either situational (environmental) causes or disposition (personality) causes. Trait theory, choice A, is a personality theory. Drive reduction theory, choice C, is a motivation theory. Fundamental attribution error, choice D, is related to attribution theory. However, the fundamental attribution error specifically describes our tendency to attribute the behaviors of others to their dispositions rather than to situational factors. The locus

CHAPTER 14

of control theory, choice E, refers to our cognitions about ourselves, not others. (Skill 1a)

552. **(D)** The fundamental attribution error specifically describes our tendency to attribute the behaviors of others to their inner dispositions (their personalities) rather than to situational (environmental) factors. Similarity, choice A, is involved in attraction research. The fundamental attribution error is a specific application of attribution theory, choice B. However, fundamental attribution error is a more specific and correct choice for this question. Social facilitation (choice C) and social loafing (choice E) are related to whether we are likely to exert an effort in different kinds of social situations. (Skill 1a)

553. **(E)** The fundamental attribution error specifically describes our tendency to attribute the behaviors of others to their inner dispositions (their personalities) rather than to situational (environmental) factors. Choice A is an incorrect summary of attribution research. Choice B refers to an irrelevant factor (luck). Choices C and D refer to factors not related to attribution theory. (Skill 1a)

554. **(C)** The peripheral route to persuasion involves using visuals and emotional appeals that aren't necessarily relevant to the central message but that will grab the attention of viewers and perhaps influence their decisions. Norm of reciprocity (choice A) and the foot-in-the-door phenomenon (choice D) are other kinds of persuasion techniques. The central route to persuasion, choice B, involves making a convincing argument using relevant facts or other details rather than emotional language or attention-grabbing details. The external locus of control, choice E, refers to whether we attribute what happens in our lives to luck or to our own efforts. (Skill 1b)

555. **(B)** The central route to persuasion uses relevant and fact-based evidence, like statistics or research findings, to try to influence viewers' decisions. This contrasts with the peripheral route to persuasion, choice C, which involves using irrelevant, emotional details in order to influence viewers. Norm of reciprocity (choice A) and the foot-in-the-door phenomenon (choice D) are other kinds of persuasion techniques. The external locus of control, choice E, refers to whether we attribute what happens in our lives to luck or to our own efforts. (Skill 1b)

556. **(D)** Using the foot-in-the-door persuasion technique involves making a small initial request and then gradually increasing that request until you reach your ultimate goal. Gradually increasing these requests increases the chance that your eventual end request will be granted. The door-in-the-face phenomenon, choice A, is the opposite technique. You ask for more

than you want at the beginning and then gradually reduce the request. Central route to persuasion (choice B), peripheral route to persuasion (choice C), and norm of reciprocity (choice E) are other kinds of persuasion techniques. (Skill 1a)

557. **(A)** Cognitive dissonance occurs when we realize that something we have done (an action) isn't consistent with the way we think or with our internal attitudes. We usually resolve this dissonance by changing our cognitions. Role playing (choice B), self-serving bias (choice C), ethnocentrism (choice D), and mere exposure effect (choice E) are not relevant to the specific dissonance between cognitions and actions. (Skill 1a)

558. **(E)** Conformity occurs when someone is surrounded by a unanimous group, all its members making the same decision, and the person conforms to the decision/opinion of the group. The social psychology concept of conformity doesn't have anything to do with genetics (choice A), personality (choice B), or operant conditioning (choice C). Choice D describes obedience, not conformity. (Skill 1a)

559. **(D)** Obedience occurs when someone follows the orders of a person who is perceived as an authority figure. The social psychology concept of obedience doesn't have anything to do with genetics (choice A), personality (choice B), or operant conditioning (choice C). Choice E describes conformity, not obedience. (Skill 1a)

560. **(B)** Social facilitation occurs when we perform a task in the presence of a group of people and the presence of others enhances our performance. Group polarization (choice A) and groupthink (choice C) refer to social principles that influence group decision making or rationale. The Yerkes-Dodson law, choice D, is similar to social facilitation. However, the Yerkes-Dodson law describes something more specific: performance is enhanced when arousal (caused by the presence of others or by other factors) is at an optimum level. Social loafing, choice E, is a principle that works in opposition to social facilitation. Social loafing is the lack of effort while in the presence of others. (Skill 1a)

561. **(E)** Social loafing occurs when we know we are in a group and that everyone is (or may be) working on the same task or toward the same goal. In this kind of situation, people have the tendency to loaf or not give as much effort as they might if they were working alone. Group polarization (choice A) and groupthink (choice C) refer to social principles that influence group decision making or rationale. Social facilitation, choice B, is almost the opposite of social loafing: sometimes the presence of others enhances our performance. The Yerkes-Dodson law, choice D, is similar to social facilitation. However, the Yerkes-Dodson law

describes something more specific: performance is enhanced when arousal (caused by the presence of others or by other factors) is at an optimum level. (Skill 1a)

562. **(C)** Deindividuation occurs when we lose our sense of restraint, feel anonymous (we are a part of the crowd), and act with a group rather than make our own decisions and use our usual internal guidelines for our behavior. Self-actualization, choice A, is part of Maslow's hierarchy of needs theory. Group polarization, choice B, describes how our attitudes may change because of conversations with a like-minded group. Self-fulfilling prophecy, choice D, describes how our beliefs about ourselves may influence how others treat us. Egocentrism, choice E, is part of Jean Piaget's cognitive development theory. (Skill 1a)

563. **(B)** If a group of people who generally agree about a controversial topic discuss that topic, they are likely to leave the discussion more polarized. In other words, at the end of the discussion they will be more convinced of their initial position than they were when the discussion began. Obedience (choice A) and deindividuation (choice C) are incorrect because they involve individuals behaving because they are following orders from an authority figure or blindly following the actions of a group. Social facilitation (choice D) and social loafing (choice E) both describe how being in a group influences whether we exert more or less effort than we would if we were alone. (Skill 1a)

564. **(A)** Groupthink occurs when a group of individuals who admire/respect each other make a poor decision because no one in the group is willing to contradict or critique the ideas of the others. Making sure that there is at least one dissenting voice in each group may help prevent group-think. Choices B, C, D, and E include factors that are not related to groupthink. (Skill 1a)

565. **(D)** Prejudice is a negative, unjustifiable attitude toward a group. Discrimination occurs when these beliefs/attitudes are acted upon— negative, unjustified behaviors are exhibited toward a group of people. The differences mentioned in choices A, B, and C are not relevant to the actual definitions of prejudice and discrimination. Choice E is incorrect because both are modern psychological terms. (Skill 1a)

566. **(E)** The mere exposure effect predicts that we will like stimuli (such as places or people) that we encounter often. We like people and places we are exposed to more frequently. Similarly (choice A) and companion-ate love (choice B) are both involved in attraction research. However, neither of them is relevant to the idea that we prefer stimuli that we are exposed to more often. Social facilitation (choice C) refers to enhanced

performance in social situations. Locus of control (choice D) relates to our explanations about the causes of outcomes in our lives—whether we attribute outcomes to causes within our control or to causes beyond our control. (Skill 1a)

567. **(C)** The norm of reciprocity (sometimes referred to as the reciprocity norm) predicts that we are more likely to help others if we perceive they have also helped us. The foot-in-the-door strategy (choice A) is a compliance strategy that is used to convince someone to agree to a request gradually. Groupthink (choice B) involves influences on group discussions. Social facilitation (choice D) refers to how social situations can sometimes enhance performance. The norm of reciprocity is an aspect of altruism research, choice E. The norm of reciprocity, choice C, is the correct choice because it answers the question more specifically than does choice E. (Skill 1a)

568. **(B)** The frustration-aggression principle predicts that increasing frustration and annoyances, which may be caused by increasing temperatures, are associated with increases in crime. Social scripts, choice A, are also associated with aggression as well as with many other behaviors. However, they are not specifically related to increasing temperatures. Operant conditioning (choice C), fundamental attribution error (choice D), and observational learning (choice E) are all concepts that might help explain individual acts of aggression. However, none are specifically related to the relationship between temperature and aggression. (Skill 1a)

569. **(A)** Ingroup bias describes our tendency to favor a group we think we belong to. We are more likely to appreciate the opinions (including social media posts) by people who we perceive are in our ingroup. Similarity theory, choice B, is related to attraction research. Groupthink, choice C, is involved in how groups make decisions. Self-fulfilling prophecy (choice D) and discrimination (choice E) are not specifically related to perceptions of others' opinions. (Skill 1a)

570. **(D)** The just-world phenomenon describes the human tendency to believe that the world is a fair place, that good actions are rewarded, and that if something bad happens to a person, he or she must have done something to deserve that outcome. Choice A, positive reinforcement, is not related to questions of morality or a sense of right and wrong. The feel-good, do-good phenomenon, choice B, predicts that doing good for others helps us feel better. Choice C, ingroup bias, describes our tendency to appreciate the opinions of people in our social group. Preconventional morality, choice E, is a stage in Kohlberg's moral development theory. However, preconventional morality involves rewards and punishments, not a sense of justice or morality. (Skill 1a)

571. **(A)** Muzafer Sherif's Robbers Cave study demonstrated that social conditions can create ingroup and outgroup biases. The study also showed that superordinate goals can help reduce those same biases. Generalization, choice B, is a process in operant or classical conditioning. One possible impact of superordinate goals might be a reduction in frustration. This is the frustration-aggression principle, choice C. However, superordinate goals do not necessarily or directly impact the relationship between frustration and aggression. Confounding variables (choice D) and selection bias (choice E) are important elements of the experimental method. (Skill 1a)

Scenarios

572. **(A)** Changing our internal thoughts and feelings (attitudes) can often influence our later actions. In this scenario, the research changed Lorenzo's attitude about motorcycles, which influenced his later action. Actions affecting attitudes, choice D, is the opposite effect. This scenario is not an example of either conformity (choice B) or obedience (choice C) because there is no unanimous group or authority figure involved. Social facilitation, choice E, refers to increased performance in social situations. (Skill 1b)

573. **(D)** Social psychology research frequently finds that what we do can impact how we feel. Once we perform an action, our attitudes about that action may change. In this scenario, for some reason Lance and Carter played basketball, which impacted their later attitude about the sport. Attitudes affecting actions, choice A, is the opposite effect. This scenario is not an example of either conformity (choice B) or obedience (choice C) because there is no unanimous group or authority figure involved. Social facilitation, choice E, refers to increased performance in social situations. (Skill 1b)

574. **(D)** Fundamental attribution error specifically describes our tendency to attribute the behaviors of others to their inner dispositions (their personalities, like being a football fan) rather than situational factors (environmental factors, like waking up with bed head). This is not an example of either stereotyping (choice A) or ingroup bias (choice C) because no one is forming an expectation about a group of people or is showing a preference toward their own group above others. Choice B is involved in this scenario; concept formation is involved in almost all kinds of cognition. However, choice D is a more specific and correct choice. Selection bias, choice E, is a term related to research methods and sample group selection. (Skill 1b)

575. **(B)** The central route to persuasion uses relevant fact-based evidence, like statistics or research findings, to try to influence viewers' decisions. This ad uses relevant evidence about health and side effects to sell vitamins. Choices A, C, and D use emotion or other compelling elements that are not relevant to the claim. Choice E is ambiguous. Not enough information is provided in this choice to determine whether it is an example of the central route to persuasion. (Skill 1b)

576. **(A)** The peripheral route to persuasion involves using visuals and emotional appeals that aren't necessarily relevant to the central message but that will grab the attention of viewers and perhaps influence their decisions. The celebrity endorsement in choice A is an example of the peripheral route to persuasion. Choices B and C are examples of the central route to persuasion. Choices D and E are somewhat ambiguous. Not enough information is provided to conclude whether these are examples of the peripheral route to persuasion. (Skill 1b)

577. **(C)** Using the foot-in-the-door persuasion technique involves making a small initial request and then gradually increasing that request toward your ultimate goal. This technique can be useful during any kind of negotiation, including political negotiations. The concepts mentioned in choices A, B, and E influence how we think and feel in social situations. They are not useful in the scenario described in the question. Choice D, self-disclosure, is involved in attraction research. (Skill 1b)

578. **(E)** Cognitive dissonance occurs when we realize that something we have done (an action) isn't consistent with the way we think or our internal attitudes. Mr. Miller was forced to work for a woman, and this action is most likely inconsistent with his previous misogynistic attitudes. Since he can't change his work situation, cognitive dissonance may have led to Mr. Miller's change in attitude. Ingroup bias, choice A, would lead Mr. Miller to be more not less biased about groups outside his ingroup. Collectivism, choice B, refers to different kinds of societies. There is no indication of an outside group goal, which is necessary for superordinate goals, choice C. A just-noticeable difference, choice D, is a sensation and perception concept and is not related to this scenario. (Skill 1b)

579. **(B)** Conformity occurs when someone is surrounded by a unanimous group, with all members making the same decision, and the person conforms to the decision/opinion of the group. Religious cults rely on a group of people who are all united in thought and attitude (and often clothing, living situations, and other contexts) that increases the pressure on new recruits to conform to the group. Absolute threshold, choice A, is a concept from sensation and perception. A variable-interval schedule, choice C, refers to an operant reinforcement schedule. Selective attention,

choice D, is a step in the memory process. Choice E, attributing the behavior of others to situational or attributional reasons, may be involved in cult groups. However, it is not likely a driving force in joining a cult. (Skill 1a)

580. **(D)** Obedience occurs when someone follows the orders of a person who is perceived as an authority figure. The effectiveness of "the look" Ms. Band uses may be due to her students' perception of her as an authority figure. Binocular disparity (choice A) and visual capture (choice B) are elements of our visual sensation and perception system. Conformity, choice C, is not likely to be involved because this scenario does not describe a unanimous group. Norms of reciprocity research, choice E, refers to a compliance technique involving giving someone a tangible reward with the expectation that he or she will be more likely to comply with your request. (Skill 1b)

581. **(C)** Social facilitation occurs when we perform a task in the presence of a group of people and when the presence of others enhances our performance. If the task comes fairly easily, the presence of others will enhance our performance. However, if the task is too difficult, being in a social situation will inhibit our performance. The explanations included in choices A, B, D, and E either are inaccurate or are not relevant to social facilitation theory. (Skill 1c)

582. **(A)** Social loafing occurs when we know we are in a group and that everyone in the group is (or may be) working on the same task or toward the same goal. In this situation, people have the tendency to loaf, or not give as much effort as they might if they were working alone. In the group task assigned by Professor Herting, some students may loaf, which complicates the grading process. Grades are a kind of operational definition, choice B, but that concept doesn't specifically relate to this scenario. Group polarization, choice C, wouldn't necessarily complicate grading because, even if the group interactions intensified some students' beliefs, this wouldn't necessarily impact the quality of the group's work, or the group grade. An availability heuristic, choice D, does not relate to the scenario. A confidence interval, choice E, is a statistical concept that doesn't relate to this scenario about grading. (Skill 1b)

583. **(E)** Deindividuation occurs when we lose our sense of restraint and act with a group rather than make our own decisions, using our usual internal guidelines for our behavior. All the social situations listed often involve acting with the group as part of enjoying the activity. None of the other concepts listed in choices A, B, C, and D have a specific connection to the social activities listed in this question. (Skill 1b)

584. **(A)** Group polarization predicts that if a group of people who generally agree about a controversial topic discuss that topic, they are likely to leave the discussion feeling more polarized, or more convinced of their initial position, than when the discussion began. Organizing the discussion groups to ensure that individuals with a variety of opinions are in each group may help prevent group polarization. No authority figures are involved, so obedience, choice B, is incorrect. Social facilitation (choice C) and deindividuation (choice E) aren't relevant to the organization of the discussion groups. Groupthink, choice D, may occur in a discussion group. However, this concept is more relevant to groups making decisions or plans rather than discussing political issues. (Skill 1b)

585. **(B)** Groupthink occurs when a group of individuals who admire and respect each other make a poor decision because no one in the group is willing to contradict or critique the ideas of others. Since the young mayor appointed people he admires to the consultation cabinet, they may have made the unwise Ice Town decision because no one in the group was willing to contradict or speak against the idea. The social psychology concepts listed in choices A and C (fundamental attribution error and cognitive dissonance) do not have any specific connection to this scenario. Fluid intelligence, choice D, relates to aging and intelligence. Long-term potentiation, choice E, describes how memories are physically stored in the brain. (Skill 1b)

Names

586. **(C)** Leon Festinger's research helped establish cognitive dissonance theory, which describes how cognitions/attitudes might change because a person's actions are in conflict with his or her attitudes. In the research study described in this question, people are compelled to perform a boring task. The researchers measure how participants' attitudes change based on the independent variable of rewards. Solomon Asch (choice A), Stanley Milgram (choice B), Philip Zimbardo (choice D), and Bibb Latane (choice E) all studied the impact of social groups on our actions/attitudes, not the cognitive changes described in the question. (Skill 1b)

587. **(D)** Solomon Asch's research investigated conformity. This occurs when someone is surrounded by a unanimous group, with all of its members making the same decision, and the person conforms to the decision/opinion of the group. Choice A is closely related to the work of Stanley Milgram. Choice B is a summary of some of the research done by John Darley and Bibb Latane. Choice C might be most interesting to

Philip Zimbardo. Choice E is an interesting social psychology question but is not associated with one particular psychologist. (Skill 1b)

588. **(B)** Stanley Milgram was interested in researching the excuses provided by Nazis during the Nuremberg trials. Milgram's research established the theory of obedience, which occurs when someone follows the orders of a person who is perceived as an authority figure. Research from Solomon Asch (choice A), Leon Festinger (choice C), Hermann Ebbinghaus (choice D), and Bibb Latane (choice E) would not be as specifically relevant to war crime trials as would Milgram's research. (Skill 1b)

589. **(D)** Philip Zimbardo's research in the Stanford prison study has been criticized for several research method flaws, including the lack of a control group, and for ethical flaws, such as not allowing participants to leave the study when they asked. The research from Solomon Asch (choice A), Elliott Aronson (choice B), Leon Festinger (choice C), and Bibb Latane (choice E) have not been criticized for the lack of a control group or for ethical issues. (Skill 3)

590. **(D)** John Darley and Bibb Latane researched altruism extensively, especially the factors that influence whether bystanders are likely to help in emergency situations. Watson and Skinner (choice A) were behaviorists. Asch and Milgram (choice B) were social psychologists who researched conformity and obedience. Festinger and Carlsmith (choice C) researched cognitive dissonance. Myers and Dewall (choice E) were coauthors of a famous introductory psychology textbook. (Skill 1a)

Research Methods

591. **(E)** The Zimbardo Stanford prison study has been criticized for a lack of precision in its research methodology. However, the closest element in the study to an independent variable is the difference between the two groups—the randomly assigned prisoner group and guard group. Choices A and B describe details of the study rather than independent variables. Choice C describes what might be called the operational definition of the dependent variable (behaviors of the participants). Choice D describes the sample group, the participants in the study. (Skill 3)

592. **(A)** The dependent variable in the Milgram obedience study was obedience. It was measured (operationally defined) by recording what level of shock each teacher administered. Choices B and C refer to elements of the research protocol, not operational definitions. Choice D is not relevant to the question. The learners in the study were confederates, not true participants. Choice E describes the dependent variable, obedience, as whether the participants who thought they were teachers obeyed the orders of the

authority figure. However, this question asks for the operational definition of the dependent variable, not a description of the dependent variable. (Skill 3)

593. **(C)** Confederates—people who pretend to be participants in the study but who are actually part of the research protocol—were essential in the Asch and Milgram studies. The confederates in the Asch study all gave the "wrong" choice to questions in order to see if the true participants would conform to these wrong choices. Milgram pretended to assign participants randomly to either the teacher or the learner role. However, all the learners were actually confederates following a script. Confederates were not used in the Zimbardo prison study. All of its participants were assigned to either the guard or the prisoner role. Choices A, B, D, and E all include incorrect information about the role of confederates in these three studies. (Skill 3)

594. **(D)** Sherif studied the impact of creating different groups on the behaviors of participants and looked for bias treatment between groups (ingroup/outgroup bias). The study involved superordinate goals, choice A, but that was not the dependent variable. Choices B and C describe elements of the experimental protocol. Choice E is inaccurate; the study did not involve this element. (Skill 3)

595. **(B)** Changing the number of confederates in the Asch study is a possible independent variable; changing this variable may cause different levels of conformity. Choices C, D, and E are not possible independent variables in the Asch study. Asch could not have manipulated these variables to determine their effect on conformity, which is the dependent variable. Choice A is not relevant to the Asch study. Instead, this is a possible independent variable for the Milgram obedience study. (Skill 3)

596. **(E)** Since social psychologists often research the impact of social situations on our behaviors, social psychologists often must create specific social situations in their experiments. In order to create these social situations, researchers often need to use confederates to assume specific social roles and deceive actual participants about the true nature of the social situation. Random sampling and assignment (choice A), independent variables (choice B), dependent variables (choice C), and the double-blind technique (choice D) are not more commonly used in social psychological research than in other areas of psychology research. (Skill 1a)

Perspectives

597. **(C)** Schemata are mental rules we use for interpreting the world. The hypothesis in the question is a cognitive psychology explanation for Asch's findings. It explains the behaviors of participants in the study using

cognitive psychology theories, such as the ways we mentally interpret and remember the world. Researchers from humanistic psychology (choice A), sociocultural psychology (choice B), behaviorism (choice D), and the biological perspective (choice E) are not likely to use the term "schemata" because they do not focus on cognitive processes as primary causes of behaviors. (Skill 1c)

598. **(A)** Maslow's hierarchy of needs is one of the most well-known elements of humanistic psychology. Humanistic psychologists believe that humans are driven to become their best selves and that we progress through consistent kinds of needs toward the ultimate goal of self-actualization. Sociocultural psychology (choice B), cognitive psychology (choice C), behaviorism (choice D), and the biological perspective (choice E) do not have any specific connection to the hierarchy of needs. (Skill 1c)

599. **(D)** Positive reinforcements are an element of operant conditioning, which is part of the overall perspective of behaviorism. Investigating the impact of positive reinforcement on behaviors across different social contexts combines the research areas of behaviorism and social psychology. The perspectives listed in choices A, B, C, and E are not likely to be specifically interested in research involving positive reinforcement. (Skill 1c)

600. **(E)** This research seems to indicate that social psychology theories, such as the fundamental attribution error, may actually be controlled by brain chemistry rather than by the interactions among cognitions, social scripts, or other social psychology concepts. In other words, the biological perspective might explain many social psychology findings. Humanistic psychology (choice A), sociocultural psychology (choice B), cognitive psychology (choice C), and behaviorism (choice D) are not likely to be specifically interested in research involving neurotransmitters. (Skill 1c)